Cost Benefit and Cost Effectiveness

STUDIES AND ANALYSIS

Cost Benefit and Cost Effectiveness

STUDIES AND ANALYSIS

EDITED BY

J. N. WOLFE

Professor of Economics in The University of Edinburgh

London

GEORGE ALLEN & UNWIN LTD

RUSKIN HOUSE MUSEUM STREET

First published in 1973

ISBN 0 04 338058 1 hardback
0 04 338059 x paper

Printed in Great Britain
in 10 point Times Roman type
by Alden & Mowbray Ltd
at the Alden Press, Oxford

Contents

PART FOUR FRONTIERS

1

Introduction

J. N. WOLFE
Professor of Economics, University of Edinburgh

1. POLITICAL ECONOMY

At least since Adam Smith, economists have directed much attention towards the development of a set of policy rules for the beneficial guidance of the economic system. The more discreet and thoughtful economists hedged their general policy prescriptions with many warnings and exceptions. Nevertheless, it was broadly true that, during the nineteenth century, economists in Britain at least were largely identified with a particular line of economic policy known variously as liberalism and *laissez-faire*. In its cruder forms this doctrine asserted that an unfettered working of the competitive price system within a background of clear laws and enforcement of contract would bring about the greatest economic benefit.

Later generations of economists have devoted themselves to the explication, limitation and undermining of this doctrine. In particular 'greatest economic benefit' was shown to imply either controversial interpersonal evaluations of the incomes received by different individuals or else simply 'Pareto optimality', i.e. a situation in which no one could gain except at somebody else's expense. Further, 'competition' in this doctrine was seen to imply perfect information, perfect markets and perfect competition. And the doctrine was seen to hold only when all externalities had been removed, all prices were in equilibrium and no disequilibrium existed in any sector.

These conditions were widely thought to be so severe that during the 1950s at least a broad consensus appeared to have emerged among economists to the effect that the economist could say very little in a general way about economic policy and that his role was to provide positive information about economic variables and their influence which could be used by the policy maker for his own purposes.

The growth of cost-benefit and cost-effectiveness analysis seems, in recent years, to have disturbed this consensus. While economists as a group are still somewhat reluctant to be identified with simple economic ideologies like *laissez-faire* or even free trade, it has become quite common and even respectable for economists to become identified with economic policy proposals at a much more detailed and micro level. The rationale for this new boldness on the part of economists is not altogether coherent but we can easily identify certain strands of thought within it.

In the first place it is certainly arguable that many or most cost-benefit applications involve redistributions of income which have no particular class bias or are unlikely to be politically sensitive.

Secondly, the question of externalities is in fact one of the issues which cost benefit normally attempts to face up to and evaluate.

Thirdly, cost-benefit exercises are often designed to deal with circumstances in which prices are out of equilibrium or in which there is monopoly present in the elements being considered.

The economist has thus increasingly become the advocate of the application of cost-benefit analysis to the economic processes, and particularly of capital formation, in those areas in which the public sector was actively involved. This identification of the economist with a policy doctrine, albeit a doctrine in the micro-economic field, is still subject to certain criticisms of a technical nature. Allowance is not ordinarily made for the possibility of disequilibrium or monopoly in other sectors than those being considered in the analysis, nor is the original distribution of income or ownership generally challenged, nor is much weight given to the effect of generalising the use of a cost-benefit decision rule upon the whole structure of incomes and prices in the economy. These are serious omissions from a puristic point of view, but it is difficult to evaluate them quantitatively. They may conceivably cancel out in practice; and it may in practice be difficult to make allowance for them even if we wish to do so.

A central point, however, is that the principal criticisms of cost-benefit analysis have not arisen from these objections but rather from certain other more obvious and less sophisticated considerations. The first of these objections is that the cost-benefit analyst is attempting to quantify the unquantifiable. The second is that he may often ignore what may seem the most important variables in the problem. These objections are contradictory; the first suggests that economists have gone too far, the second that they have not gone far enough.

The first objection is sometimes formulated by saying that the economist has no right to set a value on human life, or on suffering, or health or creativity. This objection appears to be misconceived. It is not the economist, but society, which evaluates such matters; the economist can do little more than impose consistency on such social evaluations. As a variant of this objection some people, and particularly government officials, argue that consistency of evaluations is both practical and necessary within a single government department but it is neither practical nor necessary across departments. Certainly it is true that little cross-departmental reconciliation of, say, the value of human life, has been attempted. But it is arguable that movement in this direction is merely a matter of time.

The second objection, that the economist does not evaluate enough of the factors in any given problem, is partly a question of time and resources. It is partly, however, a question of waiting for society to make up its own mind on the appropriate evaluation to be given to various factors, like the preservation of natural beauty. The need for these decisions has been made more urgent by the work of the cost-benefit analyst but a clear and acceptable consensus has not yet emerged.

The present volume contains two papers – those by Professor Peacock and Professor Williams – which survey from particular points of view the question of the political acceptability and economic rationale of cost-benefit analysis. The differences in viewpoint in these papers, and between these papers and the present introduction, will give some indication of the present areas of agreement and disagreement among economists on these subjects.

2. THEORY

It will be seen from the general discussion above concerning the relationship between welfare economics and cost-benefit analysis how great a scope there is for the further sophistication of cost-benefit studies. Among other things, the treatment of monopolies, of government intervention, of shortages and of disequilibria might be mentioned. A further and pressing point lies in the translation of cost-benefit results from partial to general equilibrium systems. An example of this problem is provided in the present volume by the discussion by Christopher Foster of the treatment of taxation in the context of cost-benefit analysis. Taxation presumably has administrative costs and may have disincentive effects; in any event it is sure to meet political objection. These problems may perhaps be sensibly ignored in a partial equilibrium analysis of a small sector. But the effects of taxation can hardly be ignored when the economy as a whole is being considered.

There are many other difficult theoretical problems associated with cost-benefit analysis, some of which are touched on here. An example is the problem of uncertainty. To what extent is the uncertainty faced by the private firm or individual to be regarded as a social uncertainty? Some of the uncertainties which the private individual faces are in fact within the power of the government to determine and make definite. Thus the uncertainty faced by someone undertaking medical education may largely be the result of a private uncertainty concerning future government policy towards health care. The government itself may be uncertain to some degree about its plans and objectives in such an area. But the determination of its policy may lie largely within its own control. Therefore, the uncertainty facing the government appears to be less than that which a well-formed individual trainee must face.

This whole question of the treatment of uncertainty in cost-benefit analysis is considered in two papers in the present volume – those by Mr Corti and Dr Thomas. The first approaches the problem from the point of view of one concerned with the problem of dealing with uncertainty in the practical context of a policy-making department. The latter considers the theoretical possibilities which may emerge from the incorporation of certain modern statistical techniques into the approach of the cost-benefit analyst.

A further frontier area, treated in detail in the last paper in the present volume, by Messrs Mansfield and Watson, concerns the development of methods for the more detailed evaluation of certain consumer preferences not easily measured through the market. The paper concentrates upon the evaluation of the benefits from economies in travel time.

Once a general measure has been established for one variable, say travel time, a process necessarily and unavoidably gets under way in which refinements of the measure are developed. Thus we may ask the value of travel time to a rich and to a poor man; to someone on a long trip or a short; to one without a car; to men, to women and to children; and so on indefinitely. The problem here is not so much the conceptualisation of differing valuations as the development of reasonably unambiguous methods for eliciting the various values involved.

3. FIELDS AND AREAS

Perhaps the two most striking original fields of widely accepted application for cost benefit were in urban rapid transport and in the development of water resources. In Britain at least the area of practical application has grown enormously. The inter-urban road system has for several years now been subjected to a test of performance based on a crude cost-benefit calculation – Time and Accident Loss (TAL). The most extensive and far-reaching studies have, however, been in the fields of airport construction.

In the present volume, two new studies of cost benefit applied to airport situations are given. These studies by Professor Heath and Professor Walters show the cost-benefit analyst in two contrasting moods, and producing two strikingly different sets of results.

The extension of the area covered by cost-benefit analysis seems, at this point, to be merely a matter of time. The introduction of programme budgeting into all aspects of central and local government administration in the UK is proceeding rapidly. Programme budgeting is not itself directly related to cost-benefit analysis. In one form it merely involves the presentation of accounts, on a programme orientated basis rather than on the basis of traditional categories of expenditure. On the other hand it is observable that the re-structuring of accounts on a programme basis leads naturally to the comparison of alternative means of achieving the same objective, and to attempts to evaluate objectives themselves. Thus it leads naturally to the extension of work both in cost effectiveness and cost benefit.

Not all economists are agreed that cost benefit is suitable for extension into the most expensive fields of public expenditure: defence, education, health and social welfare. Nevertheless, a growing body of economic opinion does favour the analysis of programmes in these terms, at any rate in the health and education fields. It will be surprising if the movement in these directions does not gather momentum during the present decade.

The most difficult problems lie in the evaluation of research and technology. This subject is discussed in detail in one of the papers in the present volume (that by Mr Jones). In spite of the optimism therein expressed, however, some economists feel that the uncertainties involved in the evaluation of the outcomes of new research and development programmes are too great to make cost-benefit appraisal sufficiently reliable at this stage. The problem is not so much a conceptual one. It really is a quasi-political one; it is not clear whether it would be wise for cost-benefit analysis, in this early stage of its acceptance, to take upon itself the further difficulty of dealing with the imponderables of technological forecasting.

4. FRONTIERS

There are many possible ways forward for cost-benefit analysis. One exciting possibility, however, is that cost-benefit valuations will be combined with other objectives and other constraints in a total systems analysis.

A simple example of such a development might be given by a model in which the building of new roads was subject to a double set of criteria, e.g. that the cost-benefit balance be appropriate, and that the total capital outlay on road construction in any one year not exceed some fixed proportion of GNP.

Another possible line of development might arise out of the extension of cost-benefit analysis into a general equilibrium setting. Present practice usually treats each proposed piece of capital investment on the assumption that all other capital installations are fixed. This leads to the possibility that a road link between *A* and *B* is acceptable, on the assumption that there is no rail link; and a rail-link proposal on the assumption that there is no road. The danger that both would be started simultaneously, and that in the event the completed rail link and road link might prove to have been inappropriate because undertaken together, cannot be excluded. That such a simple case should occur may appear unlikely. But consider the case of a road, a railroad, a new town and a regional hospital centre: these might well give quite different results if studied together than when studied separately.

Efforts in these directions must, in the present state of the art, appear somewhat tentative and informal. Nevertheless, it is possible that work along these lines may in the end prove more rewarding than the elaborations and application of simple models. The present volume contains two papers which begin the exploration of these possibilities. The first, by Professor Blake, is concerned with the evaluation of industrial promotion policies in a regional context. The second, by Professor Beesley, is devoted to the evaluation of complex urban travel patterns.

The papers in the present volume were first delivered at a conference of British economists specialising in cost-benefit analysis held in the Department of Economics of the University of Edinburgh. Thanks are due to the University of Edinburgh for providing its facilities and support for the conference. Thanks are also due to the Nuffield Foundation for its support.

Part One

POLITICAL ECONOMY

2

Cost-benefit Analysis and the Political Control of Public Investment[1]

ALAN PEACOCK
Professor of Economics, University of York

1. INTRODUCTION

The purpose of this contribution is to attempt to identify the parts of cost-benefit analysis which may be regarded as properly the concern of those who have to make political decisions, principally the legislature. As I hope to show, the 'legitimate' area of political control of such analysis is much wider than is perhaps apparent from scrutiny of existing attempts to apply cost-benefit analysis in the field of public investment decisions.[2] In practice, however, if we were to assign all decisions relating to cost-benefit analyses with a political content to the legislature, the opportunity cost in the form of administrative delay, even to the confirmed champion of Parliamentary sovereignty, could be very high. Later I offer some illustrations of the kind of Parliamentary scrutiny of the use of cost-benefit analysis which might be both feasible and desirable.

It may help the discussion if some preliminary elaboration of the problem of the division of labour between the economist as cost-benefit technician and the political authorities is provided. The general criterion for evaluating a public investment project using benefit cost analysis is allocative efficiency, that is to say a change in gross national product is the sole measure of the change in social welfare. As we shall observe later, political judgement inevitably obtrudes itself into any evaluation of costs and benefits where the

[1] I owe a debt of gratitude to my colleagues Jack Wiseman and Alan Williams with whom I have discussed several of the points in this contribution. A preliminary discussion of some points discussed in section 4 may be found in Peacock and Wiseman[10, 11].

[2] It is assumed from now on that we are using the term 'cost-benefit analysis' to apply only to public investment appraisal, that is to say we use a restrictive definition. For a discussion of the problems of defining cost-benefit analysis, see Steiner[14, pp. 57–9].

outputs are collective goods. The main point to be made at this stage of the argument is of a different order, viz. that the use of allocative efficiency as a general criterion assumes that the relevant objective function of a single decision-making body contains only one argument. The implication of this assumption must be that the community through its political representatives is indifferent, for example, to the distribution of net benefits by income level and by region. Judging from reactions to recent publicised attempts at using cost-benefit analysis, e.g. in measuring the effects of barrages across West Coast estuaries and the siting of the third London airport, this does not seem realistic.[3] There are a number of ways in which income redistribution effects may be taken care of in cost-benefit analysis which do not directly concern us in this contribution (cf. Freeman[4], Weisbrod[17]), but these generally assume that the weights to be assigned to benefits accruing to income groups or regions are either inferred from political behaviour or reflect some judgement of a *central* decision-taking body. But cost-benefiteers may also have to become increasingly interested in situations in which account has to be taken of the evaluation of costs and benefits accruing to individuals from a regional or local point of view, especially if the regional or local authorities are going to be called upon to finance particular investment projects, e.g. slum clearance.

I hope that I have been able to show that the matters I wish to discuss are professionally interesting, but are they important? I believe they are. The employment of cost-benefit analysis, with its emphasis on efficient resource-use, does not necessarily appeal to politicians or to bureaucrats with a vested interest in particular spending programmes (cf. McKean[8] Ch. 2, Schlesinger[13]). If economists commit themselves to evaluation of projects in which they unwittingly or even consciously employ an arbitrary objective function of their own, they run the danger of having their technical competence called into question. This would be unfortunate at a moment when there is increasing, if grudging, acceptance of cost benefit analysis as a tool of economic policy.

2. PROCEDURE

Our analysis must proceed to define the division of labour, as it were,

[3] The income distribution effects of costs and benefits are explicitly considered, for example, in the cost-benefit analysis of alternative sites for London's third airport[2, paras. 1.22, 29.9].

between the decision-taking authorities and the analyst (see section 2 below). Before developing this analysis, I must draw attention to the interesting flow chart, which defines the respective roles of the analyst and decision taker in cost-benefit appraisal, devised by Walsh and Williams[16]. The approach developed in this paper has been stimulated by their procedure although the emphasis is different. There is one important omission in their analysis which I suspect is deliberate. No attempt is made to sub-divide the functions of the so-called 'decision-taker' between the legislature and the executive. However, if one assumes that the political system is a necessary mechanism for the expression of consumer choices where 'market failure' obtains, it seems to me essential to explore what institutional arrangements relevant to public investment decisions will reflect these choices, and what arrangements may be 'safely' left to the executive.

Following the argument in section 3, a review is made of some of the devices which might be employed by both the legislature and the executive in order to ensure that political judgements are explicitly shown in cost-benefit studies. In section 4 I try to develop some ideas on this subject originally put forward by Jack Wiseman and myself to the Committee on Procedure of the House of Commons[10]. Section 5 contrasts the conclusions of this study with an alternative approach to the economist's role in cost-benefit analysis.

3. DEFINING THE AREA OF POLITICAL JUDGEMENTS IN COST-BENEFIT ANALYSIS

Confining ourselves to the simple case where a single project, x, is being tested as to its admittance to a government investment programme, and given no budget constraint, one may write the relevant condition for its acceptance in an adaptation of the familiar Marglin formula[4]:

$$\left\{\sum_{i=1}^{N} \frac{B_i^x - C_i^x}{(1+r)^i}\right\} - \left\{aK^x\right\} \geqslant 0$$

where:

B_i^x = gross benefits accruing from project x in the ith period,

C_i^x = gross current costs of producing the benefits in the ith period,

[4] There are many variations on the statement of the objective function in cost-benefit appraisal and the one used is only adopted for analytical convenience. See Marglin[6, Chapter 2].

r = the social time preference rate (STP),
K^x = capital cost of project x (assumed here to be incurred at once),
N = amortisation period,
a = 'shadow price' of capital.

As is obvious, the left-hand expression represents present value of the marginal social net benefits accruing from the single project, and the right-hand side, its marginal social opportunity cost. Our task is to show how each part of a formula, which has all the appearance of being a purely technical device, requires a political or value judgement to be made in order to effect rational calculation. Let us dissect each portion of it in turn:

(i) '$B^x{}_i - C^x{}_i$'. Even if we accept at the outset that we are only concerned with the objective of maximising net benefits without regard to their distribution, it is soon found that the valuation of net benefits cannot be solely the concern of the economist. The presence of externalities usually means that there are no direct or indirect methods which enable a price tag to be attached to individual benefit and cost items. The only way in which expression can be given to valuation of externalities is through the political system. (Whether such a valuation does or could be made to reflect consumer sovereignty in the Paretian sense, is not pursued here, although this issue will crop up again.) The most that the economist can be expected to do in such circumstances is to indicate in any calculations what difference is made by the explicit valuation of externalities. Whether the taste of the horse will dominate that of rabbit in the horse-and-rabbit stew, to use Down's familiar analogy, will depend on the extent to which public investment projects provide final consumption benefits to consumers directly in the form of social goods or indirectly as intermediate goods supplied to private producers whose products are valued by the market. Public investment in human capital certainly has a strong flavour of horse about it. There is therefore a rational base to politicians' distrust of economists' claims that they can determine the optimal size of health, slum clearance and education programmes (cf. Downs[3]), even if politicians may disappear behind a smokescreen of platitudes when asked to specify what adjustment should be made to economic calculations. The economist's skill in cooking the stew is more in evidence when only 'scientifically prepared' rabbit without 'random horse' is the main constituent, i.e. when intermediate inputs provided by government investment in, say, irrigation, public utilities, and transport systems are being considered. Yet there must be a few cost-benefit appraisals which do not involve at least the addition to the stew of a sprinkling of essence of horse, if not horsemeat itself.

(ii) '*N*'. An investment project may have a physical life which is relatively easy to determine, but benefits may be affected by the possibility of obsolescence as a result of technological change. Unfortunately the timing and the extent of such change cannot be predicted with certainty. The treatment of uncertainty in cost-benefit analysis cannot be gone over in detail here, but for our purposes it need only be stated that it seems generally agreed that any valuation of net benefits in which uncertainty plays a major part can only proceed if information is available on the *attitude* of the political decision-maker towards uncertain outcomes. It is true that a major part can be played in guiding the decision-maker by setting out the consequences of obsolescence and other changes on the time stream of net benefits in a form which offers a useful appreciation of the risks. The final choice depends on the policy-maker's evaluation of the penalties imposed on the community by different magnitudes of errors in calculation (see Walsh and Williams[16] pp. 14–15). The ultimate decision-rule handed over to the analyst will commonly imply an instruction about the 'cut-off' point which will depend on his judgement as to the point beyond which uncertainty is so great that benefits at any prevailing rate of discount are best regarded as zero.

(iii) '$(1+r)^i$'. The choice of a rate to discount the time stream of net benefits is one of the crucial elements in investment appraisal in the public sector, and is still a matter for furious debate. We can avoid entering the lists by concentrating on one issue only – should public investment projects be discounted at a different rate from private projects? If so, then the choice of rate is a political decision. This is clearly the case when the Pigovian assumption is made that governments are more far-sighted than private individuals and are better judges of their welfare and that of future generations than they are themselves. However, even if an imposed solution is not acceptable, and the initial assumption is made that individuals' decisions must be reflected in choices made through the political as well as the market system, it is still possible to argue that a different rate of discount for public projects would be needed. Marglin[7] argues, for instance, that people may be concerned about the economic conditions of future generations (other than heirs) and may be willing to adjust their utility functions to allow for the marginal value of consumption to future generations, *provided that others will do the same* – christened by Hirschleifer the 'Christmas Clubs for the Future' argument! In other words, this interdependence of individual decisions confers on public investments designed to benefit those who as yet have no choice in the political process the characteristics of social goods. The social rate of discount or of time preference (STP) cannot therefore be derived from any set of private time preference rates, e.g. the 'real' rate at which individuals are prepared to lend, although this is not to say that, in principle, the STP cannot or should not be influenced by voters' pressure. It will be noted in passing that this line of argument suggests that the STP would be expected to be lower than private time preference rates, although all that need be established in order to support our general position is that the STP should be *different*, and can only 'emerge', as it were, through the political process.

(iv) 'aK^x'. The calculation of the shadow price of capital, a, in its simplified form can be expressed, following Marglin[6], as follows:

$$s(p/r)+(1-s) = a$$

where: s = marginal propensity to save of private sector,
p = opportunity cost rate of transfer of £1 from the private to the public sector,
r = the STP.

The fact that the STP is used to discount the yield of marginal private investments is all that we need in order to indicate that the final component of the benefit-cost formula contains a political judgement. It will be noted that if the government were to use the private rate of discount and the capital market was perfect so that the private rate of discount equalled p, then the opportunity cost of capital would be independent of the sources of finance, i.e. foregone private investment and foregone consumption and the shadow price of capital, a, would equal unity. The importance of the political judgement which fixes STP lies in the fact that the opportunity cost per £ of resources withdrawn from private use will no longer equal £ and will generally exceed £.

So far we have been able to show that political choices enter into every part of the objective function in cost-benefit analysis without having to complicate it by introducing distributional criteria. However, if distributional effects of costs and benefits affect the value of the social welfare function, by the same token, we cannot ignore the distributional effects of the financial methods used to transfer resources from the private sector. If distributional benefits are taken account of by the use of a system of weights for incremental changes in income produced by methods of finance which require compulsory deductions from income (see Musgrave[9]). There are plenty of difficult tasks for the economist to perform in measuring the incidence of benefits and costs and of the taxes to finance projects, but his particular expertise offers no guidance on the weighting system to be adopted.

4. THE ROLE OF THE LEGISLATURE IN COST-BENEFIT DECISIONS

The evaluation of externalities, the choice of 'cut-off' period, the choice of STP rate, and the weighting of the distribution of net benefits and opportunity costs of finance – this is a formidable list of 'political' components found in an appraisal of public investment projects. Further, if these decisions were to be taken directly by some sovereign political body designed to further, in Wicksell's phrase, 'the practical realisation of the principle of voluntary consent and unanimity'[18] or the political conditions which reflect consumer sovereignty, one would be forced to examine and probably to suggest major changes in our electoral system, Parliamentary voting procedures, not to speak of designing objective functions used in investment project appraisal. Like the greedy boy who fell into a barrel of ice-cream, I do not feel equal to the occasion, however interesting it would be to try to up-date Wicksell's[18] famous attempt to design a budgetary procedure which represented a fair approximation to a pricing system for public goods. The aim of this section is much more modest, namely to propose some alterations in Parliamentary and Executive procedures, without implying major constitutional changes, but which will reveal to the public at large what political decisions are being used to guide cost-benefit analysis and who is taking them.

Such an attempt is in line with recent proposals made by the Select Committee on Procedure in its First Report[5] published in July 1969 which expressed particular concern at the lack of the development of financial procedures commensurate with the growing forward commitment entered into in government expenditures, particularly of a capital nature, and the lack of opportunity for informed public debate of forward estimates (HC 410, paras. 8 and 9, p. vii). Looking more particularly at public investment projects, it stated that the House of Commons 'should be informed of the results of analyses undertaken by the Government to show their view of the costs and benefits to individuals and to the community of particular programmes or projects such as raising the school-leaving age, or constructing the Channel Tunnel or the third London Airport – and it should know what assumptions have been made in these cost/benefit studies. Again on public investment, the House should increasingly have information so that, in addition to other considerations, it can weigh the value of benefits expected to arise in the more or less distant future – against the alternative of higher consumption and a higher standard of living now. In other words, it should be able to consider such matters as the "discount rate" applied in drawing up public investment plans'. (HC 410, para. 18, pp. x–xi).

In order to give effect to these proposals, among others, the Committee made some general recommendations on financial procedure which recognise that the present estimates procedure of the House of Commons is, to quote the famous US Congressional watchdog, Senator Proxmire, 'a classic example of an *inexplicit*, *closed*, and *uninformed* decision process' [italics his] ([5], p. vi). The House of Commons is presented before the budget with an annual projection of government expenditure over a number of years followed by the detailed estimates for individual departments. There is no supporting information showing how estimates are arrived at, for example through project evaluation, although at odd times throughout the financial year the House may receive documentation on individual cost-benefit studies but with no clear indication when these are presented or at a later date how they have been embodied in the Estimates, if at all. The Committee does not offer precise recommendations about procedure for the presentation of cost-benefit studies for scrutiny, but does recommend that the present Estimates Committee should be turned into a Select Committee on Expenditure, which would be served with a series of eight Sub-Committees of a 'functional' character. What this means is that each sub-committee would look at a particular area of government 'output', e.g. Education, but this would not limit their scrutineering to the activities of one government Department. Appraisal of cost-benefit techniques would presumably come under the rubric of enquiry into 'effectiveness of management' (HC 410, paras. 30–5).

As in the analysis of PPB systems by the Joint Economic Committee of Congress, the detailed investigation of public expenditure would impose a high opportunity cost on members of the legislature. Senator Proxmire deserves further quotation on this problem:

'Many in the legislative branch have little interest or patience for careful deliberations on budgetary matters. The careful consideration of alternatives requires much effort and concentrated study of the relative merits and demerits, the costs and the gains, of alternative policy proposals. This is hard and grubby work' ([5] p. vii). A member of the House of Commons conducting his own cost-benefit analysis with a view to advancing his political career may be even less certain than a member of Congress about investment in Select Committee membership. Given the separation of powers, great political prestige and power attaches to membership of the main Congressional Committees. While it is not unknown for politicians in the UK to win respect and possibly office, in part because they have invested their time in developing a special expertise through Committee work, they must clearly tread very warily if they are members of the party in power, in case their enthusiasm leads them to be over-critical of their Ministerial confrères.

There is an additional problem presented by more active participation in expenditure scrutiny through Committees. The Committees' efforts will be of no avail if time is not allowed for the debate by the Whole House of their findings as part of the 'budget cycle' of events. The Select Committee were obviously uncertain about the practical possibilities of this (HC 410, para. 31), and, given the continuance of the enormous pressure of Parliamentary business, it seems doubtful that any government is going to allot a large amount of further time for critical discussion of its own proposals or even that ordinary members with no special interest in financial matters will want to make further concessions which could restrict their opportunities for making their political mark. It is significant that the first debate held on the new projections of Government Expenditure prepared by the Treasury was of a high order, but few members were present.

Finally, the Select Committee put its finger on a problem which has troubled the Joint Economic Committee of Congress for many years – the availability of technical staff to offer an independent technical assessment of the expenditure proposals under Parliamentary scrutiny. At the time it reported, there were only ten clerks serving the five main Select Committees, although from time to time specialist advisers have been appointed to assist their work. It has become increasingly the practice to invite outside specialists to give written and oral evidence. Nevertheless, the expansion in the activities of the proposed Select Committee on Expenditure presupposes a concomitant increase in technical staff, and it must be agreed that it is difficult to see how the Committee could operate efficiently without them. It is a significant commentary on the state of Government financial procedure that whereas *ex-ante* appraisal of government expenditure is conducted with the help of such slender resources, *ex-post* control by the Exchequer and Audit Department headed by the Comptroller and Auditor-General, a Parliamentary official, requires a staff of about 500. No wonder the Committee asks rather wistfully in its First Report whether some of them might have their knowledge and experience put at its disposal.

I have devoted some space to commenting on the Select Committee's Report both in order to demonstrate the growing awareness in our legislature of the need to keep abreast with modern methods of investment appraisal in the public sector and also the extent of the Committee's demand for participation in the decision-making process. There is no suggestion in their recommendations that financial procedure should be substantially altered, for example by debating and voting on alternative expenditure proposals to those found in the Estimates which might follow from the proposed Select Committee on Public Expenditure's own cost-benefit appraisals. But even if Cabinet government and thus a tight and swift financial procedure is left intact, a minor concession to a belief in democratic government would require not only that Parliament is made aware how cost-benefit analyses are carried out, and how political judgements are embodied in them, but also have an assurance that these political judgements, whoever is delegated to make them, *are known to and are approved by the Government.*

One obvious step towards meeting this 'rule' would be the preparation of an Official Handbook on Cost-Benefit Procedure, available like the fully-documented volume on *National Income Statistics* to the interested public, and containing as precise guidance as is possible at this stage of our knowledge of techniques and examples of their application. This presupposes, of course, that the terms of reference for cost-benefit investigations also offer instructions on the political assumptions to be used or specify the ways in which alternative political assumptions might be made. Apparently, while this is an obvious step, it would also be a large one. It clearly requires that cost-benefit analysis is an acceptable tool of policy and this, as I have emphasised, is itself a political decision. It also requires that cost-benefit techniques are mandatory on all government Departments and are consistently applied. It is clear from the evidence presented by the Treasury and other witnesses to the Select Committee that we are a long way from meeting these requirements. One major difficulty to which attention is repeatedly drawn in contemporary discussion is the considerable cost of cost-benefit studies themselves!

There is one political judgement which, in my view, is so fundamental that I would attach some importance to explicit Parliamentary approval for it. This is the choice of a social discount rate. It will be recalled that in the passage quoted from the First Report of the Select Committee on Procedure, the Committee specifically ask to be able to consider the rate. It seems to me that it is not sufficient for Parliament simply to be able to know what the STP is and how it is arrived at, but that any change in the rate should be subject to Parliamentary sanction. This could be done very simply and without major delay if a change in rate required presentation of delegated legislation to Parliament, as does a change in the Fiduciary Issue of the Bank of England. It is perhaps no more than a symbolic gesture, but it enables limited debate of a change in STP to take place *before* it is operative[5] and therefore gives advance warning of a policy change rather than place the onus on a specialist Committee of the House to find out for itself when and why the rate has been changed.

CONCLUSION

I would not claim in this contribution that I have done anything more than spell out in some detail what is well known, viz. that government investment appraisal through cost-benefit analysis embodies important value judgements, although perhaps the attempt I have made to draw the appropriate implications for political procedures and rules may be less familiar and even mildly interesting.

I need to stress again that I have written this piece on the assumption that judgements about welfare, if they are to follow principles of Pareto optimality, require that where decisions cannot be taken through the market, we need to consider rather carefully what kind of political arrangements will approximate to the expression of *individual* choices about the allocation of resources. This approach is not necessarily acceptable to all economists.

I should like to quote at length a revealing passage from one of the accepted authorities:

[5] The appropriate statutory instrument would appear to be a Treasury Order sanctioned by an Act of Parliament which would be subject to 'negative procedure', i.e. the Order would automatically have the force of law after forty days unless amendment of the Order were called for. See Sir Bernard Cocks[1, Chapter XXII].

'The choice of maximand and constraints involves value judgments. Once a particular problem has to be faced, any reluctance to make value judgments will thus prevent the achievement of any solution at all. Hence either the economist or his employer simply has to make them, specifying maximand and constraints. (The economist will lose his job if he merely spouts highbrow agnosticism for more than the minimum period of time necessary to preserve his self-respect.)

My personal feeling is that the value judgments made by economists are, by and large, better than those made by non-economists! I therefore suggest that in most cases the economist should try to formulate maximand and at least some constraints himself and explain to his employer why he should accept them. Failing this, his job is to translate his employer's loosely formulated ideas into precise terms and demonstrate their implications.

My assertion about value judgments is not as arrogant as it sounds. For one thing, it applies only to the sort of value judgments involved in public investment decisions, and even here it does not apply to all of them . . . The point is simply that the people who are experienced at systematic thinking about a problem are usually those who make the best judgments about it. Thus, whatever their theory of aesthetics, most people are prepared in practice to accept the judgment of an art critic about the merits of a painting' (Turvey[15]).

Although coloured by a disarming frankness, Turvey's self-confessed philistinism does not appeal to me. There is an obvious flaw in his argument, and, for all its claim to offer practical wisdom, I do not believe it will help us keep our jobs. Why should economists, who may agree on the technical desiderata of cost-benefit analysis, share the same value judgements? If they disagree, why should any politician believe that any particular economist 'experienced in systematic thinking' should offer better political choices than his own? Certainly the translation of these choices into magnitudes, e.g. the weighting of benefits to income groups, which are reflected in a cost-benefit calculation is a technical matter for the economist, but this does not require him to masquerade as the fountain of wisdom for that which is good for other people. Even if his employer is uncertain of the correct political judgement to make, he may be better helped by a demonstration of the effects on any calculation of making alternative assumptions for the values of the political variables.

If I thought that Turvey's view was generally accepted by the Executive and Parliament, I do not think it would take me long to convince them that the economist was assuming their functions, but I think I have given sufficient evidence in the previous section to show that such a task of persuasion is unnecessary. In the prevailing climate of political opinion, economists would serve their profession better by seeing themselves as efficient management consultants rather than by deluding themselves that they will be publicly acclaimed as 'philosopher kings'.

REFERENCES

[1] Sir Bernard Cocks, *Erskine May's Parliamentary Procedure*. XVIIth Edition.

[2] Commission on the Third London Airport. *Papers and Proceedings*, vol. VII, HMSO, 1970.

[3] Anthony Downs, Comment on Jerome Rothenberg's Urban Renewal Programs, in Robert Dorfman (Editor), *Measuring Benefits of Government Investments*, Brookings Institution, 1965; London, George Allen & Unwin Ltd.

[4] A. Myrick Freeman III, Income distribution and planning for public investment, *American Economic Review*, June, 1967.

[5] Joint Economic Committee of US Congress, *The Analysis and Evaluation of Public Expenditures*: *The PPB System*, vol. 1, US Government Printing Office, 1969.

[6] Stephen Marglin, *Public Investment Criteria*, London, 1967.

[7] Stephen Marglin, The social rate of discount and the optimal rate of investment, *Quarterly Journal of Economics*, February, 1963.

[8] Roland N. McKean, *Public Spending*, New York, 1968.

[9] Richard A. Musgrave, Cost benefit and the theory of public finance, *Journal of Economic Literature*, September, 1969.

[10] Alan Peacock and Jack Wiseman, Measuring the efficiency of government expenditure. In A. R. Prest (Editor), *Public Sector Economics*, Manchester, 1968.

[11] Alan Peacock and Jack Wiseman, The economics of public expenditure and its consequences for parliamentary control, Appendix 2 of [12].

[12] Select Committee on Procedure, Session 1968–9, *First Report: Scrutiny of Public Expenditure and Administration*, House of Commons Paper 410, 23 July 1969.

[13] James R. Schlesinger, Systems analysis and the political process, *Journal of Law and Economics*, 1967.

[14] Peter Steiner, *Public Expenditure Budgeting*, Brookings Institution, 1969.

[15] Ralph Turvey, Present value versus internal rate of return – an essay in the theory of third best, *Economic Journal*, March 1963.

[16] H. G. Walsh and Alan Williams, *Current Issues in Cost-Benefit Analysis*, CAS Occasional Papers No. 11, HMSO, 1969.

[17] Burton A. Weisbrod, Income redistribution effects and benefit-cost analysis, In Samuel B. Chase Jr (Editor), *Problems in Public Expenditure Analysis*, Brookings Institution, 1968; London, George Allen & Unwin Ltd.

[18] Knut Wicksell, A new principle of just taxation, translated in Richard A. Musgrave and Alan Peacock (Editors), *Class in the Theory of Public Finance*, London, 1958.

3

Cost-benefit Analysis: Bastard Science? And/Or Insidious Poison in the Body Politick?

ALAN WILLIAMS

Professor of Economic Theory, University of York

1. INTRODUCTION

In the booming business of management consultancy there is no shortage of glossily packaged analytical techniques of varying degrees of power and reliability being peddled to ill-informed clients by pushful salesmen. My own early activities in this field produced a *cri du cœur* which deserves wider circulation than it has hitherto received, not only for its literary merit in the field of satirical doggerel (well up to the standards of W. S. Gilbert), but also for its aptness to a situation that is likely to be with us for some little time yet. By reproducing it here I hope that I may inspire some latter-day Arthur Sullivan to set it to music!

The Management Consultant's Lament

We showed them how to maximise the Branch's optimality,
How micro-economics had become a stern reality;
They listened with politeness but preferred their old autonomy,
Their faulty input-budgeting and massive diseconomy.
Evaluative charting could not penetrate their fallacies;
They could not see the logic of cost-benefit analysis;
Their data-handling system was in urgent need of focussing;
They had not learned the rudiments of information-processing.
Their output was unprogrammed, their retrieval rate was minimal;
Their information-network was so crude as to be criminal;
We gave them multi-access on a scheme multi-dimensional:
Their coldness was so cutting that it might have been intentional.
Our trees and algorithms were rejected with acidity;
It really is heartbreaking to encounter such stupidity.
If cybernetic doctrine cannot change their methodology,

Can't they at least be men enough to learn the terminology?

J. M. Ross
Home Office

(*O & M Bulletin*, vol. 23, No. 1, February, 1968)

Cost-benefit analysis is one of the techniques most prone to misunderstanding and misapplication in the hands of the uninitiated (not to mention the unscrupulous!). Fritz Machlup[1] has identified the following five connotations of the term 'benefit cost comparison'.

'Type No. 1. is the implicit sentiment, sans analysis, in favour of the particular project . . . Everyone with a favourite project will, when asked, assert that "of course" the benefits from it are greater than the costs . . . even if they have neither theoretical arguments nor empirical data to support such contentions.

Type No. 2, may be seen in explicit propositions about the *value* of the program, in which you impose your own value judgements upon the people of the commonwealth . . . though you do not care to say why, or to defer or refer to the opinions of others.

Type No. 3. is . . . an assumption that you and others know what society wants, what kinds of benefits it may derive from the program, and how big these benefits are. There is still no analysis, but the assumption appears to be moving closer to matters that deserve to be taken seriously.

Type No. 4. is based on theoretical analysis, where you at least state what kind of empirical information you would need to make a calculation or an estimate of the benefits and costs . . .

Type No. 5. is the actual calculation of benefits and costs in which all or much of the required information is available and analysed . . .' (pp. 150–1).

It needs to be made clear from the outset that I reserve use of the term 'cost-benefit analysis' (or CBA for brevity) to exercises of types 4 and 5, not because I object to the authoritarian/paternalistic aspects of type 3, but because I regard the crucial feature as being *explicit and formal analysis*,[1] which is still absent from type 3.

In this paper I shall argue that CBA is a natural and logical extension of systems analysis (SA), operations research (OR), and cost-effectiveness analysis (CEA), but more ambitious than them in evaluative scope and technique, and hence rather more vulnerable

[1] The qualification 'explicit and formal' is necessary here to establish a distinction from implicit and informal analysis by largely intuitive judgemental processes.

at certain (well-recognised) points. I shall then review some of the criticisms of CBA emanating from political scientists, and argue that although some of them are based on misconceptions, others are perfectly valid. Unfortunately, the valid criticisms are applicable *a fortiori* to the only alternative techniques of analysis, and all too often the argument appears to degenerate from attempts to replace poor analysis by better, to assertions that since analysis is difficult, costly and troublesome we should abandon it! It is not a conclusion I can share.

2. BASTARD SCIENCE?

Yes.

(*a*) *Is CBA different?*

I take the objective of CBA to be to assist choice (not to *make* choice, nor to *justify* past choice, nor yet to *delay* matters so that some previously chosen course of action has a greater chance of adoption, although I recognise that each of these purposes *may* also be served by the skilful employment of CBA).

There are many other techniques which also serve this same purpose, so it is necessary here to identify what (if anything) distinguishes CBA from them. Some of them are mainly concerned with the systematic exploration of what might be termed 'technical possibilities', where 'systematic' connotes being orderly and comprehensive in search, explicit in procedures, and quantitative rather than qualitative in mode of measurement. The system which is the focus of interest is 'described' or 'simulated' or 'modelled' at some level of abstraction, and the effects of various feasible changes in any controllable variable (or input) are then explored with respect to the behaviour (or output) of the system. The inputs and outputs represent the points of contact between the system and its environment, which implies that we are dealing with open systems, which in turn raises problems about defining the boundaries of the system (or of 'the problem space'). Inputs need not be commensurable with each other neither do they need outputs, nor, *a fortiori*, need inputs be commensurable with outputs. Much of the work conducted within the natural sciences and engineering, and much systems analysis and even some operations research, fall within this category, which economists would regard as logically prior (and essential) to their own role in the analytical process.

What separates this group of techniques *in principle* from the next group, is that the former are positive in orientation, rather than prescriptive. Such analyses are designed to facilitate understanding, proceeding via prediction or hypothesis tested by experiment and/or observation, with variables chosen and measured primarily so as to facilitate monitoring and replication, with suitability for manipulation for policy purposes playing a subsidiary role. When this policy manipulation becomes the central purpose of the analysis, we move more firmly into the acknowledged territory of operations research, and although in practice the differences in substance between the two kinds of exercise tend to shade off into each other in almost imperceptible gradations, this 'consultative' role needs to be regarded as something different from the 'purely scientific' role. But still it will be common to find little commensurability within or between inputs and outputs, though in applications in the field of business and governmental activities OR tends to accept as a limited basis for establishing commensurability the money values of any inputs or outputs which are conventionally so valued. But since other significant inputs and/or outputs will typically remain outside the realm of conventional financial evaluation, the result will be what is commonly called 'cost-effectiveness' analysis (CEA), 'cost' embracing all those items valued in money terms (usually inputs) and 'effectiveness' some multidimensioned pay-off exhibited without any attempt at further evaluation in commensurable terms.

The characteristic of the third group of techniques (to which cost-effectiveness studies already partly belong) is that while they too are prescriptively oriented (i.e. designed to help a client improve his situation), they try hard to render inputs and outputs commensurable. Thus the 'ideal' CBA will have all inputs and outputs evaluated in money terms (which, it should be stressed, is *not* the same as evaluating them all at market prices), though in principle any other common unit would serve equally well (e.g. years of life-expectation, utils, cowrie shells). But since it is unlikely that any but the most low-level CBA will, in the foreseeable future, succeed in evaluating all inputs and outputs in commensurable terms, the distinction between *actual* CBA and *actual* CEA will only be a matter of *degree* (and, on occasion, perhaps only a matter of *intent*).

There is one other bias distinguishing CBA from its nearest relative, CEA, which is not, as far as I can see, a matter of principle, but rather a matter of custom, generated by the differing temperaments (and cultural environments) of the respective practitioners. CEA has been dominated by mathematicians, engineers and natural scientists, and the mores of this group have laid stress on tackling only those problems where there is a good chance that quantitative analysis of existing data will point the way to immediate improvements in performance. In his survey of Operations Research, Dorfman[2] quotes one OR authority[3] in the following terms:

> 'The function of the operations research team is to assist the responsible authority of an organisation by clarifying those uncertainties in the factors on which action is based, and *only* those, which can be clarified by scientific study . . . best results will be obtained if the scientist meticulously avoids the evaluation of intangibles.'

The practitioners of CBA tend to be more ambitious, and are willing, nay anxious, to bring into systematic comparison (via 'the measuring rod of money') a much wider range of phenomena (e.g. time, life-expectation, noise and other amenity considerations) than a CEA would so treat (though they might well be mentioned, or even quantified in a CEA study, but not evaluated).

The other feature which is mentioned by Prest and Turvey[4] as a characteristic of CBA is the stress laid on 'looking at repercussions in the further, as well as the nearer, future', i.e. taking a 'long' view as well as a 'wide' one. I think that this is merely a reflection of the fact that CBA has mainly been applied to investment projects, and it is the nature of these applications which has required CBA to be moulded into the form of an investment appraisal technique, with rather long time horizons. This is certainly an important and valuable feature, but it is not inherent in the approach (as Prest and Turvey well recognise, for they observe that CBA 'can also be applied to proposed changes in laws or regulations, to new pricing schemes, and the like'). However, one of the major intellectual differences between economists and others seems to lie in the handling of time-streams of inputs and outputs, and hence the basis and role of the discount rate in CBA has proved to be an important issue, and there is no doubt that *in practice* this represents a great gulf between CBA and much CEA for even when the latter has had an important investment aspect, its practitioners have tended to accept uncritically rates of interest which have little real relevance to the problem at hand.[2]

[2] The dominance of immediate financial considerations in selecting an interest rate even in areas of long-term economic planning is well documented in *Economic Analysis of Public Investment Decisions: Interest Rate Policy and Discounting Analysis*, Hearing Before the Sub-Committee on Economy in Government of the Joint Economic Committee of the U.S. Congress, 30, 31 July and 1 August, 1968, U.S. Government Printing Office, Washington D.C., 1968.

I therefore conclude that CBA accepts, and pushes further, the scientists' preoccupation with quantification already central to OR, and pushes much further down the path already trodden by CEA towards evaluation of inputs and outputs in money terms, tending at the same time to enlarge the scope of the inputs and outputs that are brought within the area of systematic comparison.

(*b*) *Is CBA scientific?*

I do not much care for the use of the word 'scientific' in this context, because of its emotional and prejudicial overtones. I prefer to achieve what I think questioners may have in mind by asking a series of related questions:

(*a*) Is CBA systematic?
(*b*) Is CBA objective?
(*c*) Is CBA precise?

I shall offer only brief answers to these questions at this stage, but they recur in various guises in the subsequent discussion. As usual one is in the dilemma of offering answers at two levels: what is true *in principle* (and hence could conceivably be true in practice one day) and what is true *in practice* (given the present state of knowledge).

In principle, CBA *is* systematic, it imposes discipline, it requires assumptions to be explicit and evidence to be presented, it is communicable, replicable, and relies on types of evidence and analytical methods which can be challenged, validated or rejected by others in a manner consistent with the norms set by the 'scientific' sub-culture of our society. *In practice*, of course, one may find slipshod, incompetent, or dishonest, work which grossly violates these norms, and even the best studies are likely to fall short of perfection from a pure methodological viewpoint due to inadequacy of analytical resources (human and material).

Whether or not it is 'objective' is a tougher question to answer. The simple answer is 'no', both in principle and in practice, because no systematic method of analysis can be entirely culture-free, hence all are value-loaded to some extent. This is a hazard to which social science is more prone than natural science, and from which economics is certainly not exempt. *In principle* CBA is an attempt to apply the tenets of theoretical welfare economics to actual decision-making, and therefore contains within it all the methodological difficulties identified in that area of study. To take but one major instance, the use of CBA in the public sector is directed at judging whether one social state is or is not to be preferred to another. One need only glance at the literature of welfare economics[5] to be reminded that what appear at first sight to be relatively straightforward judgements about 'better' or 'worse' (e.g. judgements about the welfare implications of increased GNP per head) entail

(*a*) either postulating no conflict of interest between the affected parties, or very strong assumptions about the possibility and nature of interpersonal comparisons of utility (including the absence of that peculiar interdependence phenomenon known as envy);
(*b*) all the well-known difficulties in inferring anything conclusive from partial equilibrium analysis of a movement from one non-ideal situation to another;
(*c*) a relative ignorance (and consequent neglect) of the dynamics of economic systems;
(*d*) a tendency to concentrate undue attention upon the 'economic aspects' of problems (like the family income) at the expense of 'non-economic' aspects (like marital strife).

Just as Hamlet chided:

> 'There are more things in heaven and earth, Horatio,
> Than are dreamt of in your philosophy',

so there is no dearth of economists (not to mention lesser breeds!) ready to remind the humbler and less philosophical practitioners of CBA such as me that there is more to social policy than economics.[3] It is, of course, a weak form of defence to answer an accusation by saying 'everybody knows that', but it is the only honest answer to give in this situation. It is, however, stronger than it seems at first sight, because (i) methodological foundations that have been laid bare and discussed are safer things on which to build than those which have not yet been scrutinised, because one is aware of the risks one is taking, and (ii) no one to my knowledge has yet offered the world anything that has survived comparable scrutiny any better.

As to the third question – 'Is CBA precise?' – the answer *in principle* is 'yes, so far as the issues raised in the preceding paragraph allow', and the answer *in practice* is 'yes, so far as the data allow'. To this it may be retorted that in neither case is this 'so far' in fact very far at all, and since they are both rather severely constraining re-

[3] In the *Readings* cited in[5], the contribution by J. R. Hicks on pp. 95–9 is a brief and forthright example.

strictions this leaves us with little or no room for progress. Moreover, it might well be added, such is the strength of the influence of the scientific sub-culture within our society, that quantifiable things tend to take precedence over non-quantifiable things, and hence undue weight tends to be given to the insignificant things that CBA is able to measure with precision, while the crucial unmeasurables get neglected. One may regretfully concede this likelihood, yet still disagree as to what should be done about it. Those temperamentally and/or culturally hostile to quantification will conclude that CBA and all its works should be damned as creations of the devil, and exorcised from the 'body politick' (of which more anon), whilst those of the opposite persuasions will see it as good reason for pressing on as fast as possible with the quantification of the currently unquantifiable. Resolution of this conflict seems to me to be a deep-seated psychological and philosophical problem on which I am not competent to comment further, though I am willing to stand up and be counted amongst the quantifiers.

If forced to go back and answer the question as originally posed – 'Is CBA scientific?' I would reply guardedly 'As much as most social science, and much more than some'. But this is a theme I shall return to later.

(*c*) *The modus operandi of CBA*

In order to explore further the strength and weaknesses of CBA let us look more closely at its modus operandi, and compare it with other systematic techniques of analysis, notably systems analysis (SA) and OR.

In order to structure this discussion along lines which facilitate that comparison, I shall start with an extended quotation from Dorfman's survey of OR cited earlier, where he writes of the role of OR in business and economic administration:

> 'If an experienced operations analyst were asked to describe the problem he would most like to meet, I suspect that he would mention four characteristics: first, the objective of the operation should be clearly defined, second, the operation should be describable by a reasonably manageable model, third, the data required for estimating the parameters of the model should be readily obtainable, and fourth, current operating practice should leave plenty of room for improvement . . .' [2, pp. 64/5].

On each of these points he comments:

'... With a little care to assure that the objective function does not conflict with higher-level goals and that the measure of cost is appropriate, the definition of objectives should present little difficulty at the operating levels. More trouble is likely to occur at the executive levels, where decisions are likely to have widespread and incommensurable ramifications ...' [p. 65].

'Model building is the analyst's primary skill and contribution, and he cannot expect when he approaches a problem to find that his work has already been done for him. Thus the question is ... whether a model ... can be built in a reasonable time. The answer depends basically on whether or not the problem involves kinds of relationship that have not been established by previous scientific study ...

When he encounters such a gap the operations analyst has a choice of three options: he can proceed on the basis of a bold conjecture, he can undertake the substantive research necessary to fill the gap or he can abandon the problem as unsolvable at the current state of knowledge ... A bold conjecture is refreshing, but an insubstantial foundation for an important decision. Abandoning the project is manifestly distasteful. Undertaking fundamental research entails the usual hazard that it may not be successful, plus an unwelcome delay in arriving at a useful recommendation' (pp. 65–6).

'The third characteristic ... will be satisfied most adequately by repetitious, even routine, types of operation. If the problem being studied is non-repetitive even the statistical outlook is more doubtful, since ... statistics require a population from which a sample can be drawn ... The ... operating decisions are much less likely than broad policy and strategy decisions to be *sui generis*' (pp. 67–8).

'The final characteristic ... unfortunately works somewhat in opposition to the first three. If an operation is repetitive, well-recorded, intended to serve a well-defined goal and of a kind in which the influences of decisions on the attainment of the goal do not transcend available technical knowledge, then it is not likely that current practice will fall far short of the most efficient practice attainable ...

'... The major exception to this conclusion is problems of adapting to new circumstances or of employing novel techniques or instruments . . . An optimal situation for operations research is one in which conditions are changing too rapidly for experience to be assimilated by informal, unsystematic methods, but slowly enough to permit the formulation of a model applicable to both the recent past and relevant future, and to permit the accumulation of the data needed for estimating the parameters of the model.

On the other hand, considerable room for improvement may remain even under fairly stable technological conditions . . . The explanation in that instance probably lay in the numerousness and the complexity of the decision variables, which precluded efficient exploration of possibilities by unsystematic means' (pp. 68–9).

'The foregoing summarises the circumstances in which operations research is likely to be successful in the sense of disclosing significantly improved policies and practices. But operations research can be successful in other senses also. We have the educative value of collaborating with an analyst and looking at the problem from his viewpoint. We have seen that operations research often suggests and sometimes accomplishes valuable substantive research. In many instances the contribution . . . is to improve the planning process itself, without improving the quality of the plans . . .' (pp. 69–70).

'Finally, consider the really tough and important problems where there is no objective basis for making a usefully precise evaluation of the consequences of possible actions or policies. Contending with such imponderables is the primary responsibility of the high executive, a responsibility that cannot be delegated . . . Nevertheless, an operations research study of such a problem can help the executive by organising the data, focussing the issues, bringing out the implications of possible assumptions and hunches, delimiting the range of the inevitable uncertainty. Any detached, analytic, sceptical viewpoint can help clarify such problems, and the analyst has such a viewpoint to contribute' (pp. 70–1).

Most of those observations are equally apt as comments on the role of CBA, but because of the drive to push valuations further, and the tendency to broaden the scope of the analysis beyond the confines regarded as optimal within the OR culture, CBA finds itself persistently in the terrain which Dorfman regards as the more difficult. There is one other important feature of OR work which Dorfman surprisingly omits to mention, and which is even more characteristic of CBA, namely, that 'the problem' is not usually formulated at all clearly in the analyst's brief, and that he may well need to expend a sizeable chunk of time and effort discovering what it actually is, and getting it into an analysable shape. Over and over again one hears of cases where the problem the clients thought they had turned out not to be the problem they actually had, and any OR or CBA practitioner who accepts the client's initial formulation of the problem uncritically is heading for disaster.

This leads naturally into the vexed issue of 'objectives' and 'constraints', to which I cannot possibly do justice here. Although expressed in a form which suggests that they are concerned only with the limits of 'feasibility', 'constraints' are in principle to be interpreted as objectives cast in a form which gives them overriding priority over the variables that are actually *called* 'objectives'. 'Objectives' cast in the form of minimum target levels of performance are of precisely the same ilk as 'constraints', except that analysis is permitted to proceed with a view to discovering whether or not they can be satisfied (and if so, in what ways), whereas it is implied that no solution falling foul of a feasibility constraint (be it technological, legal, administrative, moral, political or budgetary) is worth analysing further at all. If one had faith in the capacity of the client to think through the full implications of these ostensible constraints, there would be no need to be sceptical about accepting them without discussion, but if a client had such a capacity it is unlikely that he would need an analyst anyway, so it seems to me that part of the dialogue about the nature of the problem, and about the objectives of the decision makers, must give comparable attention to the reasoning behind (and purposes served by) the postulated constraints. Even then, a counsel of perfection would be that all such constraints should be varied parametrically in order to indicate the effect on the various outcomes of shifting the boundaries of the problem, for this might well indicate that the next round of effort might more profitably be expended on extending one of the supposed 'feasibility' limits, or that others are so trivial in their impact that there is no point in expending resources to prevent them becoming more stringent.

An important and often neglected dimension in problem definition is determining who constitutes the relevant community with respect to the appraisal in question. If limited narrowly to the direct impact on the client (or client organisation) the analyst is likely to miss 'externalities' which may feed back through the system at large and affect the client indirectly (but still significantly), e.g. the generation of noise or other forms of pollution may generate countermeasures which could prove more costly than reducing the pollution in the first place but which in any event should be included in the initial analysis. More difficult still is the situation in which the client is a governmental agency which is ostensibly pursuing the interests of the community at large, and which may be confronted with difficult decisions like whether foreigners are part of the 'community at large' when determining airport location policy, or what weight consumers' interests should be given *vis-à-vis* those of producers (an acute problem for departments such as Technology and Agriculture . . . not to mention the UGC!). Because I can see little scope for incorporating redistributive or 'grand efficiency' considerations[6] in the analysis in any acceptable systematic manner at present, I would be content to see incidence calculations merely appended as exhibits to each appraisal, leaving the client to incorporate these as best he can, though I am sure there is plenty of scope for fruitful dialogue as to the principles which underlie his judgements, and eventually we should be able to discuss and analyse these too.

This redistributive aspect is one of the incommensurables I am willing to accept at present, but, I would like to pursue the general problem of incommensurability a bit further, still in the context of problem definition, through a brief excursion into the territory of systems analysis. My qualifications in this field are so small as to be derisory, but in my dilettante way I have picked up the following smattering of knowledge which seems relevant to my present purpose. General systems theory distinguishes between open and closed systems, the former being those in which there is import or export, and the latter being those in which there is none. Social systems may, in principle, be of either kind, but open systems seem typically to be more relevant for our purposes than closed ones. This says no more than that we are usually trying to assist in the optimisation of some sub-system, and we therefore need to be clear about (i) the boundaries of this sub-system, (ii) the relationships between this sub-system and its 'environment' (i.e. the rest of the system), and (iii) which of the variables are 'decision-variables' (i.e. those which can be directly manipulated).

Judging by the comments of F. E. Emery in the recent Penguin Modern Management Readings on *Systems Thinking*[7] there appears to be some dispute among systems theorists as to whether it is sufficient 'to cope with the problem by simply adding some exchange equation to the equations defining the inner system' or whether it is true (as he believes) that:

> '. . . open systems analysis cannot hope to stop with a specification of an exchange equation; it can hope to approach adequacy only when there is some characterisation of the environment. The reluctance to tackle environmental analysis appears to have arisen from the forbidding nature of two problems – (*a*) the sheer complexity of most environments and (*b*) the incommensurateness of the many heterogeneous processes that make up the system and its environment (e.g. psychological, economic, technical, meteorological).
>
> Sommerhoff had, as far back as 1950, provided a perfectly satisfactory answer to the second problem. The first problem should not have been taken so literally. Not all aspects of an environment are equally relevant to any particular system or class of systems. In economics, military theory, ecology, psychology, to name but a few, there has been a long and successful tradition of identifying and characterising global aspects of environment and relating these to adaptation.' [7, pp. 203–4].

On this 'first problem' (the choice of environmental characteristics for explicit analysis) the characteristic approach is either conventional (i.e. 'traditional'), or else subject to largely intuitive and ascientific processes of search for (and selection of) promising modifications. Only the subsequent results 'justify' one selection as against another. Thus whether the economists' conventional selection of variables is better or worse than the sociologists' or the psychologists' will depend on whether they generate results which prove more useful for the problem in hand. Part of the dispute about cost-benefit analysis and its relationship with other techniques concerns precisely this dimension, viz. the width of the range of environmental characteristics which it attempts to encompass. Nonetheless, some people argue that it is not yet wide enough, and I will return to this issue later.

The second problem, that of incommensurability of variables, is one that continues to plague cost-benefit analysis, as indeed many other evaluative techniques, so I was elated to read that it had been solved by Sommerhoff in 1950[8]. As far as I can see the solution boils down to the following statements:

1. If a set of activities, or states, are so related (whether purposively or not) to uncontrolled variations in the environment that despite

the latter some specified terminal configuration can be attained, then those activities or states are said to be 'directively correlated' with the environmental changes.

2. Since the specified terminal configuration (called the 'focal condition') could be a very particular, proximate, goal (like picking up a stone) or a very general ultimate one (like ensuring survival of the species) these focal conditions can be arranged hierarchically, and hence so can the 'directively correlated' activities or states which bring them about.

3. From which it follows that any pair of such activities or states can be made commensurate by finding the lowest level in the hierarchy of goals to which they can both be related.

This leads Sommerhoff to observe that:

> 'Apart from any other features they may have in common, any set of objectives whose states or activities are directively correlated may be thought of as a unit by virtue of their joint partnership in this single system property, and particularly on the strength of their joint relationship to a single focal condition. We thus get the conception of a set of objects which are united by the common goal of their activities'. (p. 136).

Whether or not this is a fruitful way to deal with the problem of incommensurability in biology I cannot judge, but I am sure that it is a rather empty, though formally correct, procedure in the social sciences. In economics, it is tantamount to saying, at individual level, that since individuals have preference functions, and manage to make choices, everything must be commensurable in terms of individual 'utility'. Likewise, for a society, one needs only to consult the social welfare function, and all incommensurability problems disappear. True, but unhelpful. It is always part of the analyst's job during the exploratory phases of a study to attempt to identify objectives, relate them hierarchically or otherwise as appropriate, and to find other 'directively correlated' activities (i.e. alternative courses of action) which serve the same ends and may therefore be regarded (albeit partially) as substitutes. It is frequently the case that when this process has been exhausted there are still aspects of a problem which cannot be rendered commensurable in this way (i.e. by finding some higher level index of 'effectiveness' to which the lower level indices can be systematically related; the ultimate in such indices being the social welfare function).

The economists' approach (I hesitate to call it a 'solution') is to use money values as the dimension by which as many features of a situation as possible are measured. The price mechanism provides a wealth of information which can be drawn upon for this purpose, although it needs very careful handling. McKean's rather conservative conclusion[9] is worth repeating here:

'. . . What we really face . . . is an amorphous and shifting preference function emerging (implicitly) from the political process, and a complex economy dominated by uncertainty. I have to conclude: Either market prices or imputed prices are likely to be off the mark. Where market prices do not exist, one often prefers imputed prices to no prices at all. But in what specific instances to impute prices, how far to go in refining those imputed prices, and whether to adjust market prices where they exist depends on one's judgement about the costs and worth of the information. For external effects and public goods, where no market exists at all, I would often be confident that some effort to impute prices is worthwhile. Where market prices exist, even though they are off the mark in terms of the appropriate (but dimly perceived) preference function, my personal judgement is that they are not completely unrelated to that objective function, and I would be reasonably confident only in a few instances that derived or adjusted prices would be an improvement over observed prices' (pp. 57–8).

Even this restrictive view leaves a great deal of scope for evaluative work, but it needs to be clearly understood that attempting to place a money value on non-traded 'goods' does not imply *either* that one is advocating the establishment of 'markets' in such goods *or* that one is restricting one's attention to their 'economic' attributes. Thus if I try to place a 'value' on the reduction of road accidents, I am not advocating that the victims should be required to pay for medical treatment or that they should be compensated, nor am I solely concerned with the effects on GNP[10]. The use of money as a common measuring rod in making diverse values commensurable is not to be confused with an obsession with the more sordid aspects of profit-maximisation!

I am also willing to accept that there is a role in CBA for the 'postulated' price, i.e. for a client (say a Minister of Transport) to say that for the purposes of this analysis I want variable X valued at £Y per unit (where X might be the intrinsic value of life), for then £Y represents a precise statement about the client's policy trade-off between X and the other variables in the analysis. It is 'arbitrary' in the sense that it cannot be supported by empirical evidence, but it does imply a commitment to allocate resources in a particular way for which the client will have to answer, hence it is not irresponsible, and it provides a precise focus for discussion by others (say Cabinet colleagues) who might wish to influence his judgements on this matter or modify their own. It is thus systematic, quantitative and communicable, and hence an improvement upon the casual, implicit and possibly capricious evaluation that can so easily be concealed if such matters are left to piecemeal informal judgement 'on their merits'.

3. INSIDIOUS POISON?

I earlier asserted my belief that CBA was intended to assist choice, without qualifying in any way the kind of choices I had in mind. I will now add that it will by now be obvious that it is with resource allocation decisions that CBA has been concerned. The traditional connotation of an 'allocation decision' in economics is a budgetary one, and usually also a financial one, although more recently 'manpower budgets' have been much discussed too. But some economists have recently begun to extend the application of economic models of resource-allocation to decisions which at first sight are far removed from the traditional area of discourse, as when political behaviour is seen as a 'market' for voters, or for the accumulation and enjoyment of political power rather than 'wealth'[11]. This broadening of the notion of an allocation-decision has led economists to make ever-deeper incursions into the territories of neighbouring disciplines, not simply in the role of tourists seeking information and enlightenment, but with a view to permanent colonisation. This has led to a further blurring in the delimitation of the area of applicability of resource-allocation techniques like cost-benefit analysis. It has also engendered plenty of anti-imperialistic resistance from those occupying these neighbouring territories, as they see with horror the brash and uncompromising behaviour of the parvenus!

(a) *Wildavsky's Disease: The Diagnosis*

In the vanguard of the political scientists' counter-attack is Aaron Wildavsky, whose article 'The political economy of efficiency: cost-benefit analysis, systems analysis and program budgeting'[12] should be read by all practitioners of CBA. In that article, he argues that:

'The economic model on which cost-benefit analysis depends for its validity is based on political theory. The idea that in a free society the economy is to serve the individual's consistent preferences revealed and rationally pursued in the market place. Governments are not supposed to dictate preferences nor make decisions' (p. 294).

'The dependence of cost-benefit analysis on a prior political framework does not mean that it is a useless or trivial exercise. Decisions must be made. If quantifiable economic costs and benefits are not everything, neither would a decision-maker wish to ignore them entirely. The great advantage of cost-benefit analysis, when pursued with integrity, is that some implicit judgements are made explicit and subject to analysis. Yet, for many, the omission of explicit considerations of political factors is a serious deficiency' (p. 297).

He quotes with approval the philosopher Paul Diesing who wrote [13]:

'Political rationality is the fundamental kind of reason, because it deals with the preservation and improvement of decision-structures, and decision structures are the source of all decisions . . .' (p. 203).

'. . . the political problem is always basic and prior to the others . . . This means that any suggested course of action must be evaluated first by its effects on the political structure. A course of action which corrects economic or social deficiencies but increases political difficulties must be rejected, while an action which contributes to political improvement is desirable even if it is not entirely sound from an economic or social standpoint' (p. 228).

Wildavsky then argues that:

'Once the political process becomes a focus of attention, it is evident that the principal participants may not be clear about their goals . . . The mixtures of values found in complex policies may have to be taken as packages . . . In a political structure, then, the need for support assumes central importance. Not simply the economic, but the political costs and benefits turn out to be critical' (p. 308).

This leads him to sketch out a political cost-benefit calculus to complement (and by implication to override) the economists' efforts, leading him to conclude that although:

> 'Studies based on efficiency criteria are much needed and increasingly useful . . . I would feel much better if political rationality were being pursued with the same vigour and capability as is economic efficiency. In that case I would have fewer qualms about extending efficiency studies into the decision-making apparatus' (pp. 309–10).

Thus although by implication he accepts that a broader based cost-benefit analysis would meet his objections, he sees this as a task for political scientists because 'the qualifications of efficiency experts for political systems analysis are not evident' (p. 305).

In a later article[14], Wildavsky carries the counter-attack a stage further by arguing that what the system needs is 'better policy analysis', which he delineates thus:

> '. . . policy analysis, with its emphasis upon originality, imagination and foresight, cannot be simply described. It is equivalent to what Robert N. Anthony has called strategic planning: ". . . the process of deciding on objectives of the organisation, on changes in these objectives, on the resources used to attain these objectives . . . It connotes big plans, important plans, plans with major consequences"[15]. While policy analysis is similar to a broadly conceived version of systems analysis, Yehezkel Dror has pointed up the boundaries that separate a narrow study from one with larger policy concerns. In policy analysis:
>
> "1. Much attention would be paid to the political aspects of public decision-making and public policymaking (instead of ignoring or condescendingly disregarding political aspects) . . .
>
> 2. A broad conception of decision-making and policy-making would be involved (instead of viewing all decision-making as mainly a resources allocation) . . .
>
> 3. A main emphasis would be on creativity and search for new policy alternatives, with explicit attention to encouragement of innovative thinking . . .
>
> 4. There would be extensive reliance on . . . qualitative methods . . .
>
> 5. There would be much more emphasis on futuristic thinking . . .
>
> 6. The approach would be looser and less rigid, but nevertheless systematic, one which would recognise the complexity of means–ends interdependence, the multiplicity of relevant criteria of

decision, and the partial and tentative nature of every analysis . . . [16, p. 190].

Apart from item 4, this is pretty much the agenda of those who wish to broaden the notion of an allocation decision beyond what is implied by those in item 2 and to use economic, statistical and mathematical analysis in the political field. Hence I suspect that 'policy analysis' is another bit of terminology that we need to take on board as meaning any use of evaluation techniques which attempts to incorporate the political aspect of a problem into the analysis. Or to put it more provocatively, it is 'cost-benefit analysis' writ large. Who is best qualified to conduct it as an issue I shall return to later.

(b) Wildavsky's Disease: The Cure

This is a convenient point at which to return to the role of 'constraints' in problem definition. Every analyst quickly becomes aware of the delicate nature of the dialogue which has to be pursued in order to clarify the nature, purpose and rigidity of these 'constraints', for while it is tempting to accept such constraints readily in order to keep the problem within manageable bounds (indeed it is not uncommon for the analysts to add a few of their own with this very consideration in mind!) the penalty to be paid is the danger that the problem becomes trivialised, or at any rate circumscribed to such a low level of suboptimisation that it may offer a very small pay-off to the client.

But my interest here is with a different aspect of 'feasibility', for one analyst's 'constraints' are another analyst's field for optimisation, and hence in defining and accepting such constraints one is defining and accepting the borderlines of one's discipline. I do not mean that statement to be interpreted as meaning that as an economist, I would want every economic variable left unconstrained in every problem I tackled, but rather that in a run of problems I would expect to have an opportunity of tackling every one of them as variables at one time or another. I would, not, however, have the same expectation about legal or organisational features of a problem. Here I would expect to be told (preferably after some dialogue) what assumptions to make about these aspects of the problem. Again, I must explain carefully what I do and do not mean by that statement. I do not mean that the investigation must necessarily be constrained within one specified framework of such 'feasibility' constraints. Not only would I expect alternative assumptions to be permissible, but they might well be the central feature of the analysis (for instance, in a cost-benefit analysis of alternative safety regulations).

It is at this point that I would take issue with some of Wildavsky's propositions quoted earlier about the scope of cost-benefit analysis, for he stated that it is limited in applicability to political systems which assume that 'the economy is to serve the individual's consistent preferences revealed and rationally pursued in the market place. Governments are not supposed to dictate preferences nor make decisions.' This is so patently false that if I had not had an opportunity to read and re-read this statement carefully I would not have believed it possible that such a well-informed and normally judicious observer could have made it. For while it is undoubtedly true that much of the analysis that goes into most cost-benefit studies *is* based on the assumption that the market does constitute a good guide to the value of costs and benefits, it is precisely because cost-benefit analysis may require (*a*) non-market valuations to be substituted for market valuations, and/or (*b*) valuations inferred from market behaviour to be placed on items which have no market values, and/or (*c*) the use of valuations postulated by the policy-makers or decision-makers themselves, that it is frequently criticised for precisely the opposite reason to Wildavsky's, viz. that it is too often used by governments as a (soft) justification for over-riding the (hard) realities of market![4]

But I think that a bridge can be built over this particular chasm by a careful formulation of the 'constraints' in a problem. If I am asked to conduct an optimisation exercise which involves minimising the cost of meeting a specified minimum bill of requirements, it is well known that the conventional linear programming formulation of such a problem will yield a notional (or 'shadow') price for the constrained variables (i.e. those specified in the minimum bill of requirements). Interpreted more generally, this shadow price is the value implicitly placed on the marginal unit of the constrained variable, so if one of the political 'constraints' in a problem is that group *X* must not be disadvantaged, it is, in principle, possible to compute the cost (= implicit value) of meeting that constraint. If Wildavsky's political analysts don't like that implicit valuation, they are free to replace it with a postulated value of their own, to promulgate it, to argue about it, and to justify it, etc., by whatever structure of political

[4] In a paper on cost-benefit analysis presented to the British Association for the Advancement of Science at Exeter in September 1969, I have rehearsed the case for over-riding the market in cases where the results of an orthodox financial appraisal (e.g. via DCF techniques) conflict with the results of a cost-benefit analysis[17].

rationality he approves of for the purpose. The cost-benefit analyst can then insert the postulated figure in his analysis and grind out a new set of results accordingly. The effective limit on all such shadow pricing, as McKean has pointed out[18], is the cost involved in getting the information (and judgements about how much it is worth spending for an uncertain payoff in additional information are themselves tricky optimisation exercises!). My solution, then, would be to use shadow prices, if necessary, as the vehicle by which information is carried from other analysts' territory into the realm of cost-benefit analysis, as understood by economists.

This does still leave us with a tricky problem of co-ordination, however, because we are now in the classic danger of assuming that the results of a set of sub-optimisation exercises constitute the grand optimum solution! To spell out the difficulty more fully, when I accept a restriction (based, say, on grounds of 'political unacceptability') upon the set of alternatives to be appraised, I have to assume that some political analyst has done his homework properly. But what if he reached his conclusions about what is or is not 'politically acceptable' by making some prior assumptions about the effects of various economic measures which an economist might well have been able to show to be false if asked to do so? For instance, in conducting an appraisal of alternative means of financing University education, loans to students might be excluded from consideration on grounds of 'political unacceptability' because it is implicitly assumed by the political analysts that these must have adverse effects on access to University education by women or by the children of poor families. Now the cost-benefit analyst may know this to be a false assumption, yet accept without question the restriction ruling out student loans from consideration on grounds of political unacceptability, because he may think that the declared 'political unacceptability' of student loans was based on a strong ethical aversion to usury, which, as an economist, he has no right to challenge. It is the danger that a hiatus of this kind may occur that has led many cost-benefit analysts to move into the role of general 'policy analysts'. It is very tempting to do so when you see pieces of analysis which seem (*a*) wrongly conceived, (*b*) poorly understood, and/or (*c*) misguidedly implemented (or misguidedly *not* implemented as the case may be).

Nevertheless, I wish to emphasise the dangers of succumbing to this temptation. The progress of human society has depended in very large part upon specialisation and division of labour. We all know that this has not been a costless process, in terms of growing impersonality and rigidity in the system, and its greater vulnerability to major breakdowns. But if every cost-benefit analyst has to become his client's general policy adviser, then his capacity to do technical economic or statistical work must inevitably suffer as a result, and while I recognise the dangers of compartmentalisation, I cannot accept as a solution the notion of total commitment and universal expertise (i.e. no disciplinary constraints). I would instead propagate an old-fashioned, and currently unfashionable, doctrine that there is a valid and useful role both for specialists and generalists (which distinction is not the same as that between 'professionals' and 'amateurs' respectively). It is the professional generalist who should be the general policy adviser, and whether his original discipline was economics, political science, mathematics, engineering, history or classics is not of prime importance. What is important is that he understands the nature of all the disciplines relevant to his problems, so that without necessarily being familiar with or even understanding their more intricate and esoteric parts, he can marshal and deploy them intelligently. Just as the General in charge of an army does not necessarily have to know how to fire a gun or drive a tank, so a generalist policy adviser does not necessarily have to know how to invert a matrix or how to calculate the internal rate of return on an investment project. What each does need to know are the capabilities and limitations of the forces at his disposal, their complementarity, substitutability or more complex patterns of interdependence, their relevance to his problem, and how to give instructions that cannot be misinterpreted and which will produce answers that are relevant and comprehensible. His is thus the responsibility for ensuring that no hiatus occurs and that the constraints on 'feasibility' imposed on each specialist's suboptimisation exercise are not unduly restrictive. His also is the role of 'policy analyst' as conceived by Dror and Wildavsky (mistakenly identified by them as being concerned with 'decision structures', for I see this narrower role of *political* analyst as just another specialism like that of the cost-benefit analyst)[19].

(*c*) *How to Alleviate the Lindblom–Simon Disease*

Some sharp things have also been written about the primitive and naive notions entertained by economists concerning the nature of means-ends relationships, which may be represented crudely as being that the ends are 'given' and that the economist's problem is simply to find the most efficient means of attaining them.

The first common objection to the economists' position is that people do not have clearly articulated ends, they just have vague ideas about what it would be nice to be able to do or have if . . ., and that these vague ideas get crystallised only through the process of seeking means to attain them[20]. This I regard as a semantic problem within the present context, or at any rate one mainly requiring more careful role differentiation. It seems to me to be saying no more than that there is a feedback and what the economist is saying is that his professional interest and expertise is relevant to one part of the loop, in which the assumption of 'given' ends is valid. At the next 'iteration' a different set of 'given' ends may need to be considered, but how the ends get adjusted in the light of experience is not his bailiwick.

The second objection to the economist's position is that people are not 'optimising' anything at all, but simply seeking a 'satisfactory' or 'acceptable' outcome. This position has two strands, the first being the concern with costs of search, and if that is all that is being said it amounts to saying that economists are very prone to ignore certain important costs, and hence are likely to reach misleading results. That is a fair criticism, but it is not an argument against the postulate that people are optimisers, but against the practice of inadequate optimisation. The second strand is more subtle[2], depending on the assertion that people have limited aspirations, and once these are satisfied, no further effort is devoted to them until the individual is given cause to be dissatisfied once more (i.e. until his level of aspiration is raised). Again, I reply that, as an economist, I am not interested in how levels of aspirations are raised (though if I were in the advertising business I could make a fortune if I knew!) but what the consequences are if they are whatever they are or might be. I expect the sociologists and psychologists to produce information and ideas on the value-systems of (say) corporate enterprises, and it is then up to us economists to listen attentively and attempt to work out the consequences for their economic behaviour[22]. If some systematic relationship can be established between attainment and aspirations, then if it can be cast in terms of the variables of the model by all means let us incorporate it. But if it requires a very complex apparatus of sociological and/or psychological theory to establish the linkage, then the economist may surely be permitted to say (as I did earlier) that what goes on in that part of the loop is not his concern, and he will pick up the signals again when they emerge as a fresh set of assumptions for him to make about motivation at the beginning of his segment of the loop.

(*d*) *Self on Roskillitis*[23]

This brings me finally to the objections raised by Peter Self in a recent attack[24] on the role and activities of the Roskill Commission on the third London Airport. Self distinguishes two roles which the Commission is supposed to play in this particular instance, first 'to achieve a full, fair and judicialised treatment of all objections' and second to supply a 'scientific basis for an eventual decision ... through the elaborate cost-benefit exercise of the commission's research team'. Although the former role of CBA is not without interest and significance, I shall here concentrate on Self's criticisms of the latter aspect of the Roskill Commission's activities.

In this context, the essential points made by Self are the following:

'(*a*) ... the kind of aggregate monetary figures used ... could not be made even tolerably credible or objective *upon any basis whatever*. Cost-benefit analysis gets its plausibility from the use of a common monetary standard, but the common value of the £ derives from exchange structures. Outside such situations, common values cannot be presumed ... The greater part of the figures used ... represent notional values which will never adequately be tested or validated by actual exchanges and which are highly arbitrary in the sense that a very wide range of values can plausibly be predicted, depending upon innumerable opinions and assumptions ...

(*b*) ... the framework of analysis becomes distorted by the grotesque attempt to place all factors on the same monetary basis ... such diverse items as "capital construction costs" ... which can be estimated within tolerable limits ... [and passenger surface travelling costs] ... which ... far outweigh differences in capital costs ... [and are] based upon an enormous chain of speculative analysis.

(*c*) The cost-benefit figures are incredible, not only because of the disparate basis of the items included, but because of the important items excluded. Of course, important factors often are excluded from policy judgements, but the appropriate remedy ... is to point out the missing factor with the aid of as much supporting evidence as possible ... Instead of ... being argued upon its broad merits ... [such an element] ... has to be translated into yet more items within a cost-benefit equation ... The limits of the financial quantifiable have to be stretched past absurdity, as the logic of the exercise will collapse. And once again more limited types of judgement – which ultimately in fact cannot be avoided – become confused and displaced.

(*d*) The ultimate absurdity of the whole exercise is revealed, paradoxically, through efforts to increase its rationality. Following classical welfare economics, Professor Lichfield has argued . . . that distributional values should be included in the exercise . . . But is it in any way sensible to express such factors in monetary terms? Clearly there are almost as many views upon the precise weight that is to be attached to these "distributional" . . . values as there are people in Britain. How is the Roskill Commission to proceed? Conduct a Gallup Poll of popular valuations in circumstances in which nobody will have to pay for the figure he hits upon with actual costs? Or ask the Government for directives? One only has to pose the questions to see the absurdity of such proceedings.'

Objection (*a*) is a peculiarly two-edged weapon for Self to be wielding. He appears to accept market valuations as 'objective', but not non-market values. Yet market values are merely the outcome of a large number of subjective valuations and disparately based decisions, which are on all fours with 'non-market' decisions about time savings, accident prevention, the allocation of leisure time, etc. So one possible inference from his position is that since *everything* (even market price) rests on subjective valuations (upon which it could also be said that 'there are . . . as many views . . . as there are people in Britain'), no 'objective' analysis of any sort is possible. The alternative (and opposite) inference is that the market is to be regarded as an 'objective' mechanism for reconciling conflicting valuations, but no other method is to be so regarded, least of all those which use market-type concepts and terminology (e.g. imputing a 'price' for time, or calculating the implicit 'cost' of accidents, etc.). This would be an even more extreme position than McKean's, would undermine any attempt to get away from naive financial appraisal, and surely cannot be what Self intends. If, on the other hand, he accepts the former implication, then his strictures apply as much to political science as to economics. I cannot see any way of interpreting his position which leads to a different implication from these two, and of them I would accept the former and reject the latter. But in accepting the former implication, I would assert that I am doing no more than accepting the well-recognised proposition that you cannot ascribe values without making value judgements. Market prices are acceptable if the value-premises underlying market behaviour are acceptable (e.g. accepting the prevailing distribution of economic power and the relevance of individual market-oriented valuations to the making of social judgements). Imputen prices are acceptable if it is believed that the incidental values of x to be inferred from people's associated (market) valuations of y and z are an accurate reflection of individuals' utility-maximising behaviour, and that this is the relevant consideration. Postulated prices are acceptable if it is believed that the value-premises underlying both market and imputed prices are misconceived for the purpose in hand (e.g. if one accepts the propriety of a paternalistic or collectivist basis for valuation). To say that any of these is 'arbitrary' is meaningless . . . each follows logically from a particular (but different) set of premises. The fact that each of them may be *imprecise* in the actual valuation it yields is a different point, and Self merely confuses matters by linking it with the earlier methodological points. Wide differences in actual valuations would flow from differences in methodology (e.g. whether 'market', 'imputed' or 'postulated' values are relevant), differences in methods of estimation, or differences in data. One of the advantages of formal and explicit procedures of evaluation is that it should be possible to identify which of these differences is present in any particular dispute.

Objection (*b*) appears to be saying that estimates embodying differing degrees of complexity and accuracy (which are independent dimensions!) should not be brought together. He surely does not mean it, for almost no comparisons could survive that test. If he means that likely margins of error should be indicated, one cannot disagree with him. But presumably such margins of error are needed so that they can be compared. How can they be compared unless they are in commensurable terms? What practicable alternative is there to the use of monetary units?

Objection (*c*) seems even more confused, because he appears to be saying that CBA is more likely to lead to the omission of relevant material than other modes of analysis, and at the same time that it prevents proper analysis of these excluded items by dissecting them and scrutinising each component so closely that the 'gestalt' is entirely obscured. If it is to be interpreted as an attack upon *analysis* as such (which I take to mean 'the resolution of anything complex into its simple elements' OED) then the rift between CBA (and all other analytical techniques) and the Selfs of this world is irreconcilable. If it is intended to be a more narrowly directed assault on the use of money valuations as the medium by which comparative values can be expressed, I ask once more for suggestions as to a practical alternative.

This brings me to the final quoted objection concerning distributive justice and the difficulties inherent in assessing it. His initial assertions are well-taken, but his rather lame rhetoric at the end leaves me unmoved. As I see it we are once more in the realm of choosing between 'the market' (i.e. direct observation of individual behaviour), 'imputation' (i.e. inference from associated behaviour) and 'revelation' (i.e. guidance from on high) as a source of "weights". I see none of these as inherently 'absurd', the more important issue is which of them is relevant in the particular decision-making context. From the analyst's viewpoint the cardinal sin is obscurantism – virtue lies in being explicit.

(*e*) *Is 'Roskillitis' Really Curable?*

Even if all Self's strictures on CBA were valid, however, the sad thing is that he has nothing substantive to offer in its place. He says we must return to 'planning' which he describes as offering 'multiple and interlocking perspectives which can be related in various ways'. Each of these perspectives has its own criteria of desirability, and putting them together 'cannot be free of opinion and argument'. 'But the extent of these disputes cannot be known or arbitrated unless each principal set of desiderata is investigated and classified.' In other words, objectives need to be clarified and rendered commensurable! 'In so far as these differences cannot be bridged, some ultimate valuations have inevitably to be made by somebody.'

At this point it sounds like a recipe for CBA, but he shies away from this and writes: 'In so far as the exercise involves the valuation of questions of opinion, one might suppose that truer indications could be secured through the direct collection and confrontation of the views of the interested or expert bodies. Such a process may seem to have less scientific precision than hypothesised monetary equations, but it is at least grounded in reality.' This hardly squares with his own earlier proposition that only judgements backed with cash were to be regarded as so grounded. It also elides the crucial point that the intensity of benefit or loss by each of the 'interested bodies' has still to be weighed according to *some* criterion, and he implies that 'weight of public opinion' would be the relevant consideration. He does not tell us how it is to be weighed, however, nor what sort of information the public needs in order to form an opinion, who provides it, and whether this can be done without engaging in a process essentially indistinguishable from CBA. Indeed, in his concluding paragraphs Self seems, paradoxically, to be doing no more than invoking 'the planning process' as a means of ensuring that non-market values are brought into the picture more explicitly so as to override the market values to which he ascribes such 'objectivity'! 'The claims of interested bodies must not only be checked, but sometimes overridden. However, the basis for actually doing this ought either to be the demonstrated superiority of a broader perspective – which is the real meaning of planning – or alternatively the use of some explicit valuation, such as . . . the interests of future generations in environmental protection . . .'

What Self does not seem to realise, or will not accept, is that unless such valuations are expressed directly (or indirectly[5]) in money terms they are bound to be vacuous (and therefore useless operationally). Instead he ends his polemic associating 'notional' values with 'imprecision', and castigating evaluation in money terms as a facade surreptitiously concealing value judgements rather than recognising it as a means of making them more explicit and precise. 'Greater rationality', he concludes, 'is not helped, but hindered, by the use of notional monetary figures which either conceal relevant policy judgements or else simply involve unrealistic and even artificial degrees of precision. Those who suppose otherwise are heading for a particularly dreary version of 1984.' One can only respond despairingly, that greater rationality is certainly not helped either by vacuously broad policy judgements cast in terms which defy analysis. Nor does it inspire confidence when their consequences are protected from systematic scrutiny by resort to obscurantist assertions that any attempt to turn them into empirically researchable propositions reduces them to the sordid status of terms in an equation and hence is to be resisted on some unstated (quasi-religious?) principle such as the belief that there is but one way to the truth (and although we do not know what it is, it is not CBA!).

4. CONCLUSION

In disputes of this kind two great dangers are always present. One is

[5] By 'indirectly' I have in mind expressions such as the marginal rate of social time preference, which although a pure number can be used in conjunction with variables cast in monetary terms.

that the advocates (of CBA, for instance) will oversell their product, especially as they encounter what they may (perhaps quite rightly) consider to be ill-informed resistance, both from potential clients and from those peddling rival products. This has undoubtedly occurred with CBA, and it is salutary to be reminded of the limitations of the current state of our knowledge, both in principle and in practice. The other great danger is that the perfect becomes the enemy of the good, that the acknowledged limitations of the new product are made the excuse for not abandoning old practices which have even more defects, on the curious notion that we should only change over if a *perfect* product is offered in place of the imperfect one we are already using. CBA is not the way to perfect truth, but the world is not a perfect place, and I regard it as the height of folly to react to the greater (though still incomplete) rigour which CBA requires of us by shrieking '1984' and putting our heads hopefully back into the sand (or the clouds) hoping that things will look better when we look around again in fifteen years' time. In contemplating CBA, I prefer the philosophy embodied in the answer Maurice Chevalier is alleged to have given to an interviewer who asked him how he viewed old age: 'Well, there is quite a lot wrong with it, but it isn't so bad when you consider the alternative.'

REFERENCES

[1] Fritz Machlup, In 'Comments' on a paper by Burton A. Weisbrod in Robert Dorfman (Editor), *Measuring Benefits of Government Investments*, Brookings Institution, 1965, pp. 149–57; London, George Allen & Unwin Ltd.

[2] Robert Dorfman, Operations Research, *Surveys of Economic Theory*, vol. III. *Resource Allocation*, Macmillan, London, 1966.

[3] Glen P. Camp, Operations research: the science of generalised strategies and tactics, *Textile Research Journal*, July, 1955, vol. 25, pp. 629 ff.

[4] A. R. Prest and R. Turvey, Cost-Benefit Analysis: A Survey, *Surveys of Economic Theory*, vol. III. *Resource Allocation*, Macmillan, London, 1966.

[5] For instance, Kenneth J. Arrow and Tibor Scitovsky (Editors), *Readings in Welfare Economics*, George Allen & Unwin, London, 1969.

[6] Burton A. Weisbrod, Income redistribution effects and benefit-cost analysis, In Samuel B. Chase Jr (Editor), *Problems in Public Expenditure Analysis*, Brooking Institution, 1968, London, George Allen & Unwin Ltd.

[7] *Systems Thinking: Selected Readings*, F. E. Emery (Editor), Penguin Education, X, 71, 1969.

[8] In *Analytical Biology* (Oxford University Press, 1950), an updated summary of which is included in Emery's book of readings[7], written specially by Sommerhoff and entitled 'The Abstract Characteristics of Living Systems'.

[9] McKean, The Use of Shadow Prices, In Samuel Chase Jr (Editor) *Problems in Public Expenditure Analysis*. Brookings Institution, 1968, London, George Allen & Unwin Ltd. Margolis's comments (pp. 71–7) on McKean's paper present a more radical view, more in accord with my own.

[10] That some cost-benefit analyses have given this impression is regrettable, and it has led at least one practitioner to conclude that 'cost-benefit studies deal solely with elements that can be measured in economic terms; a cost-effectiveness study considers other "benefits" in addition to those that are purely economic' (A. H. Packer, Applying Cost-Effectiveness Concepts to the Community Health System, *Operations Research*, vol. 16, No. 2. April–May, 1968, p. 250). This led him to conclude that 'The cost-benefit approach distorts the conclusions by over-emphasising morbidity among males in their maximum earning years; by underestimating prevalent problems such as neurotic conditions, common colds, and certain allegenic conditions; and by ignoring intangible costs, etc. Actual and implied costs are important dimensions of any resource allocation decision; however, the cost-effectiveness framework points (and demands) explicit consideration of variables that are measured not in dollars and cents but in terms of basic human values' (p. 251). Although I cannot deny that there is a danger that casting evaluation in money terms carries the danger Packer mentions (just as attempting any precise measure of normally unmeasured phenomena leaves the analyst open to the charge Wildavsky makes of obsessive and mindless quantification), this is not inherent in the method of analysis, but only in the way in which it may be used by some practitioners.

[11] This literature stems directly from early work by Howard Bowen (*Toward Social Economy*, New York, Rinehart, 1948) and Duncan Black (*The Theory of Committees and Elections*, London, Cambridge University Press, 1958), which itself owed much to the Voluntary Exchange Theorists (see, for instance, Knut Wicksell, A new principle of just taxation and Erik Lindahl, Just taxation – a positive solution. In R. A. Musgrave and A. T. Peacock (Editors), *Classics in the Theory of Public Finance*, London, Macmillan, 1958). Among the better known and influential recent works of this genre are Anthony Downs, *An Economic Theory of Democracy*, New York, Harper & Bros, 1957; Mancur Olson, *The Logic of Collective Action*, Cambridge, Harvard University Press, 1965, and J. M. Buchanan and Gordon Tullock, *The Calculus of Consent*, Ann Arbor, University of Michigan Press, 1962. The latest example to come to my notice is R. L. Curry Jr and L. L. Wade, *A Theory of Political Exchange*, subtitled *Economic Reasoning in Political Analysis*, Prentice-Hall Contemporary Political Theory Series, Englewood Cliffs N.J., 1968, which contains a select bibliography of relevant works. An interesting review of the methodological differences implicit in the various approaches is contained in Brian M. Barry, *Sociologists, Economists and Democracy*, London, Collier-Macmillan, 1970, which contains a much longer bibliography.

[12] *Public Administration Review*, vol. XXVI, No. 4. Dec. 1966, pp. 292–310.

[13] Paul Diesing, *Reason in Society*, Urbana, 1962.

[14] Rescuing Policy Analysis from PPBS, *Public Administration Review*, vol. XXIX, No. 2., March–April, 1969, pp. 189–92.

[15] Robert N. Anthony, *Planning and Control Systems: A Framework for Analysis*, Boston: Harvard Univ. Press, 1965, p. 16.

[16] Yehezkel Dror, Policy analysts: a new professional role in government service, *Public Administration Review*, vol. XXVII, No. 3, Sept. 1967, pp. 200–1.

[17] Alec Cairncross (editor), *The Managed Economy*, Chapter 8, Oxford, Blackwell, 1970.

[18] Roland N. McKean, The Use of Shadow Prices, in Samuel B. Chase, Jr *Problems in Public Expenditure Analysis*, Brooking Institution, 1968; London, George Allen & Unwin Ltd.

[19] This seems also to accord with the views of Charles L. Schultze, as expressed in his recent work, *The Politics and Economics of Public Spending* (Brookings Institution, 1968; London, George Allen & Unwin, Ltd, 1969), where he writes:

'There are political opportunity costs to any decision, just as real as the economic opportunity costs. Because values conflict among different groups and among themselves, securing the agreement necessary to pursue one line of action must often reduce the opportunity to pursue other lines of action . . . A civil rights bill may "cost" a housing bill . . . These costs dictate a set of efficiency criteria for political decisions equally as real and valid as the resource costs which lead to the efficiency criteria of systematic analysis' (pp. 45–7).

'. . . the purpose of advocacy process and political bargaining is to reach decisions about specific programs in the context of conflicting and vaguely known values. Systematic analysis makes a major and essential, contribution to this process by forging links between general values and specific program characteristics – links that are immediately and directly evident only in the simplest cases . . . Proceeding by trial and error is of no use unless we design the trials meaningfully, recognise the errors promptly and make the necessary corrections. Where complex issues are involved, we must rely on analysis to help. Intuition and goodwill alone will not suffice. It is not really important that the analysis will be accepted by all the participants in the bargaining process. We can hardly expect that information systems will be so complete, necessary assumptions so obviously true, or constraints so universally accepted that a good analysis can be equated with a generally accepted one. But analysis can help focus debate upon matters about which there are real differences of value, where political judgements are necessary. It can suggest superior alternatives, eliminating, or at least minimising, the number of inferior solutions. Thus, by sharpening the debate, systematic analysis can enormously improve it' (pp. 74–5).

'Analysts . . . can and should play the role of . . . partisan efficiency advocates' – the champions of analysis and efficiency. They are indeed partisans, and the ultimate decision-maker has to balance their voice against the political, tactical and other considerations . . .' (p. 96).

[20] A comprehensive and concise statement of this view is to be found in C. E. Lindblom, The science of muddling through, *Public Administration Review*, vol. XXIX, No. 1, Spring, 1959, pp. 79–88; Reprinted in *Business Strategy*, H. Igor Ansoff (Editor), Penguin Modern Management Readings, 1969.

[21] See H. A. Simon, A behavioral model of rational choice, *Quarterly Journal of Economics*, vol. 59 (1955), pp. 99–118, and Rational choice and the structure of the environment, *Psychological Review*, vol. 63 (1956), pp. 159–88.

[22] See, for instance, the work of William J. Baumol, *Business Behaviour, Value and Growth*, Revised Edition, Chapter 6, Harcourt, Brace & World, 1967; Oliver E. Williamson, *The Economics of Discretionary Behaviour: Managerial Objectives in a Theory of the Firm*, Prentice-Hall, 1964; and Richard M. Cyert and James G. March, *A Behavioural Theory of the Firm*, Prentice-Hall, 1963.

[23] In Williams' (unpublished) Medical Encyclopaedia, defined as 'the state of being inflamed by Roskill'.

[24] Nonsense on stilts: the futility of Roskill, *Political Quarterly*, July 1970 (reprinted in *New Society*, 2 July 1970).

Part Two

THEORY

4

A Note on the Treatment of Taxation in Cost-benefit Analysis[1]

C. D. FOSTER

London School of Economics and Political Science

The history of the subject has been such that there has developed no tradition of a consistent treatment of taxes and subsidies in cost-benefit analysis. Authors have used a number of approaches, often without much discussion of their rationale. But different treatments of taxation can have a significant effect on the absolute level of net benefits predicted, as later discussion in this paper of the treatment of taxation in the London Transportation Study will show; and may, in other cases, well affect the ranking of alternatives. While in principle no definitive treatment is possible, discussion of the issues should help clarify what is involved in making one set of assumptions rather than another.

Certain simplifications will be adopted. Except where there is a special point to be made, there will be no specific mention of subsidies. They may be treated as negative taxes. Neither is this paper concerned with situations where the prime motive behind expenditure decisions is redistributional. This seems common sense. Net changes in tax positions are obviously relevant to evaluating the distributional effects of investment. The problems arise when the prime concern is with the efficiency of investment.

Reading the literature suggests that authors sometimes seem to take up different positions when considering:

(i) project inputs other than capital,
(ii) capital inputs,
(iii) project outputs.

It will be convenient to begin by using the same breakdown.

NON-CAPITAL PROJECT INPUTS

Perhaps the commonest assumption made about the tax element in

[1] The idea of this paper has been further developed in 'Pecuniary Externalities in Cost-Benefit Analysis: Notes on the Treatment of Tax and Surplus' by the author.

non-capital inputs is that they should be left out. To quote Marglin 'taxes, although they represent a cost to a private concern, are not a cost from the social point of view. Consequently they are properly left out of the benefit-cost analysis of alternatives'[1]. Or as Prest and Turvey put it, most economists prefer to value inputs at their factor cost rather than their market values[2]. While extreme logic might suggest that on this principle one should eliminate the tax elements in inputs into inputs, and so on, common sense usually suggests going back no further than the first round of immediate inputs. Beyond that the economic effect of omitting tax elements is unlikely to be significant.

The most important reason given for this treatment derives from National Income accounting where taxes are treated as income transfers and rightly as irrelevant to determining the magnitude of GNP. The presupposition is that they are *not* payments for public goods and services. If they were, their value should be added to GNP. By analogy, as taxes are not real costs of an investment, they should be omitted from its evaluation. This argument survives the recognition that one cannot separate the real and distributional as completely as is traditional in National Income analysis. A change in taxation will have an effect on the allocation of resources through changing the distribution of income; and may even affect the magnitude of GNP[3]. As Mishan has pointed out, even the time-honoured poll tax is not neutral in its effect on the allocation of resources if its proceeds are redistributed, that is, if it is not paid directly back to those from which it was levied[4]. But in terms of efficiency evaluation, the changes in taxation as such are irrelevant. The right course is to evaluate the real effects of a project, given the tax policies which affect the distribution of income and efficient allocation of resources resulting from the execution of a project (and then, if one likes, evaluate the tax policies as another calculation).

Usually the tactic of 'leaving out' input taxes will do what is required. This is so if one can assume that taxes come in and go out over the margin and are taxed the same in all uses. But suppose there is a 'field' in which some or all resources are taxed at higher rate when used there, the principle that taxes are transfers would seem to lead to another treatment. We suppose we are interested in an evaluation of alternatives in Industry, *A* where tax policy is such that the inputs to those alternatives are taxed at a higher rate than in Industry, *B* from which they would be drawn. Providing one sticks to the assumption that taxes are transfers (and not prices) one would understate the benefit of the alternatives if one did not regard the increase in taxation because of the difference in the tax rates. It is, on those assumptions, a method by which government, so to speak, shares in the surplus of the project. The fact that this part of the surplus is transferred to the government through taxation is not relevant. What is, is that one measures the benefit of the project to whomsoever it accrues.

The same principle applies if one can assume that some of the resources employed in a project are genuinely 'new' and are not transferred from other uses. Any taxes on such inputs represent command over additional real resources which have been transferred to the Government through tax policy. In that case all the additional tax revenue on those inputs represents a real gain.

Thus the same principle, that one is only concerned with real gains and costs, leads to different practical treatment in the three cases. But quite often, perhaps especially in transport cost-benefit studies, the line between transferred and 'new' inputs may be drawn rather arbitrarily.

A Shadow Price of Taxation

One sometimes finds another argument why taxes should be left out. For example, Coburn, Beesley and Charlesworth wrote in the *London–Birmingham Motorway Study* that 'fuel tax will mean there will be losses in real terms because of the distorting effect of that tax. The exclusion . . . is, however, essential, since such taxes must be levied in any case and their saving represents no net benefit to the community'[5]. This may be related to the fiction of the fiscally omnipotent state which was a very common assumption until recently in discussions of underdeveloped economies (and more reasonably elsewhere). A characteristic example might be to suppose a Policy *X*, say a change in the exchange rate, which might (i) affect the magnitude of tax receipts, (ii) affect the allocation of resources and (iii) the distribution of income. The assumption of fiscal omnipotence was simply that a government could take steps to offset, if it chose, any or all of these (and therefore such side-effects could be neglected).

Provided no special weight is given government revenue, this argument is redundant in the context of cost-benefit analysis. If taxes are transfers and not real costs, then the fact that government can affect their magnitude and incidence at will cannot make them any less relevant than they already were. By assumption one is not interested in the tax changes resulting from a project, not even the net effect on government revenue, but on the real effect, however this is shared between government and the rest of the economy.

What does make a difference is if one imputes a non-unit shadow price to government revenue. To be consistent with the argument developed so far, the use of a shadow price must be justified in terms of differences in efficiency, not on distributional grounds. In fact many governments, even in developed nations, may not be omnipotent fiscally. There will be many constraints on their ability to vary the particular incidence of taxes. There may even be constraints on their ability to vary the aggregate level of tax revenue; so that a project (or perhaps more plausibly a programme of investment projects) which implied a substantial reduction in government tax receipts might imply a reduction in government revenue which could not (readily) be offset. If one is further prepared to make the assumption that the efficiency shadow price of government revenues is greater than one, it is not appropriate to 'leave out' taxes in cost-benefit analysis. The net tax change caused by the project should be measured and valued at the correct shadow price.

The *locus classicus* of the view that taxation has a value of more than unity in many underdeveloped countries is Little and Mirrlees[6]. If the value of foreign exchange is greater than its official value and if one is able to assume that domestic savings are equivalent to foreign exchange, and that marginal changes in taxation are equivalent to changes in savings, then the case for giving tax receipts a shadow price of more than unity is made. One can make a similar argument in a developed country where the exchange rate is overvalued and in which one can assume that a change in tax revenue is equivalent to a change in domestic savings and (through substitution) for foreign exchange. Presumably there could be circumstances in which the efficient shadow price of taxation was less than unity.

Taxes as prices

Another case in which it would be wrong to leave taxes out in cost-benefit analysis is in so far as they are really (efficient) prices. In some ways this possibility is the most difficult of all to handle. If a government knows it wants a tax to be regarded as a price or charge for a service, it will usually call it a price or charge. But there are many taxes which could be regarded as (more or less efficient) prices. Their legal status remains that of a tax; and there may be genuine difficulty also in deciding whether they function economically enough like a tax to be worth regarding as one.

To take a few examples: one could try to regard the weekly National Insurance contribution of an employee as a price for medical care and insurance. If one supposes a project that employs many previously unemployed, they begin to pay this 'price'. But the difference made by their payment of this 'price' on the marginal cost of providing medical care and insurance is presumably negligible (or even perverse). So it would seem pointless to regard this as a price rather than a tax.

It is obvious to even the casual reader that the authors of the government report on *Road Track Costs* re-affirmed the official view that fuel tax and other vehicle taxation was a contribution to general revenue and not to be regarded as hypothecated or as a price[7]. This position has been the official one since Winston Churchill was the first to raise the Road Fund in 1926. It affirms the principle Chancellors have adopted, that there was no relation between aggregate revenue from road-users and aggregate expenditure on roads. Highway cost-benefit studies have in general treated highway taxes as transfers and left them out[8]. But if road taxes to the user were to vary in a way which reasonably reflected variations in marginal cost, then there would be an economic case for regarding such a tax as a price whatever the legal status of the tax. In many cases a highway project which effected a net reduction in fuel use and therefore fuel tax by users by relieving congestion or shortening trips (which it could do) is unlikely to be associated with a fall in the marginal public costs of road provision.

(There may be a case for regarding some part of it as reflecting changes in marginal maintenance costs, but that would be relevant to another calculation than the one we have imagined here.) On the face of it a relation is likely to exist between changes in fuel tax and marginal social (congestion) costs of road use. It has been argued, however, that the relation is such an imperfect one that on efficiency grounds it is simply not worth regarding part of the fuel tax as a marginal cost of using the road[9].

A stronger case for regarding all or part of a tax as a marginal cost price can often be made in relation to local taxation, especially in the United States where much more effort has gone to consider the efficiency aspects of local taxation. For example, a case arose when considering the evaluation of a new rapid transit subway in the San Francisco area. Abstracting from other tax changes, it was arguable that some land previously assessed for property taxation would have been transferred to rapid transit use where it would not be so taxed.

But in so far as one could regard the property tax as a price for local public services provided, then it was relevant that the rapid transit property would not require certain local public services to be provided for it which had been provided for those it displaced. In these circumstances it was far easier to determine what share of the fall in property tax from this cause could be offset by the direct marginal benefit to the local governments concerned.

While it is often difficult to decide whether a tax is intended to be 'purely' redistributional or whether it can be regarded as a price, there seems to be a certain asymmetry in that it is often easier to decide that a subsidy is not just a transfer but is purposive. If the Federal Government makes a subvention to a city it will be usually under a title sanctioned under an Act of Congress which defined the purpose of the subsidy within limits, e.g. to promote housing of the poor. In that case it would seem wrong to leave out the subsidy from the evaluation in the sense of omitting that portion of costs covered by subsidy. Presumably, the subsidy element is intended to earn a positive return in terms of the purposes – quantifiable or not – for which it was allocated. (An alternative would be to regard it as giving the interests of specified groups more weight than their own purchasing power would give them.)

Deciding how far a tax or subsidy can be regarded as a price is therefore crucial in deciding its correct treatment in cost-benefit analysis. But it is not any 'price' that is relevant, only a 'marginal cost' price. It is well established that the rental element in a price is not relevant to evaluation[10]. In practice cost-benefit analysts tend to assume that input market prices equal marginal costs unless there is evidence to the contrary (when expenditure taxes are subtracted); and there may be no great imperfection in making this assumption. (Unemployed resources are the best-known example of marginal costs of employment being below market prices.) But it would seem to be rash to assume that in most cases taxes reflect the marginal costs of providing public services.

CAPITAL INPUTS

Where there are taxes on capital funds, presumably analysts make similar assumptions to those we have discussed in relation to non-capital inputs. The question which has been most discussed in the literature is one of shadow prices. In 1958, Eckstein and Krutilla pointed out that ordinarily part of the capital funds used in public projects came from borrowing but part from private consumption through taxation[11]. From Eckstein, a number of economists have argued the case for giving this element in the capital cost what is in effect a different weight than for capital costs financed by borrowing. A justification of this is that the marginal valuations of individuals of their marginal income when it is taken from them involuntarily may vary and vary also from the marginal return on capital as equilibriated by the capital market.

PROJECT OUTPUTS

A criticism of traditional procedures – e.g. of the U.S. Army Corps of Engineers – was that (until 1953) they 'left out' profit taxes on private water projects when comparing their net benefit with public water projects with the effect of making the return on the public projects look more attractive[12]. Since then they have shifted to a 'taxes foregone' basis, whereby they consider what taxes the project would have had to pay if it had been private. This again is compatible with the *tax as transfer* approach as outlined. The evaluation of a project should measure the benefits whoever gets them, whether or not any part is paid out as taxation. It is arguable that one should track down what happens to the equivalent in public enterprise of what would have been profits taxes: how far they result in profits or are passed on in consumer's surplus. So far as it is the latter there would seem to be as strong a case for a shadow price approach for this in reverse as there was for capital funds raised through taxation.

In summary it would seem as if the idea that one should leave taxes out has shortcomings. One is instead interested in real benefits and costs of a project however these are divided between government and the rest of the community. In practice there would seem to be something to be said for these steps:

1. Decide which taxes can be regarded as (marginal cost) prices.
2. Decide if government revenue is to have a non-unit shadow price. Ditto savings.
3. Disentangle as far as one can the tax element in 'new' inputs and surplus; and count as changes in real resources.
4. Disentangle as far as one can, changes in the tax rates of the same inputs in the project being examined and elsewhere. Treat any difference which is simply one related to this change of use as reflecting a change in real resources.
5. Simplify the treatment of other input taxes by leaving them out.

TRANSPORT PROPOSALS IN THE GREATER LONDON DEVELOPMENT PLAN

What follows is simply a comment on the treatment of taxation in the evaluation of these proposals; and is no other appraisal of them. Table 4.1 shows the incremental benefits predicted to be realised by carrying through the Plan 3, rather than the Plan 1 motorway proposals[13].

Table 4.1. Table of net benefits

	Plan 3 over Plan 1
	£m.p.a.
Benefits due to changes in journey costs	29·9
Benefits due to increased capacity	53·8
Taxation benefit	41.7
TOTAL MEASURED BENEFITS	125·4
Maintenance cost increases	3·6
TOTAL ANNUAL NET MEASURED BENEFITS	122·8

The description of the categories is not a common one in highway cost-benefit analysis and needs some explanation.

1. *Benefit Due to Changes in Journey Costs*
This is the cross-hatched area in Fig. 4.1, defined as

$$\tfrac{1}{2}(q_1+q_2)(c_1-c_2)$$

where q_1, c_1 and q_2, c_2 are the volume of trips and trip costs on the smaller (Plan 1) and larger (Plan 3) networks respectively. Trip costs are defined as time savings and vehicle operating costs excluding fuel tax.

2. *Benefit due to Increased Capacity*
The explanation of this is that *if* the MPC of travel was constant $(=C_1)$, then the volume using the road would be q_x; but because the MPC function is actually upward sloping, the equilibrium volume on the smaller network would be q_y. Not knowing the slope of the MPC curve when it turns back, they in fact assume it rises vertically so that the assumed equilibrium volume on the smaller network is q_1.

This benefit is in two parts whose explanation is quite different.

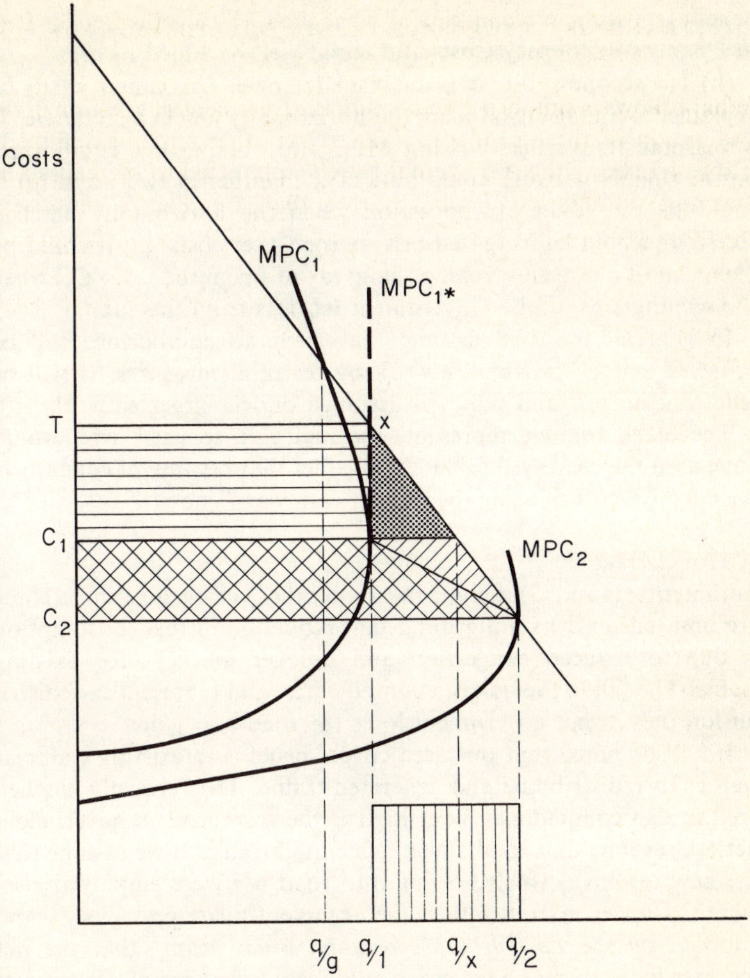

FIGURE 4.1.

(i) There is the diagonally hatched area. This represents the fact that *ex hypothesi* the traffic which was crowded off the road because of the rising MPC of congestion would have been prepared to pay at least C_1 to use the smaller network. Thus the cross-hatched area understates the benefit to them. (It is in effect that for purposes of measurement the item Benefit of Reduced Journey Costs assumed a more elastic demand curve than actually obtained. This sub-item of benefit is just the same in kind as what the LTS calls the Benefit Due to Changes in Journey Costs and could well be added to it.)

(ii) The second sub-item is the black triangle. This cannot easily be explained without introducing the horizontally hatched rectangle. If we assume the vertically rising MPC_{1*} to obtain, then equilibrium on the smaller network could hold at X in either of two ways. (*a*) It could be the result of congestion when the horizontally hatched rectangle would be increased private road-user costs. (*b*) It could be the result of a restraint (road pricing) tax of magnitude $(T-C_1)$ when the rectangle would be Government receipts from this tax.[2]

In general, the LTS assume that such an equilibrium will be achieved on the existing network by restraint measures. It will be seen that no restraint policy is assumed on the larger network.

The black triangle represents the real gain to users who would have used the road system but for the fact that because of congestion the effective cost of using the road system was T, not C_1.

3. *Tax Correction*

Both items (1) and (2) exclude fuel (and other vehicle taxation). These are omitted on the solid ground that reduction in fuel consumption is due to reduced congestion and quicker journeys for existing traffic. The fall in fuel tax is a consequence, and represents a redistribution only: what government loses the road-user gains.

It will be noted that this area covers benefits to existing traffic as well as to redistributed and generated traffic. The vertically hatched area is also counted as a benefit. It is the increment in government net tax revenue that results from generated traffic. If we assume that the new resources (fuel) flowing into road use were employed elsewhere at lower tax rates, then the argument made previously – and adopted by the *London Transportation Study* team – that the net increase in taxation is a benefit, would seem to be correct. (If some of the resources were not previously employed, it is to that extent an underestimate.)

This would only not be so if we imagined the higher tax rates on fuel not to be transfers but a price or deliberate evaluated policy. For example, if the higher than average expenditure tax rate on fuel were based on an evaluation which reckoned there were social costs offsetting the benefits from using more vehicle fuel and that to charge the higher rate of tax was a price or charge to reflect this, then

[2] This is *not* an optimal tax since it is designed to achieve maximum not economically efficient volumes.

it would be clearly wrong to treat the increased tax revenues as a benefit.[3]

4. The *London Transportation Study* does not consider the disappearance of the horizontally-hatched rectangle a benefit when the larger network is built except when *X* was reached through congestion. Then the saving in road-user costs is a real saving. It is valued at £175m per annum and increases the return in this case by 240 per cent.

But the argument of the first part of this paper suggests that to omit this when equilibrium was achieved on the larger network through road pricing or other restraint measures is wrong. The LTS argument is the standard one that what the road-user gains, the government loses. But in this case the tax is not a 'transfer' but a 'price'. As far as government is concerned, it is an efficient rent. To charge it implies a more efficient solution than not charging it from the standpoint of the economy; but it is only efficient to charge it because of the scarcity of road space. When an enlarged road network eliminates the case for charging rent, the government suffers no real loss, but the road-user makes real savings.

In this particular case it would seem that the principles adopted have led to some underestimation of the real benefits of the proposals. (Though to repeat, this is not to say that there may not be other reasons for valuing the net benefits of the proposals upwards or downwards. At issue here is only a point of taxation.)

REFERENCES

[1] In A. Maass, *Design of Water Resource Systems*, Harvard University Press, 1966, p. 210.

[2] A. Prest and R. Turvey, Cost-benefit analysis in *Surveys of Economic Theory*, vol. 3. Macmillan, 1966, p. 165.

[3] In this particular case, the position is more complicated because (i) if a price at all, fuel tax is usually thought of as a price of using the road, thus to treat it as a price at the same time as measuring benefits to road-users would run the risk of double-counting;

(ii) it is doubtful if one can regard fuel tax as a sufficiently efficient pricing system to be a price rather than a transfer. In this particular case there is also a worry that the method used may have double-counted the real benefit here. This was because although the principle of omission was accepted for all except generated traffic, the actual mechanics used were to include all indirect taxation in vehicle operating costs, thus producing a net figure change in Government revenue. This would only in any case have been an approximation to the correct magnitude, but there is some evidence that the tax correction was additional to this. However, this does not affect the principle of the argument.

[3] Cf. P. A. Samuelson, *Foundations of Economic Analysis*, Harvard University Press, 1947, pp. 243–4.

[4] E. J. Mishan, A Survey of welfare economics: 1939–59, *Economic Journal*, vol. 70, October 1960, p. 214.

[5] *Road Research Technical Report No. 46*, Department of Scientific and Industrial Research, UK 1960, p. 44.

[6] I. M. D. Little and J. A. Mirrlees, *Manual of Industrial Project Analysis in Developing Countries*, vol. 2, *Social Cost-Benefit Analysis*. Development Centre of OECD. 1969.

[7] Ministry of Transport, HMSO, 1968.

[8] Cf. Coburn *et al.* ref.[5]. But see B. V. Martin and M. Wohl, Evaluation of mutually exclusive design projects, *Highway Research Board Special Report No. 92*.

[9] On the deficiencies of fuel tax as a road price, see A. A. Walters, *The Economics of Road User Charges*, World Bank Staff Occasional Papers, no. 5, Johns Hopkins Press, 1968, pp. 194–213.

[10] The controversy goes back to Pigou's *Wealth and Welfare*, 1912. There is a good account of it in H. S. Ellis and W. Fellner, External economies and diseconomies, *American Economic Review*, 1943.

[11] J. V. Krutilla and O. Eckstein, *Multiple Purpose River Development*, Johns Hopkins Press, 1958, Ch. 4; O. Eckstein, *Water Resource Development*, Harvard University Press, 1958, p. 97; also P. O. Steiner, Choosing among alternative public investments, *American Economic Review*, Dec. 1959; M. S. Feldstein, Net social benefit calculation and the public investment decision, *Oxford Economic Papers*, March 1964.

[12] O. Eckstein, *Water Resource Development*, p. 244.

[13] The main data sources on the economic evaluation are J. O. Tressider, D. A. Meyer and T. J. Powell, The London transportation study: method and technique, *Proceedings of the Institute of Civil Engineers*, 1968, pp. 433–64; the Greater London Council, *Movement in London*, 1969; and Freeman Fox, Wilbur Smith, *London Transportation Study*, Phase 3, 1968.

5

Risk, Uncertainty and Cost Benefit: Some Notes on Practical Difficulties for Project Appraisals[1]

G. CORTI
H.M. Treasury

I

What are the phenomena of risk and uncertainty? Contemporary theory regarding the distinction made between risk and uncertainty is usually based on the work of Knight (*Risk*, *Uncertainty and Profit*, 1921). Risk is defined as situations in which the outcome is not certain but where the range of possible outcomes is known and the probabilities associated with these outcomes are known or can be estimated with some accuracy. Uncertainty relates to those situations where either the range of out turns is known, but where probabilities cannot be estimated accurately, or where even the range of possible outcomes is not known.

Situations of pure risk, hence refer to contingencies which can be protected against by the normal insurance practice of pooling. For this to be so, risk situations are characterised by a considerable degree of past experience. Uncertainty on the other hand relates to situations in some sense unique and of which there is very little certain knowledge of some or all significant aspects.

The usefulness of a risk-uncertainty distinction is, however, open to question in practice. There is no sharp dividing line on one side of which are situations of pure risk and on the other uncertainty. Rather the two extremes of pure risk and pure uncertainty merge into an intermediate 'mix' in most cases.

Let us consider a few of the major elements of risk and uncertainty.

(*a*) *Technology*

Technological change and development can substantially or drastic-

[1] Mr P. Gray helped with the preparation of this paper and Mr J. M. Bridgeman, Mr B. D. Cullen, Mr B. Denning and Mr J. Bowman offered constructive suggestions on early drafts of various parts of the paper.

ally affect the earning power of an investment project by suddenly cutting it short. This is particularly important for projects with a long expected life. Technological changes might occur either in techniques of production for a given commodity or through the development of completely new products which substitute for the original product as railways displaced canals.

(*b*) *Competition*

There are a great number of risks and uncertainties operating within a competitive framework. The action of a competitor in reply to or in anticipation of a major investment programme cannot be accurately predicted, but it can greatly affect the return. Indeed the essence of a competitive economic system is to inject uncertainty.

(*c*) *Government Action*

Particular steps taken by the government in its general economic policy can have important sectoral impacts which may alter the expected returns from an investment.

(*d*) *Differential Inflation*

There may arise unforeseen increases in costs, significantly above the general rate of inflation, in a particular investment project. Such differential inflation is very hard to predict and could be regarded as an example of

(*e*) *Snags*

A large variety of unpredictable events may occur during the life of an investment project. Some examples are strikes, exchange rate changes, takeovers of suppliers or customers and the occurrence of technological 'bugs' during design or construction.

Besides the width of the range of uncertainties implicit in analysing the future, in some cases these increase over time; time having an accumulating effect on some uncertainties.

However, it is possible to overdo things. What part of the capital invested in a given project is at risk? Because an investment is subject to a great variety of uncertainties it does not mean that all the capital is at risk. The relevant portion at risk, is that which could not be recovered if the project were abandoned. How far have the capital assets the valuable quality of flexibility? How far can they be used elsewhere or for other purposes? For instance, part at least of the

NCB's plant pools must have these attributes. In a similar way not all the positive cash flows resulting from a project need be at risk; long term sales contracts produce a safe as opposed to a risk portion. So knowledge of what proportion of the capital and income and expenditure flows are actually at risk is of importance in appraising uncertainty. This leads us very naturally to consider methodology.

Sensitivity analysis is a desirable first step in the appraisal of risk and uncertainty. As is well known, this is a method of testing the sensitivity of the merit of an investment. It involves revising estimates of uncertain assumptions and variables and ascertaining how such revision affects the expected profitability of a project. The idea is that management must become aware of the financial consequences of all likely outcomes before being able to make a reasoned evaluation of the worth of a project. Should management be convinced that the more important variables will not fall in the critical range such a project is termed 'fail safe' by Merrett and Sykes, that is, clearly profitable on all reasonable and likely assumptions. Although sensitivity analysis is an important first step because it concentrates attention on those factors most likely to affect the outcome, it is not a decision process in itself, except in identifying 'fail safe' projects.

The net present values which are the usual result of sensitivity analysis do not, however, take full account of all the knowledge which is available to the decision maker: some assumptions are more likely than others to prove right. The whole question of the treatment of risk and uncertainty is essentially therefore how you incorporate such additional information as you have about possible outcomes into the decision process. There are two basic elements in this: the use of analysis, usually involving the estimation of probabilities, and the use of various decision criteria. In some cases these elements are complementary.

Having obtained the various possible outcomes it is necessary to assign the probabilities of each outcome actually occurring. It is perhaps easiest to consider handling firstly where there is knowledge of probabilities, i.e. situations of 'risk' as opposed to complete uncertainty. Having weighted possible outcomes by the assigned probabilities it is possible to derive the expected monetary value of a project (that is the average of each possible outcome multiplied by its probability). This result now incorporates an allowance for risk.

Even where reasonably objective probabilities can be assigned, this type of result is criticised as being unsatisfactory because it is expressed in money terms. It is pointed out, quite correctly, that different people attach different values to the same amount of money. Ministers will probably take the view that it would be worth paying more for a barrage or barrier to protect London from a tidal surge of the Thames than would be justified by a straight calculation of the loss and multiplying it by the probability of its occurrence. It is argued, therefore, that the expected value of an investment should be expressed in utility terms to account for differing attitudes both to risk and money values. At a theoretical level this is perfect: at a practical level its application is open to severe doubt. Each manager certainly possesses his own 'utility map' – discovering it is a different matter. The approach usually suggested is to confront managers with a large series of alternatives, find out preferences and hence construct a utility function and use it to weight the outcomes. Utility functions are open to objection that any irrational choice makes them rather meaningless. Are we entitled to say that we are perfectly rational?

But uncertainty exists and must be considered. A distinction is often made between objective and subjective probabilities. It has been advocated by some that in areas of uncertainty the decision maker should substitute his subjective probability. It is hard, however, to make a sharp distinction, and cases in which it is possible to assign purely objective probabilities are by no means a majority. The aim should be to try to be as objective as possible by drawing on all possible information: some elements of subjective judgement are, however, almost certain to be necessary. In many cases you may be able to ask an engineer or a marketing manager drawing on their experience and such information as they have, to say what they think the odds are on something happening. If one is prepared to accept such judgements, and the key question is whose judgements, it is then possible to use the expected value criterion. Now real misapprehension can arise from using too much, or not recognising, subjective judgement in assigning probabilities. The effect is then merely to transfer the original uncertainty connected with possible outcomes to the probabilities attached thereto. The danger is either that both the analyst and his managerial colleagues will think there is a scientific basis for a 'right' decision, or that the manager knowing that subjective elements are included says 'its all guesswork' and flings analysis, and thus a lot of knowledge, away.

Where there is no confidence in assigning probabilities, that is in conditions of great uncertainty (of actual outcome, not of possible outcomes), a variety of decision rules – developments of game theory

– have been developed to aid management. These alternative decision rules which do not use subjective probability and thus avoid this rather doubtful stage in the analysis, are on the other hand open to the criticism that you are not making full use of the knowledge which is available to you within the organisation. The appropriate criterion varies for the person concerned – it is dependent on the individual's (or possibly the firm or corporation) attitude toward uncertainty. The more commonly discussed are Maxi-Min, Laplace, Minimax Regret and Maxi-Max in ascending order of optimism or 'risk loving'.

An apparently completely different approach to risk treatment from those above is to make adjustments to the *discount rate* used in net present value calculations. Adoption of a higher discount rate will cause a fall in the net present value of a project and hence build into the calculations an allowance for risk.

The rationale behind the discounting process is to allow for differences in the timing of cash flow, but not for risk, and this argues for the use of a risk free or time preference interest rate. The obvious problem here is the definition and identification of a 'risk free' rate of discount. For appraisal of nationalised industry investment, and much other public sector investment as well, the government has formulated a discount rate which we term 'low risk'. It has the advantage of being based on observation and the obvious disadvantage that 'low risk' is undefinable.

'Loading' the discount rate above a risk-free or low-risk rate as an allowance for risk is satisfactory in only a few cases. Increasing the rate assumes that risks are increasing into the future, that is risks are primarily a function of time. Changing the discount rate is a passable procedure when this is so, but it is a poor measure of many types of uncertainty which do not have this characteristic, such as consumer acceptance of product. In cases of great uncertainty this method appears to provide an 'easy escape' to the problem, but nevertheless is liable to lead to considerable distortions in the analysis, for example, by discriminating against capital-intensive and long-term projects. It has the attraction of simplicity.

The pay-back approach is a further easy, rule-of-thumb approach to the treatment of risk and uncertainty. Its appeal is limited to cases involving a particular type of risk – 'risk of a sudden cataclysm' involving an abrupt halt to cash flows. Where there is such a threat, for example, from technological developments, it is desirable to have a quick return from an investment project.

A similar approach to pay-back is to shorten the life of the project being appraised. If a particular investment project is expected to 'run' for thirty years, risk can be allowed for in the present value calculations by arbitrarily reducing the length of project appraisal to say, twenty years.

The arguments against the pay-back method are familiar and the arbitrariness of shortening the length of project appraisal is obvious. It is quite another matter in constructing alternative likely paths for cash flows to consider some in which the economic life of the project is considerably shorter than the most probable outcome.

But none of the 'easy' methods of dealing with risk avoid (indeed they positively obscure) defining the manager or the corporation's attitude towards risk or uncertainty. Of course by the very nature of the problem we are considering, judgement cannot be avoided in the majority of cases. But the advantage of the decision rules we considered earlier is that they cause one to reflect consciously, what standard of decision am I applying and is it appropriate to the firm or corporation's circumstances?

II

In autumn, 1969, there was a seminar on investment appraisal with board members of nationalised industries. In order not to keep the discussion on risk and uncertainty at too abstract a level enquiries about risk appraisal were made of a few contacts in private industry. Some were managing directors and the others directors or senior managers. None was working as an economist or an operational research specialist. The industries they were engaged in are engineering, oil, textiles and shipping. Five of the firms are very large indeed, the others medium-sized. All the firms use discounted cash flow methods for project appraisal. Only one specifically mentioned sensitivity analysis, but it can be inferred that others used it. The favourite method of analysis was to examine three or more sets of outcomes and then to try and assign probabilities thereto. There are some traces of confusion here because in some cases probabilities in the form of most likely outcomes seem to have been assigned before the analysis. All bar one of the firms did not employ a specifically risk loaded discounting rate; and the reason for the one firm doing so was specially related to international operations. One firm was considering using simulation techniques. When it came to decisions, all the managers referred to the degree of personal judgement remaining for the manager and especially for top management after the analyses were carried out. It was especially interesting that terms like optimism, pessimism and confidence were scattered throughout the replies received. Clearly none of the firms concerned has consciously sat down and said for instance, we will employ a minimax regret criterion of decision taking. Put this way it would of course sound bizarre if any of them had. But some interesting thoughts were prompted by the replies and by contrasting the position of these managers with those in the nationalised industries. The interest centred not so much on use of technique as on decision taking within the actual organisation.

Firstly, attitudes towards risk. It was noticeable that in talking to all levels of management in private enterprise firms an attitude towards risk taking pretty soon emerged; its major determinant being the attitude of top management. One was not concerned here with foolhardiness – not facing uncertainties – but some firms will always play it safe, others will consciously take more chances. How far in other organisations did Boards give guidance to other management levels on risk acceptance or aversion? How far should they give such guidance? How far did staffs think that positive mistakes will be identified and negative mistakes ignored?

Secondly, different methods of dealing with risk analysis had been outlined very briefly. Down to what size a project should one apply elaborate analysis? When do short-cut imperfect methods become the only practical measure? Obviously there comes a small size of investment project at which the game of elaborate appraisal is not worth the candle. Short-cut methods then become necessary. But there are two difficulties. How does one ensure a consistent attitude towards risk between the larger and smaller cases? How does one ensure that risks are not lost sight of when a lot of small investment projects are inter-connected or subject to the same risk.

Thirdly, who assesses risk within very large organisations? The usual first answer one gets to this question is that it is dependent on the size of the project. The larger the project, the higher the level at which it is considered; the smaller the more it can be delegated. But is this right? Because project appraisal is rightly delegated in very large organisations does it mean that all risks can be delegated? Which uncertainties and contingencies lie within the purview of subordinate management levels in the organisation which are properly taken account of by top management? It is not suggested that a lot more projects should be referred to top management. It is suggested that top management must guide, in some cases instruct, subordinate levels on the allowance to be made for some risks or uncertainties.

Risks which are peculiar to an individual project are very much the responsibility of the managers specifically concerned. But risks related to the whole economic health of the entity, firm or corporation, cannot be left without a clear allocation of responsibility, acknowledged by everyone. If this is not done then it could happen that each level of analyst and decision taker might take the risk into account so that over provision was made for it. Alternatively and possibly more likely in large hierarchal organisations no one may make allowance for aggregate risk particularly in respect of major changes in technology or the emergence of substitutional products. Kolb[1] challenges received American doctrine for many of public utilities: that is, that they are low-risk industries. In his view the gas industry in the United States comes out of the matter well because of its inherent flexibility. Yet in Britain the gas industry has gone through two technological revolutions in less than a decade. How much allowance for the second, not entirely unforeseeable contingency was made when decisions were being taken on the first?

One important point that emerged from the discussion that Autumn was the importance of feeding back into the organisation's general strategy the conclusions that emerged from considering individual projects.

Conversely, it was necessary to ensure that major uncertainties were appraised at the strategic decision stage when they could not be coped with at the individual project stage. The view taken about the riskiness of an individual railway project, or about the absorption rate of natural gas in a particular area, should be related to thinking on railway investment and the natural gas programme as a whole. This amounted to no more and *no less* than saying that organisations needed to check that the base line of their thinking was still valid.

This leads to an even more difficult and contentious question which seems to have received too little consideration in the literature. What happens when the risks involved are so large, so aggregated that they are important socially for the whole community? Who considers these possibilities? This is not a problem of who pays *ex post* or even of who takes the decision, but rather of who faces the uncertainties and who ensures that they are faced? An example might be with us soon in the field of inter-urban transport where various possible competing systems can be contemplated – improved motorways and roads; improved cars and buses; improved airports and airport links;

vertical take-off aircraft; tracked hovercraft; advanced passenger trains.

Investment appraisal can never be better than the figures which have to be employed. Since these figures relate to the future they will almost always have a measure of uncertainty about them. Furthermore the decisions must be made within continuing organisations: not as isolated abstract exercises. In practical terms, having regard to difficulties actually encountered, the following conclusions are drawn.

(*a*) Sensitivity analysis is a useful first step for identifying factors most likely to affect the outcome.

(*b*) The better way of proceeding is to attach probabilities and expected values, as far as possible, to alternate likely paths for cash flows for the assessment. It is worth establishing how practical it is to get this process on to a routine basis, particularly with the aid of computers.

(*c*) It is necessary to be as clear as possible about what are the objective and subjective elements entering into assumptions, projections and weighting.

(*d*) Although analysis and decision-taking judgement are frequently inter-related, the two must not be confused and the judgement element faced on its own. Decision rules may help with this.

(*e*) Top management should define its attitude towards risk and communicate this to subordinate managers.

(*f*) Some risks will affect the whole economic well-being of an organisation and yet lie outside the purview of most of its managers. Top management should instruct or guide all its managers on how to treat these risks. These are in the main risks and uncertainties affecting or determining overall strategy.

III

So far these notes have not sought to define closely the framework within which the project analysis and decision-taking were being made. Is it taking place on a conventional basis of 'cash' values, or private returns, or in a framework of social returns and costs, on cost-benefit analysis? Certainly, as one moves from a conventional analysis, whether carried out in a profit maximising or cost minimising area, towards a social cost-benefit appraisal, the problems arising out of risk and uncertainty do not diminish. This difficulty was noted by Prest and Turvey in the concluding section of their *Cost Benefit Analysis: A Survey*.

Two practical examples of work intended to provide a background to decision-taking in fields when social costs could be important are worth discussing briefly. The first is concerned with the Hartlepools Power Station. On 21 August 1968, the Minister of Power announced that the government had consented to the CEGB's application to build an additional nuclear power station at Hartlepool with a capacity of 1250 MW. The government announcement stated that careful and sympathetic consideration had been given to the case for a coal-fired station and in examining the choice between the different fuels they took full account of the wider economic factors including in particular the effect of the decision on employment. There was some public interest in the decision which, despite a disclaimer, was regarded as important for the future choice between coal and nuclear power stations. The decision was difficult and important enough on its own terms, however, and was reached by the Minister on the basis of a good deal of work done in government, involving consultation with both the CEGB and the NCB. The nature of this work was not and has not been made public: though there is a brief description in the report of the SCNI on Ministerial Control of Nationalised Industries.

In November 1969, Mr G. K. Jones[2] drew three conclusions of which only two need concern us here. These are:

(*a*) The outcome of the analysis is heavily dependent on the values assigned to major factors. Given the uncertainties of estimation it is essential to employ sensitivity analysis to provide a range of possible outcomes, rather than to produce a single figure.

(*b*) Employment effects, when considered solely from a purely economic viewpoint, seem highly significant and on a wide range of assumptions about duration of unemployment are sufficient to alter the outcome of the analysis.

As regards the first conclusion this is not in question as far as it goes. The elements identified by Mr Jones as being important are capital cost (but not station life), system simulation, that is running stations in order of merit, the discount rate, unemployment, the cost of coal and intangibles. All of these elements were considered in the work leading up to the decision. Present values for alternative choices both for the station and the system were estimated and sensitivity analysis was employed. As regards Mr Jones's second conclusion, unquestionably if a social cost-benefit analysis of a project is being carried out, regard should be had to the relevance of employment and unemployment effects. A power station which could affect the employment of miners in an area of above-average unemployment certainly warrants examination of this factor. Two methods of calculation may be attempted.

(*a*) To assume that the opportunity cost of idle labour would be zero and to set about estimating on various assumptions the length of time for which men might be unemployed, having regard especially to age, training and location.

(*b*) To employ an 'unemployment relative' for shadow pricing the labour which would be affected in the area (at rates depending on the relative, varying from 100 per cent to zero) and to make various assumptions about the relative rates of unemployment nationally and in the area for estimating the relative.

Both methods entail making assumptions about unemployment rates over long periods, in this case for twenty to thirty years from 1975 *onwards*. It is possible that unemployment in the relevant area at levels warranting some reduction in the accounting cost of coal can be predicted for periods from a minimum of seven to a maximum of nearly forty years in the future. But with what degree of certainty? Calculations on a variety of estimates should be carried out and these should allow for employment effects as well as unemployment – a nuclear power station requires extra labour during construction, as compared with a conventional station. In fact very great variations in the effect on employment and unemployment were eventually tested. Furthermore, it is at least arguable that the final choice of which assumptions are the most probable for the future, or the most acceptable, on this count, must involve a considerable amount of judgement, including a substantial amount of political judgement.

Reflection on the nature of forecasts of the main variables – capital and appropriate mining costs, system simulation, discount rate and employment – immediately indicates firstly that all the elements of risk and uncertainty, exemplified previously, are present in greater or lesser degree, secondly that a number of these elements are likely to involve subjective elements of judgement (not to mention that some are emotionally charged and rightly so; when we proceed from economics through analysis to decision-taking we are dealing with people). Mr Jones does not discuss whether some attempt should be made to gauge the relative probabilities of the various out turns. It would seem wrong to aggregate all favourable or unfavourable out turns – depending on one's point of view for what is favourable or unfavourable – and this might be the outcome of leaving the matter at the sensitivity stage. If this is to be avoided and the decision does not lie in the fail-safe range as defined above, then the prescriptions set out above, or at least those at IIa to d would have to be applied. How far this will clarify the decision cannot be certain, elements of judgement must remain. In brief, one can agree with Mr Jones's first conclusion, because in fact sensitivity analysis was applied; but more than this is and was necessary for a decision.

The second example concerns the Third London Airport Study. Here indeed is a massive piece of work: probably the largest cost benefit – or is it social cost minimising study? – to date in Britain. The work of the Commission and its research team will provide an invaluable basis for the decision, will we ever need a TLAP,* and if so, when? The critical variables seem to be associated with or contained in traffic forecasts. Traffic forecasts contain at least two variables in turn, that is the relative growth of demand by air travellers and aircraft size. Both of these contain considerable elements of risk and uncertainty – consider the elements set out earlier in this paper. Other variables could affect the significance of different traffic forecasts, for instance different management regimes or differential pricing systems. (Thereafter the questions of evaluation of time – discussed at length in the report – would arise.) Let us suppose, however, that the two variables bearing on traffic forecasts are critical. We are not entirely without knowledge of either the history or the prospects for these variables. There is much risk and some uncertainty in projecting them. It should be possible, though difficult and contentious, to assign probabilities to various outcomes for demand and aircraft size. It would then be possible to calculate probabilities of TLAP ever being needed or being needed at various future time horizons. If the outcome showed that TLAP would be needed, then the costs and benefits of acceleration or delay could be weighted by the probabilities related to future periods of time. Passenger demand is indeed forecast and probabilities are attached thereto by the Working Party on Traffic and Capacity Forecasts. Then the research team set out in Table 28.19 air traffic movement, and probabilities for various forecasts at future dates are attached thereto, giving

* Maplin

expected costs. But it is difficult to discern how they have treated the relationships between passenger growth and aircraft size, so that air traffic movement is not dealt with entirely clearly. We may assume that these matters have occurred to Mr F. Thompson and his team and we may hope that their work and thoughts on this aspect of the TLAP debate will be made available not only to those concerned with making the decision but also to the public who were so interested as to cause the Commission.

How do these two examples measure up against the conclusions drawn earlier? In both cases sensitivity analysis was applied. Let us re-pose the question. When we are dealing with risks which are so large and so aggregated that they are important for the community, who faces the uncertainty and who ensures that they are faced? The answer would seem to have to be the government. But this answer seems to raise questions about the manner in which we should look at and study the largest project appraisals. May I suggest that there is a need for more cross-disciplinary analysis in these fields? In the earlier part of the paper, in the context of the firm or trading organisations, it became necessary to pose questions which were prompted by business studies including those on business organisation and behaviour, in addition to those derived from economics and operational research. So in extending analysis to consider social cost benefits in the actual field of decision-taking, that is where risk and uncertainty exist, it would seem highly desirable to go further and to associate with the disciplines already identified studies in government, in the widest sense, and administration. How else are we going to avoid applying analysis based on a distinction between private and social returns with insufficient parallel diffentiation between the social organisations concerned? How else ensure that the degree of risk propensity or aversion is appropriate to and reflects the many interests concerned?

REFERENCES

[1] Burton A. Kolb, *The Rise and Fall of Public Utilities – An Appraisal of Risk*.

[2] G. K. Jones, *Cost-benefit analysis of the Choice between Nuclear and Other Fuels*.

See also: Alan Williams, Output budgeting and the contribution of micro-economics to efficiency in Government.

6

The Assessment of Project Worth with Applications to Research and Development

H. THOMAS
London Graduate School of Business Studies

DISCUSSION

There is a need at this time to re-evaluate and discuss the methodological issues involved in the method of rational decision-making known as cost-benefit analysis. There are many theoretical problems associated with the improvement of cost-benefit techniques arising in part at least from the degree of arbitrariness which is inherent in such studies.

The best known of British cost-benefit studies are the studies which were carried out to help justify decisions to build the Victoria Line[1] and the M1. Recently, of course, cost-benefit analysis has been applied to the difficult task of deciding upon the location of the third London Airport and has inevitably come under fire (see, for example, P. Self[2]) from critics of the method who resent the degree of arbitrariness involved in numerical quantifications of, in particular, social costs and benefits.

Whilst these techniques can be criticised for giving 'soft' numbers there are certain clear advantages which they offer. First, they force the decision-maker to recognise that the investment project under consideration has cost-benefit elements which cannot easily be expressed in cash terms but which inevitably affect the worth of the project. Second, by forcing the decision-maker to clinically dissect the elements of the decision problem it will tend to reduce the arbitrariness of governmental decision-making and the extent to which decision-making can be affected by particular political pressure groups and interests. Third, and this is an important point, they have a proven record of success. Despite the at times carping criticism of Roskill (see, for example, K. Richardson[3]), it can fairly be said that the cost-benefit analysis exercise has at least reduced the dimensionality of the decision-maker's decision problem and enabled him to see the choice between the subset of feasible alternative sites more clearly. Fourth, it gives the interested parties in the planning process the chance of full involvement in the process of decision-making.

Cost-benefit analysis thus has a purpose both at the governmental planning level and at the micro level of the firm. Whilst the analysis becomes more complicated at the governmental level because of the large number of externalities involved (e.g. social factors) the principles involved in the cost-benefit exercise are similar at both macro and micro levels. In this paper we discuss general methodological considerations of cost-benefit analysis in relation to private investment in research and development and contrast cost-benefit procedures with decision theory analysis.

INTRODUCTION

Professor Howard Raiffa[4] quotes a speech by Admiral Rickover to the Committee on Appropriations, House of Representatives in the United States, which neatly summarises some of the unfavourable aspects of cost-benefit (or effectiveness) studies. The most useful extract for our purposes follows:

> 'The basis for using cost-effectiveness studies as the rationale on which to make a decision is the assumption that the important factors can be expressed in numerical form and that a correct judgement of the situation can then be calculated mathematically. But for most complex situations this is an unrealistic assumption. Frankly, I have no more faith in the ability of the social scientists to quantify military effectiveness than I do in numerologists to calculate the future . . .'

The essence of Rickover's argument is that it is unwise to surrender the cost-benefit analysis to analysts who have not sufficient experience in the military area. He has some justification for being cautious in the light of the available evidence about cost overruns in military research and development. The studies carried out by Marshall and Meckling[5], Peck and Scherer[6] and Summers[7] on military research and development projects show that initial estimates of cost are far too small in relation to actual final values.

This finding is also broadly true of commercial research and development as evidenced by the studies of Meadows[8], Allen and November[9] and Thomas[10], though Mansfield's study[11] shows little evidence of estimate inaccuracy. In addition the Thomas study shows that engineers find difficulty in estimating the benefit variables (e.g. sales, price and market life) for research and development projects.

Rickover's reaction to the above evidence would probably be to conclude that we should abandon any analysis. The more sensible reaction to the problems of uncertainty is to try to improve the methods of analysis. Let us suppose for expository purposes that our problem is to assess the worth of R & D projects in industrial R & D and decide which projects to undertake.

In the discussion which follows we carry through a decision analysis procedure for R & D projects. We first consider the crucial issues of our decision problem – the assessment of project worth and a number of allied measurement problems. We then turn to the second phase of the decision analysis, namely the determination of the criterion or objective by means of which we shall discriminate between projects. Once we have answers to these phases of the analysis we shall present the results of the decision analysis and contrast it with a non-mathematical decision analysis model suggested by Churchman and Ackoff[12].

THE ASSESSMENT OF PROJECT WORTH

Many models have been proposed in the literature for simplifying appraisals of project worth. These range from check lists of desirable properties that a project should possess and from which a score is obtained to more sophisticated financial appraisals. Mottley and Newman[13], for example, suggest that a project should be graded in terms of five factors: promise of success (P), time of completion (T), cost of project (C), strategic need (N), and market gain (M). They suggest that the project should be evaluated on each factor and a total value score be obtained for the project by means of the following convention. Each factor is given a score of 1, 2 or 3 (a low value indicating high potential and vice-versa) and the total value score is obtained by multiplying the project factor scores together. It is clear immediately that such a method is not very valuable because of the weaknesses of the scoring procedures and the equal weights given to each of the five factors (which are assumed to exhaust the desirable properties for a project). Dean[14] also presents the range of available financial measures. We shall concentrate in this paper on capital budgeting criteria such as the net present value (NPV) of a project. Our justification for NPV comes from Turvey[15].

We assume initially that a financial objective is reasonable for R & D project analysis and consider ways of incorporating and allowing for uncertainty in our financial measures of project worth. Before we do this we should outline the logic of our decision analysis procedure in terms of an idealised decision tree diagram. The decision tree shown in Fig. 6.1 shows a set of possible decisions (indicated by square boxes □) and chance events (indicated by ○) which might occur during the life of an R & D project.

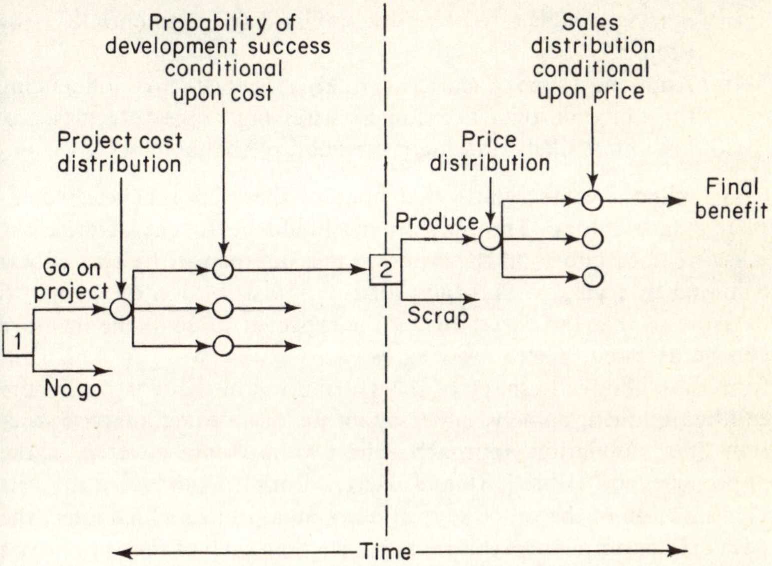

FIGURE 6.1.

A diagram such as the one above depicts no more than the futurity of possible decisions and chance events that the decision-maker feels may occur during the life of the R & D project. It is thus a logical flow diagram of future possibilities and is useful for the decision analyst in identifying uncertain quantities such as cost, price, sales etc. for which marginal and conditional probability assessments will have to be obtained from the decision-maker. Although there are severe problems in obtaining such subjective marginal and conditional probability measures we shall not consider them here. Reference can, however, be made to either [10] or [16].

With the decision-flow diagram as a logical basis for our present analysis we turn for the moment to a consideration of how we incorporate uncertainty into capital investment analysis. Uncertainty to the firm is the possibility of unpredicted fluctuations in the cash flow pattern occurring on a given project. Hertz[17] in a classic article on capital investment analysis discusses a number of efforts which have been made to cope with uncertainty. They comprise:

(i) More accurate forecasts of cash flows.
(ii) Empirical, subjective adjustments to some of the factors influencing the outcome of a decision.
(iii) Setting a high rate of return standard for a potentially risky project.
(iv) Applying a type of sensitivity analysis to the factors influencing the outcome of a decision by assessing range forecasts, say low, most likely and highest values, of the factors.

He suggests quite rightly that none of these approaches is completely satisfactory. The major aim should be to characterise the effect of uncertainty on the criterion measure of worth. This is best achieved by trying to find the probability distribution of the worth measure so that the variability of the expected value of the measure can be assessed. There are clearly two possible ways in which information about the shape of the distribution of the worth measure can be obtained, namely, either by means of an exact analytic solution or a simulation approach. The two ways are covered in the approaches of Hillier[18] and Hertz. Both methods require the identification of the set of key variables on a project which affect the cash flow pattern. Once this set is known then each of the approaches can produce an approximation to the distribution of the worth measure. In the next section we turn to a detailed statistical consideration of both approaches.

A STATISTICAL TREATMENT OF UNCERTAINTY ON FINANCIAL MEASURES OF WORTH

Measures Based on the Probability Distribution of NPV or IRR

In our treatment of the two possible approaches for obtaining the probability distribution of NPV and IRR we will first consider the rationale of each approach and then give the flow diagrams and mathematical derivations. In later sections we shall present some results of the use of such measures on a sample of operational projects.

The simulation approach

We shall consider first of all the work of Hertz and Hess and Quigley [19] who first derived the simulation approach commonly known as risk analysis.

The steps in the procedure are as follows:

(i) Identify the set of significant key input factors for the investment decision under consideration.

(ii) Obtain estimates of the range of values for each of the factors (e.g. selling price of final product, investment cost, etc.) and within that range the likelihood of occurrence of each value. In essence, therefore, we must obtain information about the likely probability distribution of each key factor.

Since these factors are often interdependent we must try to estimate and quantify the correlations between them. These correlations are introduced by means of conditional probability distributions. Thus, if we sample a value from the distribution of one key variable the value obtained will determine which of several conditional distributions should be sampled to give the value of another variable.

(iii) Logically, in our treatment of correlation effects it was necessary in step (ii) to indicate how they would be tackled before discussing the sampling procedure. However, this third phase consists of selecting at random from each of the relevant distributions a value for each of the key factors and allowing for correlation effects as in step (ii).

(iv) The sample values on each iteration should then be used to calculate the cash flows over the time periods of the project's life. From these cash flows the measure of worth (say, NPV) of the project, is determined.

(v) This procedure is repeated for a set of iterations sufficient to establish the shape of the NPV distribution for the project.

The risk-analysis approach has become popular since its development largely because of its simplicity in application and its ability to handle a wide range of possible distributions on the significant factors underlying the investment decision. Further, very few assumptions have to be made in setting up this type of simulation model. However, the simulation approach is an imprecise technique because it provides only an approximation to the true probability distribution and is not adequate for describing the extreme points or tails of the distribution. Simulation methods are also cumbersome and time-consuming, because of the problems of developing the model, preparing the input data, developing computer programs and completing the simulated runs. Risk analysis is most useful as a sensitivity analysis mechanism and as a means for incorporating into the analysis analytically difficult skew distributions on the key factors underlying the investment decision.

The Analytical Approach

Hillier[20, 21, 22, 23] and Wagle[24] have been responsible for the development of an alternative exact analytic approach for measuring the worth of an individual project. The initial stages in the procedure are similar to those of the Hertz approach in that we must identify the set of significant input factors for the investment decision and estimate their means, variances and the nature of the association between some of them. Hillier then makes the assumption that the probability of cash flows of various magnitudes occurring in a given year can be described by the normal distribution. With this assumption we can show that the distribution of possible values of an investment project's present worth will also be approximately normally distributed. This method is very flexible and simple for obtaining the distribution of a project's NPV but less suitable for obtaining the distribution of the internal rate of return criterion. If the NPV distribution is normal and obtained with some discount rate r then the equation $P(\text{IRR} > r) = P(\text{NPV} > 0)$, where P denotes 'probability of', can be used to give a point on the cumulative distribution of the IRR criterion. Several points on the cumulative distribution can then be obtained from the equation above by considering different values for the discount rate r in the NPV calculation. In this way from the points obtained the cumulative and probability density functions of the IRR criterion can be approximated.

In situations where the distribution of IRR is required it can be seen that the analytical calculation is quite time-consuming whereas the simulation model can give the IRR distribution directly. Further, if the NPV distribution is not normal the equation above cannot be used to derive points on the cumulative distribution of the IRR function. Despite this difficulty, in situations when the assumptions of the analytic model hold approximately it should give a quicker, cheaper and more accurate (at least as far as the tails of the distribution are concerned) measure than the equivalent simulation approach. Because of the costly and time-consuming nature of the simulation method it is only likely to prove effective when the assumption of normally distributed cash flows is not realistic.

The choice of approach is thus a function of the nature of the investment decision and the types of probability distributions which appear to characterise the uncertainties in the key input factors. A method which is valuable to decision makers in determining the choice between approaches is sensitivity analysis. For example, if we wanted to question the assumption of normality of each of the cash flow distributions when the decision makers assess slightly skew distributions for these cash flows we can set up two simulation runs with normal distributions for cash flows in one case and skew distributions in the other case. From the results we could then determine the rough effect of skewness on the shape of the overall criterion distribution, NPV or IRR.

Detailed Consideration of the Analytical Approach

The analytical model presented here to derive the probability distributions of NPV and IRR is reproduced from Wagle's paper with certain notational alterations.

Suppose first that an investment decision problem is characterised by m sources of cash flows $S_1, \ldots, S_m$ and let the random variable Y_{tk} denote the cash flow in the tth year from the kth source S_k. Assume that Y_{tk} has a finite mean μ_{tk} and variance $\sigma^2{}_{tk}$.

Now let the net cash flow in the tth year be denoted by V_t.

Then

$$V_t = \sum_{k=1}^{m} Y_{tk}$$

and

$$E(V_t) = \sum_{k=1}^{m} \mu_{tk} = W_t$$

$$V(V_t) = \sum_{k=1}^{m} \sigma_{tk}^2 + 2\sum_{k \neq j} \text{cov}\,(Y_{tk}, Y_{tj}).$$

If the project life is assumed to be n years then

$$\text{NPV}_n(i) = \sum_{t=0}^{n} \left[\frac{V_t}{(1+i)^t}\right].$$

Where (i) NPV_n denotes the net present value over a project life of n years, and (ii) $100i\%$ denotes the rate of discount or cost of capital to the firm then

$$E[\text{NPV}_n(i)] = \sum_{t=0}^{n} \frac{W_t}{(1+i)^t} = \text{W}_n(i)(\text{say})$$

$$V[\mathrm{NPV}_n(i)] = \sum_{t=0}^{n} \frac{V(V_t)}{(1+i)^{2t}} + 2\sum_{t \neq t^1} \frac{\operatorname{cov}(V_t, V_t^1)}{(1+i)t+t^1}$$

$$= R_n^{\,2}(i)\,(\text{say})$$

Thus for fixed n the expressions above give the values of the mean and variance of NPV.

These expressions can be amended if n the project life is itself variable – a case which occurs frequently in practice. If n has some discrete probability distribution and P_n denotes the probability of the project life being n years, then

$$E[\mathrm{NPV}(i)] = \sum_{n=N_1}^{N_2} P_n \cdot E[\mathrm{NPV}_n(i)]$$

$$= \sum_{n=N_1}^{N_2} P_n \cdot W_n(i)$$

$$E[\mathrm{NPV}^2(i)] = \sum_{n=N_1}^{N_2} P_n \cdot E[\mathrm{NPV}_n^2(i)]$$

and

$$V[\mathrm{NPV}(i)] = \sum_{n=N_1}^{N_2} P_n \cdot E[\mathrm{NPV}_n^2(i)] - \left(\sum_{n=N_1}^{N_2} P_n \cdot E[\mathrm{NPV}_n(i)]\right)$$

$$= \sum_{n=N_1}^{N_2} P_n R_n^2(i) + \sum_{n=N_1}^{N_2} P_n[W_n(i) - E\,W_n(i)]^2$$

give the values for the mean and variance of the NPV criterion function.

In the derivation of the formula for the mean and variance of the net present value criterion we have omitted discussion of two critical problems which we are not able to consider here.[1]

(i) The conditions under which the distribution of net present value follows the normal distribution.

(ii) The formulae for the mean and variance of net present value require estimates of the means and variances of the various cash flows and of the covariances between them.

Having outlined the essence of the simulation and analytical approaches we discuss and present the results of the simulation approach on a sample of industrial R & D projects.

[1] The interested reader will find full details in Hillier[18] or Wagle[24].

The Simulation Approach and a Discussion of the Results

The simulation approach was undertaken for the following reasons:

(i) To assess the sensitivity of the normality assumption for the final criterion function to non-normality in the cash flow distributions making up the particular investment project.

(ii) To assess the reasonableness of characterising uncertainty about particular parameters in terms of probability distributions on those parameters. For example, do decision-makers think in probabilistic terms and how sensitive is the final result to the subjective input distributions of different decision-makers?

(iii) To give some evidence on the general structure of a capital budgeting problem in the R D area. For example, what do the distributions of IRR and payback, which are difficult to obtain analytically, look like?

The first factor is important because if it appears that the normal assumption for the NPV distribution is robust against non-normality of various forms in the cash flow distributions, then the simulation approach is considerably inferior to any of the analytical approaches outlined in the previous section for obtaining a measure of worth for a project simply, cheaply and efficiently.

The second factor is important because both the analytical and simulation approaches depend upon the accurate estimation of cash flow distributions from decision-makers and often these are obtained on a subjective basis. If it appears from the evidence that measures of worth vary in value according to which decision-maker assessed the cash flow distributions, then our measure of worth depends heavily upon the estimation ability of the particular decision-maker.

The third factor is valuable to aid the further statistical development of financial criteria of worth in the area of capital budgeting.

Clearly, the basic disadvantage of a simulation is its cost of implementation and routine calculation. The development of the simulation approach is only justifiable here insofar as it helps us to determine the relevance of existing analytical approaches. If these analytical models are useful then they would obviously be used to determine the worth measure as the first stage in our decision analysis procedure.

We will thus consider successively the structure of the model, a discussion of the computer programming work and a consideration of the final results and their bearing upon the issues about analytical versus simulation approaches raised earlier.

MODEL STRUCTURE

We follow the basic cash flow structure of the model outlined earlier. We assume as a first approximation that the net cash flows in successive years of a project's life are statistically independent. Further, the economic factors making up the net cash flow pattern are assumed to be independently distributed. These assumptions, whilst restrictive, are necessary to limit the amount of subjective information to be derived from a particular decision-maker. They can gradually be relaxed.

The basic economic factors considered in the evaluation of a particular R & D project comprise estimates of development cost per year of the project's life, production and sales costs when at the point of commercial sale, the price at which the product will be sold and the quantity which will be sold per year of the project's life. These estimates are considered in relation to the decision-maker's subjective distribution about the length of the project's life cycle.

Once estimates of the relevant economic factors have been obtained the appropriate measure of the project's worth, i.e. NPV, IRR or payback can be obtained. Thus, if the project is assumed to have a fixed project life the simulation approach consists of generating a value for each of the relevant economic factors from the appropriate probability distribution and so obtaining a value for the net cash flow in each year of the project's life. Then, the measure of worth is calculated from the project for the first iteration of values from the appropriate probability distributions and from repeated iterations of this process a distribution of values for the measure of worth is obtained. Thus, distributions for NPV, IRR and payback can be generated and graphed.

The distributions obtained in this way are statistical estimates and not exact results. Given both time and cost constraints, it was decided that 150 iterations would be sufficient to obtain a reasonable approximation to the true mean and variance of the profitability measure.

DATA

The data base for our analysis of research and development projects consisted of a potential sample of fifteen projects from Firm *A* and 8 projects from Firm *B*. In some cases, by the time the fieldwork measurements of the probability distributions on the underlying factors had been started, the list of potential prospective projects had been reduced because initial preliminary review had detected one or two relatively unprofitable research projects amongst the portfolios of fifteen or eight. In fact, the initial review analysis was of a similar type to the Churchman–Ackoff model which was carried out on the same data base of eight projects for *B* and 15 projects for *A*. Further, since the time involved in obtaining the subjective input measures from the decision-makers was considerable, it was decided to evaluate the sample of projects in Firm *A* most intensively.

Certain steps were followed in obtaining data for our models. These were:

(i) Identification of the relevant decision-makers in firms *A* and *B* – this is the same first stage analysis as in the implementation of the C–A model.
(ii) Evaluation of appropriate probability distributions from decision-makers.
(iii) Fitting possible theoretical probability distributions to the decision-makers' probability distributions.

The problems involved in obtaining these probability distributions and transferring them into equivalent theoretical distributions with known parameters are not taken up here. Finally, it should be noted that the data are not presented in detail here because of the need to maintain the anonymity of the co-operating firms.[2]

ANALYSES AND RESULTS

It should be noted that the time involved in each simulation run was approximately two to three minutes. This meant that a fully comprehensive programme of simulation runs was not carried out because of time and cost constraints.

(i) *All Normal Analysis*

For each project under consideration in *A* and *B*, normal distributions with appropriate parameters were fitted to the distributions assessed by different decision-makers on the underlying economic factors. Given the fact of the independence of these factor distributions it follows that the final criterion function NPV is in this instance normally distributed.

[2] Working papers containing details of the data may be obtained by bona-fide researchers from the author.

Table 6.1. Firm *A*, decision-maker 1, DM;1_A.

Project	Length of life (years)	IRR (%) Mean (S.D.)	(Years) Payback Mean (S.D.)	NPV at 10% (£) Mean (S.D.)	NPV at 15% (£) Mean (S.D.)	NPV at 20% (£) Mean (S.D.)	NPV at 25% (£) Mean (S.D.)
01	7	126·40 (3·95)	2·53 (0·04)	224750·25 (7735·27)	177891·06 (6273·63)	142163·16 (5183·60)	114536·31 (4320·83)
02	4		1·70 (0·08)	241574·81 (207515·5)	204928·81 (18364·87)	174653·19 (16398·62)	149435·62 (14734·66)
02	5	140·23 (12·68)	1·68 (0·07)	287407·25 (21601·30)	241748·12 (18795·00)	204526·37 (16795·46)	173893·94 (14393·09)
02	6	138·82 (13·31)	1·70 (0·08)	307244·75 (21980·25)	256668·00 (19343·36)	215831·25 (17182·66)	182512·06 (15371·20)
03	7	242·27 (8·50)	2·25 (0·02)	847168·69 (27414·72)	679080·06 (22103·64)	550615·00 (13148·94)	451069·50 (15077·94)
04	7	61·18 (3·37)	3·40 (0·09)	30023·27 (1573·22)	22404·97 (1321·43)	16711·98 (1119·31)	12407·14 (964·13)
05	5	79·19 (3·98)	2·70 (0·05)	103578·75 (7232·00)	82895·75 (6128·98)	66458·50 (5225·32)	53278·18 (4489·47)
05	6	85·92 (3·63)	2·72 (0·08)	143929·81 (7545·21)	114851·12 (6303·92)	90930·81 (5358·06)	72630·19 (4592·86)
05	7	92·30 (3·33)	2·72 (0·08)	196037·75 (8536·27)	153748·25 (6994·76)	121417·06 (5839·66)	96383·62 (4939·21)
08	3	> 500%	1·07 (0·01)	332566·69 (21526·84)	298725·56 (19312·31)	269625·5 (17424·93)	244434·06 (15827·29)
08	4	> 500%	1·07 (0·01)	442844·25 (24098·02)	390890·56 (21349·54)	347231·00 (14034·38)	310231·25 (17125·23)
10	3	506·50 (31·47)	1·21 (0·02)	207502·81 (8913·48)	183480·50 (8002·81)	163081·12 (7171·43)	145635·50 (6435·10)
10	4	526·50 (22·72)	1·21 (0·01)	350226·00 (12544·00)	302973·31 (10752·00)	263877·62 (9413·00)	231254·50 (8245·32)

Table 6.2. Decision-maker 1_B.

Project	Length of life (years)	IRR (%) Mean (S.D.)	Payback Mean (S.D.)	NPV at 10% (£) Mean (S.D.)	NPV at 15% (£) Mean (S.D.)	NPV at 20% (£) Mean (S.D.)	NPV at 25% (£) Mean (S.D.)
04		2·16	2·98	−6583·18	−5933·16	−5374·98	−4892·34
		(6·95)	(0·16)	(2009·45)	(1803·65)	(1627·90)	(1476·70)
08		444·71	2·15	341332·31	280068·69	233177·56	194277·74
		(140·63)	(0·22)	(109320·69)	(90637·00)	(76074·19)	(64566·93)
Decision-maker 2_B*							
08		199·73	2·37	83102·31	67626·87	55557·86	46031·62
		(55·21)	(0·26)	(28568·53)	(23532·35)	(19653·44)	(16850·91)

* An alternative evaluation for project 2*B* was obtained from the marketing manager in the firm.

Table 6.3. Firm *A*, decision-maker 2, DM;2_A.

Project	Length of life (years)	IRR (%) Mean (S.D.)	Payback Mean (S.D.)	NPV at 10% (£) Mean (S.D.)	NPV at 15% (£) Mean (S.D.)	NPV at 20% (£) Mean (S.D.)	NPV at 25% (£) Mean (S.D.)
02	3	41·62	2·06	26018·14	19787·99	14579·86	10202·60
		(15·34)	(0·23)	(12486·37)	(11304·25)	(10286·72)	(9404·92)
02	4	77·60	1·99	79432·81	65463·97	53921·07	44312·50
		(13·53)	(0·15)	(15143·40)	(13451·82)	(12035·66)	(10837·70)
02	5	90·38	2·00	126438·06	103774·00	85424·94	70432·00
		(11·73)	(0·15)	(16084·64)	(14105·86)	(12485·58)	(11142·25)
02	6	97·86	1·99	172256·19	139829·06	114128·62	93528·50
		(11·77)	(0·15)	(19827·09)	(17093·75)	(14897·57)	(13122·81)
02	7	36·97	4·35	96308·12	64575·75	41542·98	24644·39
		(1·89)	(0·09)	(7548·20)	(5944·60)	(4777·04)	(3917·91)
03	7	233·75	2·28	782198·87	627294·50	508785·87	416867·19
		(6·65)	(0·02)	(27117·88)	(21951·91)	(18074·76)	(15077·94)
04	7	178·46	2·43	129682·19	103423·44	83377·06	67863·94
		(8·05)	(0·03)	(4132·34)	(3349·47)	(2793·66)	(2343·66)
05	7	92·35	2·65	227217·06	177733·19	140046·27	110968·37
		(3·34)	(0·08)	(8804·82)	(7248·40)	(6084·37)	(5158·25)

Table 6.4. Firm *A*, decision-maker 3, DM;3_A.

Project	Length of life (years)	IRR (%) Mean (S.D.)	Payback Mean (S.D.)	NPV at 10% (£) Mean (S.D.)	NPV at 15% (£) Mean (S.D.)	NPV at 20% (£) Mean (S.D.)	NPV at 25% (£) Mean (S.D.)
06	4	40·59	3·03	177776·81	131073·44	93835·56	63949·38
		(16·93)	(0·32)	(102635·19)	(88110·25)	(76202·87)	(66354·44)
06	5	56·92	3·00	361974·50	278682·62	213245·81	161390·37
		(10·78)	(0·26)	(89755·25)	(76475·44)	(65711·44)	(56898·52)
06	6	64·11	2·97	525625·25	404049·44	310412·00	237517·19
		(10·03)	(0·27)	(106396·25)	(89080·62)	(75410·12)	(6444·73)
06	7	67·18	3·01	671624·62	510521·87	389032·50	296221·06
		(9·69)	(0·28)	(125638·06)	(103083·12)	(85735·60)	(72133·37)
06	8	101·44	2·59	1498318·00	1157742·00	903978·00	711898·00
		(5·49)	(0·12)	(89117·37)	(72675·12)	(60124·58)	(50450·84)

Table 6.5. Firm *A*, decision-maker 4, DM;4_A.

Project	Length of life (years)	IRR (%) Mean (S.D)	Payback Mean (S.D.)	NPV at 10% (£) Mean (S.D.)	NPV at 15% (£) Mean (S.D.)	NPV at 20% (£) Mean (S.D.)	NPV at 25% (£) Mean (S.D.)
02	3	−4·08	2·87	−11219·93	−14719·54	−16259·61	−18394·79
(run 1)*		(18·14)	(0·16)	(+14719·70)	(12968·23)	(11495·42)	(10247·88)
02	3	−2·20	2·96	−11040·69	−14022·69	−16391·54	−18272·62
(run 2)		(5·91)	(0·07)	(5422·57)	(4437·91)	(4523·93)	(4167·37)
02	4	12·37	3·22	3014·63	−2198·90	−6387·83	−9714·16
(run 1)*		(11·74)	(0·5)	(12825·58)	(11289·07)	(10000·25)	(8911·28)
02	4	12·63	3·14	2894·92	−2364·92	−6513·96	−9843·42
(run 2)		(4·99)	(0·24)	(5373·44)	(5373·44)	(4372·76)	(4018·66)
02	5	15·13	3·49	6497·69	404·28	−4419·11	−8256·21
(run 1)*		(11·10)	(0·74)	(13557·10)	(11893·68)	(10502·84)	(9330·85)
02	5	16·96	3·23	943·49	−4114·52	−8148·22	−11376·18
(run 2)		(4·81)	(0·28)	(5118·80)	(4579·48)	(4126·45)	(3742·35)
06	5	105·30	2·57	881574·37	713935·87	581270·87	475253·94
		(6·65)	(0·07)	(81321·00)	(67848·69)	(57180·34)	(48656·84)
06	6	107·89	2·58	1036561·37	832361·12	672758·25	546645·44
		(5·92)	(0·07)	(79089·06)	(65442·43)	(54782·20)	(46323·98)
06	7	107·94	2·58	1109396·00	884228·44	710084·44	573755·25
		(6·62)	(0·07)	(92040·44)	(76304·69)	(63947·75)	(54106·92)
07	3	4·07	2·88	−5680·40	−9542·51	−12639·83	−15127·84
		(7·68)	(0·12)	(7785·22)	(6672·34)	(5988·22)	(5408·16)
07	5	38·26	2·91	47110·27	33957·37	23515·70	15162·16
		(5·80)	(0·17)	(9928·05)	(8625·91)	(7563·82)	(6688·96)
07	6	27·49	3·28	31532·95	19676·25	10373·49	3026·40
		(5·44)	(0·20)	(9708·32)	(8494·93)	(7500·94)	(6678·80)

Table 6.5. (continued)

Project	Length of life (years)	IRR (%) Mean (S.D.)	Payback Mean (S.D.)	NPV at 10% (£) Mean (S.D.)	NPV at 15% (£) Mean (S.D.)	NPV at 20% (£) Mean (S.D.)	NPV at 25% (£) Mean (S.D.)
10	3	26·74	2·53	12655·69	7652·96	3547·03	161·34
		(14·67)	(0·20)	(10654·57)	(9902·01)	(9256·92)	(8698·27)
10	4	54·30	2·51	50789·48	39636·50	30578·67	23169·31
		(14·70)	(0·18)	(11301·14)	(10354·18)	(9572·68)	(8918·00)
10	5	61·31	2·51	70762·37	55647·80	43543·93	23766·78
		(12·29)	(0·18)	(10233·80)	(9288·67)	(8527·65)	(7904·26)

* We present here for 02 the simulation results from two runs of the same model. This provides some guidelines for the accuracy of results from simulation experiments.

This part of the analysis could, therefore, have been performed by the analytical approach more simply except for the fact that it is much easier to generate the IRR distribution by a Monte Carlo method.

The purpose of this initial analysis was twofold. First, to find the extent to which the parameters and shape of the final criterion distribution on the same project varied when more than one decision-maker assessed the various subjective inputs. Second, to compare roughly the financial measures of worth for given projects obtained here with the results given by the C–A model. It should be noted that each decision-maker DM;1_A, etc. is the same person as in the C–A analysis.

We present the results of this analysis for each decision-maker in Tables 6.1 to 6.5.

(ii) *Churchman–Ackoff Analysis*

Our justification for the Churchman–Ackoff (C–A) model is that it rationalises the decision structure of the decision maker. Further, it is an example of a decision theoretic approach based on the notion that R & D or investment decisions in general are made with reference to an effective subset of business objectives which has been suggested by writers such as Drucker[25]. In essence, the decision criterion in such a formulation is multi-dimensional and a weighted function of the set of objectives.

The basis of the C–A model is as follows:

1. Suppose that at some moment in time, the decision-maker assigns a relevant set of objectives ($O_1, \ldots, O_n$) for his decision problem.
2. Suppose also that he has a number of alternative research projects ($R_1, \ldots, R_k$) which need to be evaluated.
3. The decision-maker then constructs a $(k \times n)$ matrix with alternative projects as rows and objectives as columns.

$$\begin{array}{lccc} & O_1 & \ldots & O_n \\ \text{Weights} & W_1 & \ldots & W_n \\ R_1 & & \ldots & \\ \cdot & & \ldots & \qquad = (M) \\ \cdot & & \ldots & \\ \cdot & & \ldots & \\ R_n & & \ldots & \end{array}$$

The cells in the matrix are assigned values between 0 and 1

according to the extent to which each R_i satisfies each of the objectives.

4. The decision-maker is also asked to estimate a positive weight W_i to each objective subject to the restriction that

$$\sum_{i=1}^{n} W_i = 1$$

in order to establish the priority between objectives. Let W be the $(n \times 1)$ column vector of weights.

5. The procedure is then to calculate a weighted objective score for each project R_i by obtaining the $(k \times 1)$ row vector S by matrix multiplication i.e.

$$S = M \times W$$
$$(k \times 1) = (k \times n)\,(n \times 1)$$

This weighted objective score is the criterion by which preliminary project decisions should be made. There are a number of problems with this procedure which are concerned with the validity of the procedures to obtain weights for objectives and values for the cells in the M matrix. The procedure is an attempt to provide an objective criterion at the expense of somewhat arbitrary measurement of objective weightings. Further, there are basic problems with using objectives as a basis for decision[26, 27]. First, a person's objectives change and evolve through time. Second, a person is not always certain what his objectives really are, aside from the problem of whether he will reveal them to a third person. Clearly such uncertainty of purpose on the part of the decision-maker is a problem for a normative model.

Table 6.6 shows the results of the C–A model applied to the sample of projects in firms A and B described earlier.

DISCUSSION of Results of All Normal and C–A Analyses

A number of conclusions are immediately apparent from the analysis. First, in cases where more than one decision-maker was responsible for evaluating a project, the measures of IRR, NPV and payback differ and often quite considerably. (See, for example, 02 where decision-makers 1 and 2 find it profitable and 4 finds it unprofitable in IRR and NPV terms.) The immediate question that this finding raises is which evaluation is not relevant? Should the decision-maker most directly responsible for a given project be assigned the responsibility for the evaluation or is the senior engineer

Table 6.6.

Firm *B*

	DM;*B*	
Projects	Scores	Rank
1	20·77	6
2	15·78	8
3	20·89	5
4	24·59	3=
5	24·59	3=
6	28·29	1=
7	28·29	1=
8	18·90	7

Firm *A*

	DM;1*A*		DM;2*A*		DM;3*A*		DM;4*A*	
Projects	Scores	Rank	Scores	Rank	Scores	Rank	Scores	Rank
1	28·34	6	42·59	2	30·40	6	39·68	4
2	23·51	8	31·03	7	35·15	4	19·93	8
3	38·91	2	35·34	4	37·31	3	41·85	3
4	18·35	10	32·14	6	—		57·54	2
5	28·34	6=	39·64	3	—		37·68	4=
6	31·20	5	28·88	8	31·62	5	38·28	6
7	—		12·29	11	40·11	2	16·26	9
8	44·57	1	44·25	1	—		58·60	1
9	—		34·97	5	28·09	7	—	
10	35·95	3	23·51	10	—		24·92	7
11	—		—		4·25	8	−0·5	10
12	20·38	9	11·08	12	3·97	9	−3·86	12
13	—		8·82	13	—		−1·24	11
14	33·17	4	8·81	14	—		—	
15	—		27·93	9	43·43	1	—	

Note. 1. DM;*B* Denotes Decision Maker in Firm *B*, DM;1*A*, 2*A*, 3*A* and 4*A* represent the four decision-makers in Firm *A*.
2. Blanks in the table indicate cases where the relevant decision-makers did not feel able to evaluate the worth of a project because of inadequate knowledge of its nature.

somewhat detached from the project likely to give a better evaluation? The issues raised here are complex but the finding does throw into open debate the usefulness of the probabilistic analysis method because of its dependence upon the accuracy of the initial prior evaluations on the underlying economic factors.

Second, in comparing the C–A and simulation analyses we find that they rank the projects in approximately the same order.

Third, we include in our results for decision-maker 4 the NPV,IRR and payback values for two separate runs of the simulation programme for project 02 with exactly the same parameters for the input distributions. The purpose of showing the results from the two runs is to emphasise strongly that simulation results are statistical estimates. It is clear that the mean values of NPV,IRR and payback do not differ appreciably between the two runs, yet the standard deviations differ appreciably. This finding is to be expected from the simulation method because sampling theory (under normal assumptions) tells us that estimates of the mean of a distribution are reasonably precise. However, when we require estimates which characterise the shape and tails of the probability distribution simulation results tend to be imprecise.

Fourth, the present value and IRR criteria are certainly a function of the length of the life cycle and planning horizon for a project. Generally, the longer the life cycle, the greater the present worth. However, this is dependent upon the exact nature of the cash flow pattern over the project's life cycle.

(iii) *Non-normal Analysis*

Since decision-makers do not always assess symmetrical distributions of the normal type for unknown input factors, the simulation approach can prove to be more flexible than existing analytical approaches which depend for their strength on identically distributed input factors and particularly those which follow the normal distribution. The purpose of the analysis here is to suggest some of the range of probability distributions which can be fitted to the economic input factors, e.g. rectangular, lognormal and beta when they are not normally distributed. If the number of input factors was n, say, and we used four possible probability distributions to characterise them then the number of possible simulations for our cash flow model would be 4^n in general. Clearly, it is impractical and costly to consider all possible combinations of the underlying cash flows in our analysis and so we must seek some compromise.

It is suggested here that a reasonable method to allow for non-normality on a given factor is to fit the appropriate beta distribution to the data since the beta distribution is widely used and suggested as an approximation to a skew distribution[28] and is implied in the work of Hertz[29] when he asks decision-makers to make three 'guesstimates' about a given probability distribution. Some preliminary work was also undertaken with the lognormal distribution but this will not be described here.

Having allowed for non-normality by fitting the relevant beta distribution we used this approach to test the sensitivity of the assumed normal form for the distribution of the NPV criterion to non-normality in the input factor distributions. It is recognised that this is an imprecise test because simulation methods do not provide reliable estimates for the tails of distributions.

In our consideration of the effect of non-normality on the normality of the final criterion function, NPV, we shall present the extreme case where all non-normal distributions of factors are considered to be beta distributions, i.e. the all-beta analysis and draw conclusions about normality of NPV from this analysis alone.

The immediate conclusions which could be drawn from the all-beta analysis were as follows:

(i) the effect of non-normality in the input distributions on the mean value, of payback, NPV and IRR is of a very small order in nearly every case. Sometimes the effect on the standard deviation of the three criteria distributions is to reduce its size but never to increase its size.

(ii) From inspection of the graphs of the NPV and IRR distributions, it is clear that they would be approximated well in most cases by normal distributions.

(iii) the distribution of payback appears to follow one of two types – a very concentrated normal distribution or one with a long right tail but very concentrated at the left side of the distribution (the lower bound for payback). Thus, there is some justification for Weingartner's[30] assertion that under certain assumptions about the distribution of net revenue over time, the probability distribution of the payback period is approximately normal.

If this is the case then Weingartner's conclusion that the payback measure is robust to uncertainties in the estimation and projection of cash flows should follow. Unfortunately, it appears that payback is equally prone to errors in forecasts of cash flows, as can be seen from the evidence in this section and also in the earlier section for project 02 where payback varies from 1·7 to over 3 years.

Hence, it is apparent from the analysis presented here that the assumption of normality for the NPV criterion distribution is very reasonable in cases where the underlying economic factors are independently, non-normally distributed. In the all-beta analysis case just noted we would expect that identically independently distributed beta variables for the economic factors would have an NPV distribution that is normal. But when we analysed combinations of independently normally and beta distributed variables for the underlying economic factors the assumption of normality for NPV and IRR still holds.

Therefore, Hillier's basic analytical method for obtaining the NPV distribution would seem to hold under a variety of alternative conditions. One set of conditions not considered here is the effect of statistically dependent economic factor distributions on the form of the final criterion function. For the moment, as a first approximation, it is reasonable to say that the assumption of normality of NPV holds and so Hillier's analytical approach should be used in developing the NPV distribution exactly and simply in practical decision analysis applications.

Further Areas of Development

As we have seen the correlation between C–A method and the simulation method is quite good. However, both methods suffer from measurement problems but have particular virtues which should, if possible, be used to develop another measure. For example, the C–A approach adopts a multi-dimensional criterion function as the discriminator between projects. The dimensions are the objectives and the criterion function is a weighted function of these objectives. Whilst this multi-dimensionality is valuable the difficulties of measuring the weights to be assigned to objectives and the project scores seriously invalidate the method.

The Bayesian decision analyst would suggest that the path to improvement lies in evaluating the decision-maker's preference or utility function for money by means of the Von Neumann/Morgenstern standard gamble and transferring expected monetary values, NPV's, into utility equivalents. These utility values should then be used to rank projects and discriminate between them.

Whilst the decision theorist is correct it is often the case that R & D projects should be evaluated in terms of a number of criteria. In the Rand Corporation work on R & D performance, cost and time were stressed as relevant for evaluating alternative projects. We, therefore, suggest that the major aim of the decision analysis procedure should be to develop a utility function for all achievable performance, cost and time triplets that would reflect the decision-maker's ordinal preferences among such alternatives.

In the consideration of applied R & D projects an adequate measure for performance is the expected financial rate of return. The decision analysis approaches outlined earlier provide methods by which rates of return can be obtained from the blend of uncertain cost, market and social factors which make up the projects.

Once measures for the attributes (performance, costs, time) of projects are available, we must develop methods for assessing preferences amongst alternatives in terms of these attributes. Raiffa[4] provides some guidelines but as yet the field requires much detailed research.

The position taken in this final section is a Bayesian one. One of the cornerstones of Bayesian decision analysis is that probability assessments by decision-makers in decision problems can be considered separately from assessments of the decision-maker's preference or utility structure. This position is arguable but on its foundations rests much of the potentially useful research that can be further done in decision and cost/benefit analyses.

SUMMARY AND CONCLUSIONS

This chapter has largely been a methodological review with some illustrations of methods. At the same time it has not been a comprehensive review as, for example, the learning process and utility aspects of decision analysis are considered fully elsewhere (see Thomas[10]).

The main conclusion is that the analytical NPV method suggested by Hillier[18] is the most useful model for assessing a project's worth in financial terms. Some measurement problems were encountered in obtaining subjective probabilities for uncertain factors and because decision-makers did not always agree on probability assessments for the same projects.

We feel that, even though the C–A model develops a weighted attribute score for a project, formal decision analysis procedures for the assessment of multi-attributed utility functions need to be developed and integrated with the worth assessment procedures. An outline of the structure of such methods is given in the paper and developed more fully elsewhere (Thomas[31]).

REFERENCES

[1] See C. D. Foster and M. E. Beesley, Estimating the social benefit of constructing an underground railway in London, *Journal of the Royal Statistical Society*, A, 1963, pp. 46–94.

[2] P. Self, Nonsense on stilts: the futility of Roskill, *New Society*, 2 July 1970.

[3] K. Richardson, Flaws in Roskill's airy arithmetic, *Sunday Times Business News*, 24 January 1971.

[4] H. Raiffa, *Decision Analysis*, Addison-Wesley, 1968 p. 270.

[5] A. W. Marshall and W. H. Meckling, Predictability of costs, time and success of development, RAND Corporation Paper, p. 1821, Santa Monica, 1959.

[6] M. J. Peck and F. M. Scherer, *The Weapons Acquisition Process*, Harvard, 1962.

[7] R. Summers, Cost estimates as predictors of actual costs in T. Marschak (Editor), *Strategy for R & D*, Springer-Verlag, 1968.

[8] D. Meadows, Estimate accuracy and project selection models in industrial research, *Industrial Management Review*, vol. 8, No. 3, Spring 1968.

[9] D. H. Allen and P. J. November, A practical study of the accuracy of forecasts in novel projects, Tripartite Chemical Engineering Conference, Montreal, September 1968.

[10] H. Thomas, Econometric and decision analysis studies in research and development in the electronics industry, Unpublished Ph.D. Thesis, Edinburgh, 1970, Chapters 6–8.

[11] E. Mansfield and R. Brandenberg, The allocation, characteristics, and outcome of the firm's R & D portfolio: a case study, *Journal of Business*, October 1966.

[12] C. W. Churchman, *Introduction to Operations Research*, John Wiley, 1957.

[13] C. M. Mottley and R. D. Newman, The selection of projects for industrial research, *Operations Research*, 1959, pp. 740–51.

[14] B. V. Dean, *Evaluating, Selecting and Controlling Research and Development Projects*, AMA Research Study, 1968.

[15] R. Turvey, Present value versus internal rate of return, *Economic Journal*, March 1963.

[16] R. L. Winkler, The quantification of judgement: some methodological suggestions, *Journal of the American Statistical Association*, **62** (1967), 1105–20.

[17] D. B. Hertz, *Risk Analysis in Capital Investment*, Harvard Business Review 1967.

[18] F. S. Hillier, *The Evaluation of Risky Interrelated Investments*, North-Holland, 1969.

[19] S. W. Hess and H. A. Quigley, *Analysis of Risk in Investments using Monte-Carlo Techniques*, Chemical Engineering Symposium Series, 42. American Institute of Chemical Engineering, 1963, p. 55.

[20] F. S. Hillier and D. V. Heebink, Evaluating risky capital investments, *California Management Review*, Winger 1965.

[21] F. S. Hillier, Derivation of probabilistic information for the evaluation of risky investments, *Managements Science*, **9,** pp. 43–57, 1963.

[22] F. S. Hillier, Supplement to 'Derivation of probabilistic information for the evaluation of risky investments', Communications to the Editor, *Management Science*, **11,** pp. 485–7, 1965.

[23] F. S. Hillier, Evaluation of risky interrelated investments, Technical Report No. 73, Contract Nour – 225(53), Office of Naval Research, United States (1963).

[24] B. V. Wagle, A statistical analysis of risk in capital investment projects, *Operational Research Quarterly*, **18,** No. 1, March 1967.

[25] P. F. Drucker, *The Practice of Management*, Harper, 1961.

[26] See Bennis *et al. The Planning of Change*, Holt, Rinehart and Winston, New York, 1961.

[27] R. Lippitt, Dimensions of the Consultant's Job, *Journal of Social Issues.*

[28] See D. G. Malcolm, J. H. Roseboom, and C. E. Clark, Application of a technique for research and development program evaluation, *Operations Research*, September – October 1959, pp. 646–69.

[29] D. B. Hertz, Investment policies that pay off, *Harvard Business Review*, February 1968.

[30] See H. M. Weingartner, Payback period and capital budgeting decisions, *Management Science*, B, 602, **15,** No. 12, August 1969.

[31] H. Thomas, An alternative method of measuring project worth. Unpublished Working Paper, London Business School, 1970.

Part Three

FIELDS AND AREAS

7

A Cost-benefit Study of Alternative Runway Investments at Edinburgh (Turnhouse) Airport[1]

J. B. HEATH AND W. N. OULTON

Department of Trade and Industry

1. INTRODUCTION

This paper is a study of alternative runway investments at Turnhouse Airport, undertaken for Ministers in a decision context by the Economic Services Division, Department of Trade and Industry. It is one of a number of cost-benefit studies relating to airports being conducted by the Department of Trade and Industry, some of which contributed to the present work (such as the costs and benefits of improving instrument landing systems), while others were aided by the lessons of this study (such as the subsequent analysis relating to proposed new investment at Aldergrove Airport (Belfast)).

In this case the main problem was (and continues to be) that the airport at Turnhouse is operationally unsatisfactory. The diversion rate is exceptionally high, partly because the existing runway is aligned across the prevailing wind, but mainly due to the frequency of poor visibility conditions. Diversions rates for Turnhouse, Abbotsinch, Prestwick and Heathrow Airports are given in Table 7.1. These high diversion rates have led to continuous public protest, especially by local businessmen, and pilots themselves regard the airport as one of the least satisfactory in the country. Moreover, some of the larger aircraft which the airlines plan to operate from Turnhouse in the future, the Trident 3B in particular, could not use the airport without restrictions on the payload which they could carry. The question, therefore, was how best to deal with this situation.

It should be added at this point that there are a number of other

[1] Mr J. R. W. F. Graham, Head of the Aviation Economics Branch, and Mr M. J. Cook also made major contributions towards this study, and we are grateful for the help provided by the Scottish Office.

Table 7.1. Percentage diversion rates (average 1965–9)

Heathrow	0·35	
Prestwick	0·01	
Abbotsinch	0·82	(1966–9 only)
Turnhouse	2·52	

relevant considerations which are not analysed in this report. One matter relates to the future role of Turnhouse Airport in relation to Abbotsinch and Prestwick, especially in the context of the possibility of developing a Central Scottish Airport, on which at the time parallel work was being undertaken with the present study. Another issue not pursued here relates to the profitability of Turnhouse, and to the fact that it is currently run at a substantial loss to the owners (at present the Department of Trade and Industry), and clearly this raises questions about who should pay for any improvements at the airport and about pricing policy (of course a different pricing policy would affect future demand, but this matter was bound up with further complications concerning the negotiations being conducted at the time for transfer of the Airport to the British Airports Authority, and the conditions of the transfer). And there is a military presence at Turnhouse Airport which introduced some further constraints on the study. Also not included in the present paper was another exercise on alternative means of improving the terminal buildings at Turnhouse (this was omitted only because methodologically the issues are less interesting than those relating to the runway problem).

Thus the problem was not a clean exercise in public sector investment appraisal; there were many peripheral complications which were time-consuming (because the precise constraints which they imposed were not at all self-evident), and which in the decision context were clearly important. In our experience almost every cost-benefit study we have undertaken in a decision context has been subject to some such complications, and sometimes these are more difficult to handle than the cost-benefit appraisals themselves.

2. THE PRINCIPAL ALTERNATIVES

After initial study of the problem, which included examining earlier reports, talking with appropriate technical experts and visiting the site, six quite different ways of dealing with the situation were identified. One obvious possibility (closing the airport, transferring all passengers to Abbotsinch Airport and converting the existing airport to alternative uses) was examined in the context of parallel studies relating to the proposal for a Central Scottish Airport, and for various reasons was rejected. A preliminary analysis enabled some possibilities to be ruled out without difficulty, and ultimately concentrated attention on the following three principal possibilities:

1. Do nothing. In practice, for safety reasons, the existing runway would have to be re-surfaced. This would minimise the cost to the owners of the Airport, but the community costs of diversions would rise over time with the growth in traffic.

2. (*a*) To extend the present runway by 1,000 feet on the North-Western end, and by 200 feet on the South-Eastern end, to demolish or reduce in height Carlowrie House and the surrounding trees; it was thought that this investment could be completed by 1 January 1973.

(*b*) The same as 2(*a*) above, but with completion by 1 January 1975.

3. (*a*) To build a 7,700 feet new runway, to be operational by 1 January 1973, on a new alignment.

(*b*) To build a new runway to be operational by 1 January 1975.

It is the details of these three possibilities which are reported in this paper.

3. SOME PRINCIPAL ASSUMPTIONS

In all our cost-benefit work we make explicit decisions (in consultation with our clients) as to which is the relevant community for the purposes of analysis – *whose* costs and benefits are to be included. In the present case, given the political context of the decision, at one stage we were urged to confine the study to the Scottish community, but given that the vast majority of the air traffic at the airport is with England and Northern Ireland, the United Kingdom community as a whole was clearly the more relevant. Moreover, given the importance of foreign owned enterprise in Scotland, it was thought that the welfare of foreigners travelling to and from the airport could reasonably be identified with that of the UK community, and so time savings by foreigners were included in the analysis.

Next came the usual problem of the choice of discount rate. Since we were concerned only with the use of real resources, we took the appropriate discount rate to be determined by the opportunity cost of these resources; and the government has decided that in the general case this should be 10 per cent (actually 8 per cent in the initial phases of the study); this was also the rate used in other cost-benefit studies. While it is possible to argue that some other rate should have been chosen, at least choosing a common rate throughout all government work ensures some consistency in resource allocation within that sector, even though the overall levels may be thought incorrect. Ordinarily, of course, tests for the sensitivity of the conclusions to different discount rates are made in studies of this kind, since one would not wish the outcome to be determined solely by the choice of a rate which is difficult to justify with complete confidence.

The time horizon for forecasts was determined essentially by the rate of technological change in aviation, and by the extreme difficulty of visualising the likely magnitudes of many basic parameters more than about fifteen years ahead – some would say that even fifteen years is too long. In the event 1985 was taken as the terminal date, which coincided with other forecasts for the London area which were used extensively in preparing the specific forecasts for Turnhouse. All costs and benefits were expressed in constant 1969 prices, and attributed to the year in which they might be expected to occur. Finally, the decision rule was taken as the highest positive (or lowest negative) estimate of the most likely net present value of the overall costs and benefits to the United Kingdom community. In addition the internal rate of return was calculated.

4. THE FORECASTS

A carefully constructed forecast is generally essential if a cost-benefit analysis is to be meaningful. The forecasts of terminal passengers used in this cost-benefit study were constructed by examining the market composition of traffic at Turnhouse, and its trend in the past. Much use was made of work done recently on forecasts for the London area by the Department of Trade and Industry in conjunction with other Departments and representatives of aviation interests. This has involved the construction of econometric models, which were used in testing hypotheses about the extent to which growth rates are declining. However, since no entirely satisfactory econometric model came out of the work on the London area, neither the London area nor the Turnhouse forecast has employed an explicitly mathematical model. But the qualitative answers, given through the models which were developed, did influence the judgements which were made about growth rates in particular markets.

Of course, forecasting for a single, small airport is more hazardous than forecasting for two large ones, as in the London area. International and charter traffic is comparatively undeveloped at Turnhouse, and forecasting is always more difficult if the base is small. Nevertheless, we were helped by the fact that nearly 80 per cent of terminal passengers at Turnhouse are on a single route – to and from London, and so the conclusions reached in the London area forecast about the growth of domestic traffic can reasonably be applied to passengers on this route at Turnhouse.

The basic procedure in the forecasts was to split the traffic into its component markets, and then to apply the growth rates agreed for the London area forecasts to each market; proper allowance was made for some identifiable differences, such as the higher proportion of charter traffic at Edinburgh which is on international services. Examination of past trends had suggested that the pattern of growth at Edinburgh could be expected to remain similar to the pattern of growth in the London area, thus making this procedure quite reasonable. No specific allowance was made for special factors operating in the Edinburgh area in the 'most likely' forecast, such as population shifts, both because such shifts seemed unlikely to affect the forecasts substantially and because the influence of conditions in the London area seemed at least as important as those in Scotland.

The 'most likely' forecasts, which imply an annual average growth rate of 8·5 per cent, are shown in Table 7.2.

Table 7.2. Forecast of terminal passengers at Turnhouse (thousands)

1967 (actual)	600	1978	1470
1970 (forecast)	766	1979	1595
1971	831	1980	1731
1972	902	1981	1877
1973	978	1982	2036
1974	1061	1983	2208
1975	1151	1984	2394
1976	1249	1985	2597
1977	1355		

But this forecast should be regarded as the centre of a range. This range was difficult to determine on any systematic basis (for instance the date of the introduction of an Advanced Passenger Train on the London–Edinburgh route, and its effects on air traffic, is very uncertain). Nevertheless, a 'low' of 5 per cent per annum and a 'high' of

13 per cent were assumed in the sensitivity tests. The 5 per cent was based on the overall growth in traffic.

After careful reconsideration of the evidence about the likelihood of there being a significant growth in traffic which is being frustrated by the present rate of cross-wind diversions at Turnhouse (these being the only ones that would be virtually eliminated by the new runway, visibility diversions being unaffected), it was decided not to produce a separate forecast for traffic with the new runway. The difference seemed likely to be well within the margins of error to be expected from a forecast of this type. But to cover the possibility that there could be a large frustrated demand, the sensitivity tests included deliberately rather high (13 per cent) growth rate assumption – much higher than seems at all realistic even with the most optimistic generation of new traffic (this implied over 5·4 million passengers at Turnhouse in 1985, as compared with the 'most likely' forecast of 2·6 million; 5·4 million passengers is twice as many as Gatwick handles today, and is approaching half as much currently as at Heathrow).

5. ASSUMPTIONS FOR THE COST ESTIMATES

The costs associated with three alternative projects may be categorised as follows:

(*a*) *Construction Costs*. The capital costs of planning, designing and constructing the new runway, or the runway extension, and their associated engineering works, or the re-surfacing of the existing runway, at the dates stated.

(*b*) *Recurring Costs*. The operating costs of the airport.

(*c*) *Costs of Diversions*. These were estimated for alternatives 1, 2(*a*) and 2(*b*) where cross-wind diversions would be in excess of those expected from the new runway. Diversions due to poor visibility would be the same on each alternative, and are discussed separately in section 6, on All Weather Operations.

(*d*) *Cost of Airport Closure*. Alternatives 2(*a*) and 2(*b*) involve also regrading the present runway; this would effectively close the airport for some months, and would cause all commercial flights to be diverted to another airport (assumed to be Glasgow).

(*e*) *Cost of Weight Restrictions*. Adopting the first alternative would mean continuing indefinitely the weight restrictions for certain types of commercial aircraft; this cost would fall on the UK community insofar as the capital resources represented by UK owned aircraft would be under-utilised. The other alternatives involve weight restrictions only until the improved or the new runway becomes operational.

A set of 'most likely' assumptions was developed to enable these costs to be estimated.

(a) Construction Costs

The first alternative to 'do nothing' would involve strengthening and resurfacing the existing runway (which we understood could be undertaken at night without interruption of traffic); we were advised that this might cost up to £0·55 million. In the absence of a full engineering feasibility study, the second alternative was estimated to cost £2·18 million for the runway extensions and for the regrading of the present runway which would also be necessary. The new runway (the third alternative) was estimated to cost £4·09 million (all at 1969 prices).

(b) Recurring Costs

Station direct costs at Turnhouse were £254,000 in 1967–8. To undertake a minor runway improvement or to extend the existing runway is assumed not to increase these running costs by any detectable amount. But the new runway, which would be in addition to the present runway, is assumed to involve extra running costs of £20,000 per annum.

(c) Costs of Diversions

Diversion costs are the costs per passenger of an unexpected diversion, multiplied by the diversion rate, multiplied by the forecasts of traffic. The costs per passenger and the forecasts used are the same for each proposal, but the diversion rates differ (the possibility that generated traffic would be greater with the new runway than with the extension is taken in with the sensitivity testing). The following discussion refers specifically to *unexpected* diversions as a result of adverse *wind* conditions at Turnhouse; poor visibility diversions, which tend to occur at particular times of the day, and planned diversions, e.g. as a result of temporary airport closure, will incur a slightly different pattern of costs.

(i) *The costs per passenger* are made up of two elements: those borne directly by the individual passenger, and those borne by the airline (which ultimately passes them on to the passenger). Diversions are assumed to be always to Abbotsinch, the passengers then being ferried to Edinburgh by coach. The additional time for the coach trip was assumed to be two hours. This may be generous because the time lost would be only from touchdown at Glasgow to Edinburgh *Airport* (not the City Centre), and because the completion of the Edinburgh–Glasgow motorway during the time horizon of this study may reduce travel times. There is no evidence that, unlike poor visibility diversions, cross-wind diversions affect one category of passenger more than another; they appear to occur randomly distributed. There may be some loss of time to people other than passengers, for example, when a business meeting is delayed or when a chauffeur or other person is meeting an aircraft. However, we do not know what number of people are so affected or by how much; insofar as this is not covered by the time and value assumptions, and by the sensitivity tests, they may be taken as included in the extra 5 per cent for passengers' incidental costs mentioned below.

The value of time used in this study is a weighted average of the values of leisure and business time. The value of leisure time used is the average value established by the Ministry of Transport. This is not the same as the value of leisure time as perceived by leisure air travellers since the latter are likely to have higher incomes than the national average. But where the beneficiaries do not pay for the services they enjoy, as is the case here, the distribution of income will tend to become unequal if perceived leisure time values are employed. This is because investment will tend to be concentrated on schemes which favour higher income groups, because such schemes will show larger benefits than similar schemes which favour lower income groups. We followed Ministry of Transport practice in using the national average value of leisure time.

The value of business time was based on the survey of the incomes of air travellers carried out by the Roskill Commission. If it were assumed that all time spent travelling is lost, then marginal productivity theory would indicate that the value of business time is simply the average wage of businessmen (plus perhaps some associated labour costs borne by the firms). But in the case of executives, who are the business travellers involved here, it did not seem reasonable to say that all time spent travelling was lost. For an executive is still able to read, to discuss with colleagues or just simply to think, when travelling, though not with the same efficiency as when at the office. In the absence of any firm empirical evidence, any assumption must be to some extent arbitrary. We assumed that the value of business time was half the average wage of businessmen. Following again the practice of the Ministry of Transport, the values of leisure and business time were increased at 3 per cent and 3·25 per cent per annum respectively to take account of the expected rise in real incomes and productivity.

In order to calculate the weighted average of business and leisure time values, it was necessary to know the proportions travelling for business and leisure purposes. A recent origin and destination survey indicated that the proportion of business travellers was 70 per cent. Because each business passenger was assumed to pursue a leisure activity at the end of his return journey, it follows that 35 per cent of passengers will lose business time and 65 per cent will lose leisure time as a result of a diversion. As these proportions were assumed constant, the average value of time may be overstated in future years, since the business proportion of total traffic is likely to fall. (This becomes particularly important when the high values of passenger growth are inserted in the sensitivity tests. It seems quite impossible that the bulk of the growth could come from business passengers.)

An objection to our methodology is that the theory of time valuation has been developed to cover situations where the loss of time is expected. It is not clear what adjustments ought to be made to cover unexpected time losses, as here. As a result of these assumptions, the

Table 7.3. Values of time in old pence per hour

1970	127	1978	164
1971	131	1979	169
1972	136	1980	174
1973	140	1981	180
1974	144	1982	185
1975	149	1983	191
1976	154	1984	197
1977	159	1985	204

values of time used in this study are shown in Table 7.3. While we accept that there may be other incidental costs involved with diversions which would have to be borne by individual passengers these would probably be not much more than the normal rates of incidental expenditure of any journey. But nevertheless we have added on 5 per cent to cover such costs, and also possible costs to non-passengers as mentioned earlier.

The airlines' costs concerned with diversions mainly result from the extra flying time of aircraft, and the costs of moving the passengers between Glasgow and Edinburgh. Diversions were assumed to be always to Abbotsinch and to involve an extra eight minutes in the air. Cruising costs were obtained from the BEA Accounts. There may be additional costs caused by the air crew working over their hours quota and an entirely new crew being called out to replace them. Also cabin crews' time on a diversion is a dead loss and would probably incur overtime payments. The problem is that this may or may not be a penalty to BEA depending entirely on the crew rosters, and although these extra duties may have been taken into account in the rostering process, just as similar allowances are made when scheduling the aircraft, nevertheless, we included an additional 11*s* 0*d* per passenger (approximately equal to two hours of crew time) to cover these extra costs.

All passengers involved in a diversion, whether they are the passengers initially involved on a London–Edinburgh flight or the passengers on the next flight who have to be repositioned to Abbotsinch, were assumed to be transferred by coach between the two airports. Data on coach costs was obtained from BEA. The coaches would probably have to return empty in order to avoid further delays to passengers and have been costed accordingly. This methodology covers cancellations as well as diversions, on the assumption that a cancellation does not cost more than a diversion.

Airlines also incur some other small losses on unexpected diversions. Food which is waiting at Edinburgh to be put on to aircraft for the return flight to London is lost, and a small allowance was made for this, again using information supplied by BEA. On flights to London which are diverted there will be a small cost to BEA incurred by those passengers interlining at Heathrow who miss their onward connections. This is not a very common occurrence, and since it would affect only a small fraction of the 10 per cent of total passengers mentioned above who are the London-bound interline passengers it may be ignored (the main cost here would be a transfer payment between BEA and the hotel and catering industry in any event). There would be no costs on ground and maintenance staff since these costs would not fall if diversions were eliminated. (There might, of course, be a saving if BEA knew in advance when diversions were going to take place.) Finally it could be argued that diversions cause the capital of an airline, mainly the aircraft, to be underutilised. But BEA maintain two standby aircraft to deal with the disruption to their schedule, of which diversions at Turnhouse are only a tiny part. It is highly unlikely that eliminating the latter would reduce the number of standbys required, since aircraft are unfortunately indivisible.

The total diversion cost *per passenger*, on the basis of the previous paragraphs is shown in Table 7.4.

Table 7.4.

	£		£
1970	2·72	1978	3·04
1971	2·75	1979	3·08
1972	2·80	1980	3·13
1973	2·83	1981	3·18
1974	2·87	1982	3·22
1975	2·91	1983	3·28
1976	2·95	1984	3·33
1977	3·00	1985	3·39

(ii) *Diversion rates* for the first alternative (to do nothing), based on the number of passengers, are assumed to be 3 per cent for 1970 rising to 6·8 per cent for 1971 and 8·1 per cent thereafter. These figures include diversions due to poor visibility, and are based on the 'most likely' assumptions. In the main calculations, however, visibility diversions have been excluded because they are common to all projects (but see section 6 below). The increases over time are due to the larger number of passengers per aircraft that are expected to be operating on the London route in the future. Of course, largely because of visibility diversions, in alternatives 2(*a*) and 2(*b*) the rate remains at 3 per cent throughout, and in alternatives 3(*a*) and 3(*b*) the rate is 2 per cent throughout (and the costs of these are not included in the main calculations). These rates cover diversions from all other causes and include cancellations as well as diversions.

(*d*) *Cost of Airport Closure*

It is assumed as being 'most likely' that alternatives 2(*a*) and 2(*b*) would require the airport to be closed for six months. If this is done in the spring and autumn months it will affect about half the annual traffic. Airline cost is taken to be zero (it might even save the airline's money if the traffic is concentrated), since these diversions could be planned well in advance. The extra passenger time involved will be less than in the case of unexpected diversions, so 1½ hours' diversion time was used instead of 2 hours. The value of time is assumed to be the same. The coach cost will also be less since the coaches need not return empty. We have therefore taken the coach cost as half that of the unexpected diversion case. Closure cost per passenger will therefore be £1·09 if the airport is closed in 1972 and £1·14 if the airport is closed in 1974 (corresponding to opening dates of the extension of 1973 and 1975). The lost airport revenues at Turnhouse would be approximately equal to the gain at Abbotsinch and the result would be simply an income transfer.

(e) Cost of Weight Restrictions

The simplifying assumption has been made that weight restriction costs will affect only the London route. All passengers of this route are assumed to travel by BEA (i.e. BUA is ignored, though weight restrictions on BUA's aircraft might be less than on BEA's), and BEA is assumed to continue to use the Trident 3B from Spring 1971 (i.e. three-quarters of that year is affected by weight restrictions) up to and including 1985.

The cost of weight restrictions depends on how the airline reacts to the situation. If it does nothing but continues to make the same number of flights as before, its load factor will tend to rise, since the number of seats on offer has been reduced. This will mean that some passengers will not be able to travel at the time of their choice or may have to travel by another mode. In both cases there is a loss to the community. We considered it more likely, however, that the airline will wish to keep its load factor at the previous level before weight restrictions were introduced in order to maintain its competitive position. This means that it must increase its frequency. We have also assumed that passenger demand will be constant, at least for small variations in the number of flights, provided that the number of seats offered is constant. The cost to the community of weight restrictions is then the number of extra flights the airline has to make, multiplied by the variable cost of a flight. It can easily be seen that the number of extra flights necessary to maintain the same load factor is given by:

$$Pn/[LN(N-n)]$$

where P is total passengers, L is the load factor, n is the original seating capacity of the aircraft and n is the number of seats unusable through weight restrictions. P was derived from the forecasts and values of L, N and n together with cost data for the Trident 3B were obtained from discussion with BEA.

6. ALL WEATHER CAPABILITY

In this section and the one that follows two issues are discussed that were of considerable interest and relevance to the present study, but which were not included in the main cost-benefit analysis. The first one relates to the navigational aids which an airport may possess.

It is difficult to summarise briefly the range of problems and issues concerned with the costs and benefits of installing instrument landing systems (ILS) with a capability for all-weather operations (AWO), which were relevant to the Turnhouse decision (the ILS is the system of guidance beams and monitors, both on the ground and in the air, and is only part of the total system which would enable an airport to have an AWO capability). Many new types of aircraft (including the Trident and the VC10) are fitted with equipment which will enable these aircraft to achieve a certain degree of automatic guidance and control during landing, but the use of this equipment would depend upon there being corresponding installations and other ancillary equipment in operation on the ground. There are certification procedures for both aircraft and airports which would permit landing operations down to certain decision heights (below which the pilot has to assume control, and if the visibility conditions are not adequate he has to initiate a missed approach technique). But advanced instrument landing systems, besides enabling aircraft to operate in adverse visibility, also are believed to improve the safety of operations of aircraft in good visibility, because less judgement is required of the pilot.

However, decisions about installing the necessary equipment in aircraft are made by the airlines, while decisions about installing the associated ground equipment and making the other changes necessary for all weather operations are undertaken by airport authorities, and it does not follow that because an aircraft type operating to a particular airport has a certain capability for assisted or automatic landing in poor visibility that that airport should of necessity have all the equipment which would enable it to do so. This was an important issue at Turnhouse. The problem was complicated by the fact that under proposal 1 it would be technically impossible with existing equipment to enable the airport to have a capability for Category II or Category III AWO (the provisional requirements for Category II operations at an airport in the UK have been promulated in 'United Kingdom Provisional Operating Requirements for All Weather Operations Category II', Board of Trade, CAP321, HMSO 1969; it permits operations down to a decision height of 100 feet and a visual reference of 1200 feet – with a high probability of approach success). And with proposal 2(*a*) and 2(*b*), a Category II AWO capability might only be feasible if another 900 feet of runway were added to the proposed extension, and if certain physical obstructions were removed (these obstructions would be likely to deflect the ILS beam, and cause the system to be unreliable). But there would be no certainty that even these measures would enable the airport to operate down to Category II conditions, and trial-and-error tests would be necessary under the proposed conditions. However, if the new runway were built (proposals 3(*a*) and 3(*b*)), then it is thought that this new runway would have Category II ILS from the beginning (the existing airport has only Category I ILS), although not necessarily a capability for Category II AWO.

At the time of the study, it appeared to us (largely on the basis of other cost-benefit studies of AWO being conducted separately) as though the extra costs of achieving a Category II AWO capability would be most likely to exceed the benefits from so doing under any of the proposals under consideration (the benefits being compounded of a reduction in diversions due to adverse visibility, and an improvement in safety during all conditions of visibility). For this reason the costs and benefits of installing ILS systems with an All Weather capability was specifically excluded from the study, in order to keep the various alternatives on a common basis. But it seemed clear that there was considerable doubt as to whether any improved ILS embodying the current technology could be installed with Category II capability or better under the extended runway proposal, whereas under the new runway proposal the airport could have full Category II – and perhaps Category III – capability if required.

7. REGIONAL DEVELOPMENT FACTORS

The second factor which occupied much attention, but which eventually was excluded from the study, concerned the possible effect of airport development and improved regional air services on the economic development of the region, and the consequent benefits which might accrue. The point was put to us, and argued with some force, that the improvement in the means of physical communication that would follow from improvements at Turnhouse Airport would promote faster regional growth, and that this should be counted as a benefit to the community in the analysis. Although, so far as we are aware, no relationships of this kind have ever been examined in any rigorous way in the past, the following points would appear to be relevant.

First, there is the obvious point that more traffic at Turnhouse would mean a larger value added in southern Scotland due directly to the increased airport activity (and its income multiplier effects), although whether the social rate of return would be higher in this marginal investment than in the best alternative would require quantification. But as already indicated, this factor is probably rather trivial. More important may be the effects of improved airport operations on plant location, and, more generally, on regional investment and growth.

Airports as a Factor in Determining Plant Location

The first issue is whether an improved means of physical communication would affect plant location, and the second question is whether this should be counted as a benefit in the analysis, and if so how it should be quantified.

Surveys indicate that airports do affect plant location decisions, but the extent of this and the circumstances in which location is most likely to be affected are very uncertain. *A priori*, the availability of air services could be important in determining the choice between two locations where other circumstances, such as the area having a suitable infrastructure, would be comparable; if the area is generally suitable, then *within that area* the location of the airport may well affect plant location decisions. However, where an important element, such as a suitable pool of skilled labour or the right supporting industry, is lacking, the availability of air services may not be sufficient to induce the firm to choose that location. We concluded that although an *improvement* to airport facilities could affect plant location as between one regime and another, the effect was likely to be much smaller than in the airport/no airport situation, and that in the context of the magnitude of improvements envisaged at Turnhouse its significance in the UK context seemed likely to be trivial. Even if the present and future state of Turnhouse Airport were to discourage some industrial activity from locating itself in the general catchment area of Edinburgh, enterprises wishing to locate in Scotland would have the alternatives of locating near Prestwick or Abbotsinch. The main effect, therefore, might be on re-location within Scotland, and perhaps elsewhere within the United Kingdom. Thus, although there would be some implied benefit to a firm from locating in the Edinburgh area as compared with its second best choice, the effect would be marginal, and to some extent included in the larger income generated by the airport itself. Intuitively, we did not see that this could be a significant factor.

Improved Communications and a Faster Rate of Growth

One hypothesis about improvements in transport communications and their effects on regional development is that new opportunities are provided for the developing region to sell to markets which were previously not accessible, or were too costly to reach. In effect, the tariff on exports from this region to other parts of the country (and overseas) is reduced. However, the developing region also becomes an accessible market for firms elsewhere, and the change in the region's balance of trade would not be easy to identify. The results would depend upon the magnitudes of relative prices and of elasticities of demand and supply, both in the short and the long term, and the problem of evaluation is closely similar to that which would be relevant to identifying the effects of tariff reductions between nations. All that we can be sure of is that the effects of growth, and on the levels of real income in the UK community as a whole, would be very uncertain.

But insofar as the social costs of increased activity in the catchment area around Turnhouse Airport would be less than their private costs (although the reverse may well be true at the London end of the communication link), any net gain would appear to be relevant. But again, the magnitude of this resulting from an improvement in the service reliability at Turnhouse Airport seemed likely to be very small.

Improved Communications and Labour Mobility

The work of Makower, Marschak and Robinson (1939–40) pioneered the study of unemployment and regional mobility. More recent studies confirm their conclusion that there is a positive and significant relationship between the rate of unemployment in a region, and the rate of outflow of labour from that region. *A priori*, therefore, one may suppose that improvements in the ease and reliability of transport modes may encourage and facilitate the migration of labour from areas of high unemployment. A good example of labour (and expenditure) migration is given by the Severn Bridge project. On completion of the bridge, subsequent surveys indicated that there was an outflow of labour from the Cardiff area into the Bristol area, in search of new job opportunities. Furthermore, there was a significant transfer of expenditure by the population of the Cardiff area from their own region to the Bristol area, with a consequent downwards pressure on the level of commercial activity in the already relatively depressed region. The work of Myrdal (*Economic Theory and Underdeveloped Regions*, 1957) tends to confirm this example, and he states that the region of buoyant industrial activity and high growth rate will generally attract resources from the less favoured regions.

All of this led us to conclude that we would not be justified in including any specific element for the supposed net benefit effect of improvements to Turnhouse Airport on the regional growth of real income.

8. THE RESULTS AND SENSITIVITY TESTS

The main results are given in the following tables. Table 7.5 shows the basic data used in the study, derived in the ways described earlier. Tables 7.6, 7.7 and 7.8 show respectively the weight restriction costs on the old runway, cross-wind diversion costs on the old and on the extended runway, under the three sets of assumptions listed below. Tables 7.9, 7.10 and 7.11 give consolidated summaries of the costs

Table 7.5. Basic parameters (most likely assumptions)

	Forecast of terminal passengers (thousands)	Value of time (£s decimal) per hour	Closure cost per passenger (£s decimal)	Diversions cost per passenger (£s decimal)
1970	766	0·53	1·04	2·72
1971	831	0·55	1·06	2·75
1972	902	0·57	1·09	2·80
1973	978	0·58	1·12	2·83
1974	1061	0·60	1·14	2·87
1975	1151	0·62	1·17	2·91
1976	1249	0·64	1·20	2·95
1977	1355	0·66	1·24	3·00
1978	1470	0·68	1·27	3·04
1979	1595	0·70	1·30	3·08
1980	1731	0·73	1·33	3·13
1981	1877	0·75	1·37	3·18
1982	2036	0·77	1·40	3·22
1983	2208	0·80	1·44	3·28
1984	2394	0·82	1·47	3·33
1985	2597	0·85	1·52	3·39

of the various alternatives, again under the three sets of assumptions. These results are summarised in Table 7.12.

The three sets of assumptions used are:

(*a*) '*Most Likely*' *Assumptions*

1. Passenger growth as forecast at 8½ per cent per annum.
2. Value of time as given in Table 7.5, col. 2.
3. Closure for regrading the existing runway takes six months.
4. Cross-wind diversions result in the extended runway diversion rate being 1 per cent greater than for the new runway.
5. The excess running costs of the new runway over the other solutions is £20,000 per annum.

(*b*) *Assumptions Favourable to the Extended Runway* (*proposal 2*)

1. Passenger traffic grows at 5 per cent per annum.
2. Total closure and diversion costs are reduced by 25 per cent per passenger.
3. Closure for regrading takes four months.
4. Diversion rates on the extended runway are 0·75 per cent more than on the new runway.
5. The excess running costs of the new runway is £40,000 per annum.

The 5 per cent assumption for the growth of passenger traffic is based upon the approximate rate at which other forms of travel are growing, which is lower than for air traffic generally. This assumed 'lower bound' growth in passenger traffic would reduce the cost of weight restrictions on the extended runway proposal, and the annual costs of cross-wind diversions, as compared with the 'most likely' assumptions.

The assumption that closure for regrading would take only four months (instead of six months) is based upon the possibility that quick-drying concrete could be used, or that the use of aluminium heating foil to decrease the setting time for concrete would be feasible (see *The Engineer*, 30 October 1969). Moreover, the closure time might also cause fewer diversions if the regrading could take place during the winter months (concrete is laid for runways during sub-zero temperatures in Canada, although it is not thought that this would be feasible in this country).

The 25 per cent variation is the same range as used by the Commission on the Third London Airport (Papers and Proceedings, Volume VII *The Sensitivity Tests*).

(c) *Assumptions Favourable to the New Runway* (*proposal 3*)

1. Passenger traffic grows at 13 per cent per annum.
2. Closure and diversion costs per passenger are increased by 25 per cent.
3. Closure for regrading takes nine months.
4. Diversion rates on the extended runway are 1·25 per cent more than the new runway.
5. The excess running costs of the new runway are zero.

Table 7.6. Weight restriction costs on the old runway (£m PV in 1970)

	Most likely		Most favourable to the new runway		Most favourable to the extension	
	Annual	Cumulated	Annual	Cumulated	Annual	Cumulated
1970	0	0	0	0	0	0
1971	0·064	0·064	0·076	0·076	0·057	0·057
1972	0·085	0·149	0·104	0·180	0·072	0·128
1973	0·083	0·232	0·107	0·286	0·069	0·197
1974	0·082	0·315	0·110	0·396	0·066	0·263
1975	0·257	0·572	0·356	0·752	0·198	0·461
1976	0·253	0·825	0·366	1·118	0·189	0·649
1977	0·250	1·075	0·376	1·494	0·181	0·830
1978	0·246	1·322	0·386	1·880	0·172	1·002
1979	0·243	1·565	0·397	2·277	0·165	1·167
1980	0·240	1·805	0·407	2·684	0·157	1·323
1981	0·237	2·041	0·419	3·103	0·150	1·473
1982	0·233	2·275	0·431	3·533	0·143	1·617
1983	0·230	2·505	0·441	3·975	0·136	1·753
1984	0·226	2·731	0·453	4·428	0·130	1·883
1985	0·224	2·955	0·467	4·894	0·124	2·007

A high passenger forecast would increase the cost of weight restrictions and of diversions. Thus we have taken the main assumption favourable to the new runway as being a passenger growth rate of 13 per cent per annum, a rate in excess of the growth of UK international air traffic as a whole. This assumption is asymmetrical – that is, the 'upper bound' forecast is rather higher in relation to the 'most likely' than is the 'lower bound' lower than the 'most likely'. The 'upper bound' forecast is probably very implausibly large. It seems to us most unlikely that, even taking account of the prospective industrial growth at Grangemouth and elsewhere the growth rate of air passengers could *be sustained as an annual average* as high as 13 per cent per annum up to 1985. It seems most improbable that inter-

Table 7.7. Cross-wind diversion costs on the old runway (£m PV in 1970)

	Most likely		Most favourable to the new runway		Most favourable to the extension	
	Annual	Cumulated	Annual	Cumulated	Annual	Cumulated
1970	0·019	0·019	0·027	0·027	0·013	0·013
1971	0·091	0·110	0·134	0·161	0·060	0·073
1972	0·116	0·226	0·177	0·338	0·074	0·147
1973	0·115	0·341	0·184	0·522	0·078	0·225
1974	0·115	0·456	0·192	0·714	0·069	0·294
1975	0·115	0·571	0·200	0·914	0·067	0·361
1976	0·115	0·686	0·208	1·122	0·064	0·425
1977	0·116	0·802	0·217	1·339	0·063	0·488
1978	0·116	0·918	0·226	1·565	0·061	0·549
1979	0·116	1·034	0·236	1·801	0·059	0·608
1980	0·116	1·150	0·245	2·046	0·056	0·664
1981	0·116	1·266	0·257	2·303	0·055	0·719
1982	0·116	1·382	0·263	2·566	0·053	0·772
1983	0·116	1·498	0·279	2·845	0·052	0·824
1984	0·116	1·614	0·291	3·136	0·050	0·874
1985	0·117	1·731	0·305	3·441	0·049	0·923

Table 7.8. Cross-wind diversion costs on the extended runway (£m PV in 1970)

	Most likely		Most favourable to the new runway		Most favourable to the extension	
	Annual	Cumulated	Annual	Cumulated	Annual	Cumulated
1973	0·019	0·019	0·030	0·030	0·013	0·013
1974	0·019	0·038	0·031	0·061	0·011	0·024
1975	0·019	0·057	0·033	0·094	0·011	0·035
1976	0·019	0·076	0·034	0·128	0·011	0·046
1977	0·019	0·095	0·036	0·164	0·010	0·056
1978	0·019	0·114	0·037	0·201	0·010	0·066
1979	0·019	0·133	0·039	0·240	0·010	0·076
1980	0·019	0·152	0·040	0·280	0·009	0·085
1981	0·019	0·171	0·042	0·322	0·009	0·094
1982	0·019	0·190	0·043	0·365	0·009	0·103
1983	0·019	0·209	0·046	0·411	0·008	0·111
1984	0·019	0·228	0·048	0·459	0·008	0·119
1985	0·019	0·247	0·050	0·509	0·008	0·127

Table 7.9. Summary of costs (most likely assumptions) (£m PV in 1970)

	Do nothing	Extension opening 1 Jan. 1973	New runway opening 1 Jan. 1973	Extension opening 1 Jan. 1975	New runway opening 1 Jan. 1975
Capital costs	0·50	1·64	3·07	1·35	2·54
Closure costs	—	0·37	—	0·38	—
Cross-wind diversion costs on OR	1·73	0·23	0·23	0·46	0·46
Weight restriction costs on OR	2·96	0·11	0·15	0·27	0·32
Cross-wind diversion costs on ER	—	0·25	—	0·21	—
Extra running costs on NR	—	—	0·11	—	0·08
Total	5·19	2·60	3·56	2·67	3·40

national traffic (which is growing faster than domestic traffic) could ever be so important at Turnhouse that the overall growth rate would anywhere near approach the international rate; nevertheless, as explained earlier, a high forecast was used to include the possibility of a substantial amount of generated traffic from the better facilities that a new runway would provide.

The assumed closure time for regrading was nine months; this was

Table 7.10. Summary of costs (assumptions most favourable to the new runway (£m PV in 1970)

	Do nothing	Extension opening 1 Jan. 1973	New runway opening 1 Jan. 1973	Extension opening 1 Jan. 1975	New runway opening 1 Jan. 1975
Capital costs	0·50	1·64	3·07	1·35	2·54
Closure costs	—	0·85	—	0·94	—
Cross-wind diversion costs on OR	3·44	0·34	0·34	0·71	0·71
Weight restriction costs on OR	4·89	0·15	0·18	0·37	0·40
Cross-wind diversion costs on ER	—	0·51	—	0·45	—
Extra running costs on NR	—	—	—	—	—
Total	8·83	3·49	3·59	3·82	3·65

to take account of the possibility of under-estimation and that some completely unexpected circumstances might arise which would delay the engineering works beyond what would normally be thought reasonable.

Since each of the three sets of assumptions applies its forecasted growth of traffic over each of the three projects in the same way, and since implicitly it has been assumed that landing fees would be invariant as to the forecasted growth in traffic and as to the project chosen, the airport revenues for each set of assumptions will be the same as between projects, and may therefore be omitted. The results therefore show net costs, and to minimise net cost becomes the object of the exercise.

Table 7.11. Summary of costs (assumption most favourable to the extension) (£m PV in 1970)

	No nothing	Extension opening 1 Jan. 1973	New runway opening 1 Jan. 1973	Extension opening 1 Jan. 1975	New runway opening 1 Jan. 1975
Capital costs	0·50	1·64	3·07	1·35	2·54
Closure costs	—	0·16	—	0·15	—
Cross-wind diversion costs on OR	0·92	0·15	0·15	0·29	0·29
Weight restriction costs on OR	2·01	0·08	0·13	0·22	0·26
Cross-wind diversion costs on ER	—	0·13	—	0·10	—
Extra running costs on NR	—	—	0·21	—	0·16
Total	3·43	2·16	3·56	2·11	3·25

The results are summarised in Table 7.12. On the 'most likely' assumptions, the lowest net cost is achieved by Project 2, whichever of the two starting dates is assumed. On the set of assumptions most favourable to Project 2, that project is, of course, still the least cost, while on the assumptions most favourable to Project 3, Project 2 is the least cost if the starting date is taken as 1 January 1973, and Project 3 is the least cost if the starting date is taken as 1 January 1975. But the differences between Projects 2 and 3 are, under this set of assumptions, not large.

However, it must not be forgotten that to choose Project 2 would most likely pre-empt the possibility of being able to introduce

Category II all-weather operations at the airport, or at least not without considerable extra expenditure (though our preliminary calculations suggested that it would be uneconomic to do so even on the new runway).

Table 7.12. Turnhouse cost-benefit study results (£m PV in 1970)

Alternative		Assumptions favourable to:		
		Project 2	'Most likely'	Project 3
1	'Do nothing'	3·43	5·19	8·83
2(*a*)	Extension 1973	2·16	2·60	3·49
2(*b*)	Extension 1975	2·11	2·67	3·82
3(*a*)	New runway 1973	3·56	3·56	3·59
3(*b*)	New runway 1975	3·25	3·40	3·65

It may be mentioned that in addition to the above results, calculations were made of the Internal Rate of Return on the various projects, and Project 2 again emerged as the best. In the IRR calculation incremental rates of return were also made – the rate of discount that would equate the extra costs and benefits of Project 2 over Project 1, and of Project 3 over Project 2. Under two of the three sets of assumptions, the incremental internal rate of return of Project 3 over Project 2 turned out to be either negative or impossible to calculate (since the extra annual costs exceeded the extra annual benefits).

Finally, on the question of aircraft noise and the costs that this would impose upon the community, it was thought that each proposal would give rise to approximately the same noise costs, and in consequence these were ignored. Later, however, it transpired that the noise costs would be somewhat greater if the new runway were built than if either of the other two courses of action were taken. At the Public Inquiry that was held after this study was completed, what attracted most attention was not whether the total noise costs would be greater or smaller if the new runway were built, but the fact that a group of people – mainly in the higher income brackets – would be subject to aircraft noise where virtually none exists at present. The fact that some other people would suffer less aircraft noise than at present seemed of much less significance.

8

Investment in Airports and the Economist's Role. John F. Kennedy International Airport: an Example and some Comparisons[1]

A. A. WALTERS

Cassel Professor of Money and Banking, London School of Economics and Political Science

I

After the many months of public hearings at stage V of the Roskill Commission no one doubts that airports are not only very big business, but are also everyone's business. A new airport such as that envisioned in the proposed TLA is probably the largest single piece of transport investment ever to have been seriously contemplated. (The order is £500 to £600 million at 1968 prices, and much further capital spending will be associated with it.) It also provides a focus for development, population growth, industry and commerce. And on the other side, it is a source of noise pollution and it results in the destruction of villages, and traditional patterns of rural life. Jetports, like urban motorways, are relatively new phenomena and although vast and rapidly growing numbers of people are enjoying the incomparable speed and safety of jet airplanes, the population affected by airports seem to have much more difficulty in adjusting to their new and often deteriorated environment. Fears have spread. Conservationists are taking a hard line; indeed a typical 'over-reaction' seems to have set in.[2]

The role of the economist in this process of decision-making is

[1] Much of the material in this study has been culled from the following: *Jamaica Bay and Kennedy Airport*, vols. I and II, National Academy of Science, Washington, 1971.

[2] These words were written before the government's decision on a third London airport was announced. It would be quite wrong to imagine that the London decision was made on environmental grounds. It was not. It was designed to serve the interests of a small group of politically important and wealthy people.

bound to be a central one. The organisation of the evidence and its interpretation are typically tasks which the economist, with a suitable training, can do better than any other discipline. The continuous quest for alternatives foregone, new solutions and their consequences, and for suitable standards for judging the value of decisions gives the economist an unusual chance to apply in practice the principles and imaginative reasoning which he professes. Rivals there are a-plenty. On the one side there is the super generalist – the planner. His eclectic sweep includes all – even aesthetics and moral welfare. But the planner pays a high price for his omnipresence; there is no analytical discipline, nor are there well-established propositions of planning. Planning cannot serve as an integrating core for such decisions. On the other sides there are the particular disciplines such as engineering which offer at least the hard-headed alternative of configurations of hardware and concrete. But the limitations of engineers in dealing with the behavioural and financial aspects of decision-making are well known.[3] It seems therefore that economics can usefully serve as the integrative discipline. In practice one is driven to this conclusion by the great convenience of using the monetary unit of account and by the fact that the economist specialises in the valuation procedure. Just as the accountant has become the integrator of information for business decisions, so the economist is becoming the architect of information for public investment decisions.

I will now discuss perhaps the best publicised case of airport congestion and 'frustrated' solutions in the West – the New York Airport System (NYAS) and in particular the case of John F. Kennedy International Airport (KIA) on Jamaica Bay. NYAS consists essentially of three large commercial airports at Newark, New Jersey, La Guardia and KIA, together with one or two small airports such as Islip (on Long Island) and Teterboro (mainly for general aviation). The main commercial airports of NYAS – and we may conveniently restrict NYAS to these three from now on – are situated relatively close to one another and to the Central Business District Manhattan.[4] In spite of their proximity to one another they achieve a large number of operations both per day and during their peak hours of operation. This is partly due to the fact that the main runways of the three airports are parallel and do not very much interfere with one another's ILS approach paths, and partly because they operate for

[3] This does not mean that some firms of engineering consultants do not have splendid economic assistance. Many do.

[4] There are only some nine miles or eleven miles between runways.

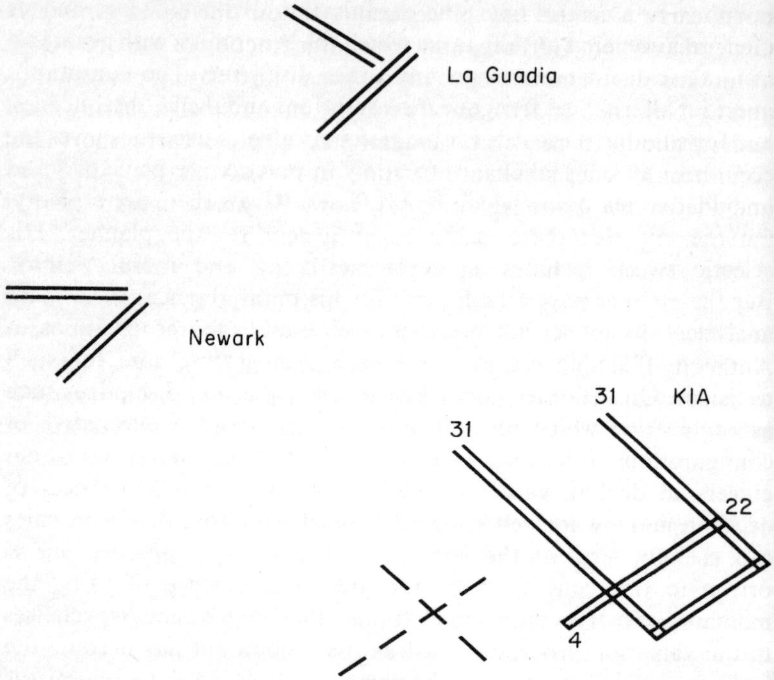

FIGURE 8.1.

much of the time under visual flight rules (VFR) rather than instrument flight rules (IFR). Under IFR conditions we may calculate the capacity of NYAS to handle operations (either on take-off or landing) by assessing the capacity of a runway and by multiplying by the number of duty runways. Calculations appearing in Vol. VII of Roskill V indicate that the approximate capacity of a runway is about 42 operations an hour. And there are normally four runways in operation (one each at Newark and La Guardia and two at KIA) so this gives a capacity of about 170 movements an hour.[5]

The three airports in NYAS do specialise to some extent on certain kinds of traffic. KIA concentrates primarily on long haul and international traffic. La Guardia cannot accommodate four-engine jets, so its 727s, DC9s etc., are employed on short- and medium-distance services. Newark, again restricted to domestic flights, does rather more longish distance operations than La Guardia. But all three air-

[5] Some reservations appear about this figure below.

ports carry a mixed bag of general aviation (including air taxis). General aviation (GA) accounts for a large fraction of the operations at La Guardia – amounting to more than a third during peak hours – and at Newark. At KIA the fraction is much smaller during peak hours – about 10 per cent. Similarly all airports carry short-haul commercial feeder services by airlines such as Mohawk, Alleghany and Piedmont. All these airplanes, however small, use up the 170 movement capacity of the NYAS runways during the IRF conditions.

Congestion has been building up for some years in the NYAS. Airlines or operators for a long time were allowed to schedule flights at will, without the leave of CAB, FAA or Port of New York Authority (PONYA). There was a marked peak at KIA that was due to an excessive number of scheduled operations – and particularly landings – in the afternoon when the transatlantic services arrive. The capacity of KIA to handle arrivals is severely limited under certain wind conditions (NE or SW) which occur about 12 per cent of the time since the capacity 4–22 runway system is limited by the fact that the two runways are only 3,000 feet apart and cannot be operated independently. Normally under IFR one can then handle a maximum of about thirty-five landings and fifteen take-offs. During these hours in 1967 there were sometimes more than eighty operations scheduled. Leaving aside the unscheduled traffic which demanded service, the excess demand gave rise to long queues, diversions, domino effects at Chicago, Boston, D.C., and so on.

Some quantitative idea of the delay experienced can be seen from the survey by Carlin and Park[1]. The average peak hour delay under IFR conditions of arrivals was over an hour, and the delay to departures was more than twenty minutes. The delays were rather less at Newark and considerably less at La Guardia. Yet at both delays nearly all exceeded the standard of four minutes which is widely regarded as the 'acceptable' amount of delay.[6] Whether or not this is an appropriate standard, it is clear that the delays in the NYAS were too long by any standard.

Congestion of course induces its own unfortunate solution. Operators unwilling to take pot luck at KIA tended to move to other airports which were less crowded such as Dulles, Boston and Philadelphia. People tried trains or got out the car. But the PONYA and FAA also tried their hand – or perhaps one should say made some moves – towards a solution. These took the form of:

[6] To be strict the average delay should not exceed four minutes in the thirty busiest hours of the year.

1. Raising the minimum landing fee at NYAS for the use of duty runways during peak periods, and
2. introducing a 'scheduling committee' of participating airlines to ration a quota of flights among the competing users.

These were the short-run policies. The long-run policies took the form of:

3. Seeking a site for a fourth jetport, and
4. extending JFK into Jamaica Bay (together with some minor extensions to Newark).

In this paper I will deal mainly with (1) and (4) but I shall have occasion to refer to (2) and (3).

II

Perhaps the most astonishing feature of the NYAS is the system of landing fees. These are recorded before August 1968 in Table 8.1. The landing fee is primarily determined by the weight of the aircraft –

Table 8.1. Schedule of charges for use of public landing areas (1968, prior to 1 August)

	$ Kennedy	La Guardia	Newark
1. Charge (c/1000 lb) per:			
Air carrier takeoff (max. takeoff weight)	24	*	38
Air carrier landing (max. landing weight)	*	104	*
Non-lessee takeoff (max. takeoff weight)	35†	95†	38†
2. Charge ($) per takeoff and landing for:			
707, Series 300	78	*	135
727, Series 100	38	142	61
DC-9, Series 10	21	85	33
FH-227 (air carrier)	10	45	17
DC-3 (non-lessee)	9	24	10
Lear Jet (Model 25)	5	14	6
Aero Commander (500 V)	5‡	6	5‡
Cessna 172	5‡	5†	5†

Notes: * Not applicable. † Subject to $ minimum charge per aircraft. ‡ Determined by the $5 minimum rather than aircraft weight.

Sources: Port of New York Authority, Aviation Department, and aircraft weights from William Green, *The Observer's Book of Basic Aircraft, Civil* (London, Frederick Warner, 1967).

at a fixed rate per gross pound of weight. Unlike the fees at London airports there is no variation according to the distance travelled or whether the flight is domestic or international. A second feature is the curious relationship of landing fees between the airports in the NYAS. The price at KIA is approximately four times the price at La Guardia. In fact the progression of landing fees is *negatively* related to the degree of congestion at the airports in NYAS. There seems therefore to be an *a priori* case for getting the relativities right. A third feature of the landing fees is that they seem too 'low' relative to albeit back-of-the-envelope calculations of the costs of extending capacity; even intuitively it seems that, for example, $5 for landing an aircraft at KIA etc., is small beer (and less than the cost of parking one's car!)

The principles of fixing the general level of landing fees are good solid 'recover-your-costs' rules of accounting. PONYA pays a small nominal lease rent to the City of New York for KIA, for example, and since the basic construction work took place some twenty years ago, the historic cost of the runways is now small. Consequently the landing fees are low at KIA. But at La Guardia substantial reconstruction of the runways was carried out at great expense some three years ago. The higher landing fees reflect the need to recover these costs.

The second principle of pricing reflects of course the time-honoured rule of charging-what-the-traffic-will-bear. This was no doubt a useful principle when the airport had much spare runway capacity, so that discrimination between traffic enabled the airport authority to expand runway use and to cover its costs. But such excess capacity days had long disappeared and the principle was redundant. A small aircraft on a duty runway occupies as much airspace and runway as a 747.[7] The case for landing fee discrimination, at least during peak hours, no longer exists.

One small hesitant faltering step was taken by the PONYA in 1968 towards a more rational pricing system – a small step for the critical economist but a huge step for PONYA. This was the raising of the minimum landing fee from $5 to $25 for the use of duty runways during peak hours. The main effect was on general aviation which faced this nominally five-fold increase in fee. In practice, however, the new fee could be avoided at KIA and Newark to some extent by the use of non-duty runways (normally under VFR con-

[7] It may be claimed that a propeller aircraft will occupy more airspace because it is the odd man out in the approach speeds on the landing path.

ditions). With the newly discovered attraction of non-duty runways for GA at KIA (for 70 per cent of landings) the average fee for landing during peak periods was only $11.[8] (Unfortunately the use of non-duty runways does conflict to some extent with the use by other aircraft of duty runways – they wait for intersecting or crossing paths – so the dichotomy may not be as clear as one would at first expect.)

The effects of these increased fees were quite dramatic. The general aviation traffic at KIA and Newark fell by 44 per cent whereas that at La Guardia fell by 57 per cent – comparing in each case the June/July seasonal and hourly peaks. It may seem quite unprincipled to use only two observations to calculate a demand curve, but they are actual observations in an experimental situation. It seems worthwhile simply to fit a line through what one may calculate as the free demand-price points in the two situations.[9] If we extrapolate the line back to the axis it cuts it between $40 and $110 according to the assumptions made. Thus I conjecture that a landing fee of $100 would see only trivial amounts of general aviation using NYAS. It is worthwhile giving some estimate of the relief which would ensue such a change.

The amount of general aviation at peak periods in July 1969 was between 12 and 20 per cent of the total number of aircraft movements:

NYAS July 1969

Hour	Departures air carrier	GA	Arrivals air carrier	GA	Total
1600–1659	60	13	76	14	163
1900–1959	73	10	77	10	170.

Perhaps even more significant was the high number of landings of general aviation during the peak landing period at KIA:

Hour	Departures air carrier	GA	Arrivals air carrier	GA	Total
1600–1659	23	5	38	6	72.

Such a virtual suppression of general aviation would clearly increase air carrier capacity by at least 10 per cent. If air carrier scheduled operations did not change (i.e. did not expand in a Parkinsonian way to fill up the slots) there would be considerable reduction in delays.

[8] Probably the figure at Newark should be higher than $11.

[9] Some calculation must be made of what demand would be without the constraint of congestion.

This is particularly the case at KIA for the critical arrivals peak at 1600–1659. Arrival delays would average about 10 minutes instead of the much higher values of over an hour that were experienced in bad IFR conditions in 1967–8 and the lower values of half an hour of 1969. The savings in delays would approximate to some $12,000–15,000 an hour – which indicates a marginal cost of operation in the region of $1,000 per aircraft movement. It must be emphasised that these numbers are very rough 'ball-park' orders of magnitude. But they are surely all that is needed. Spurious accuracy would be out of place. There is no need to know the exact weight of the elephant in order to kill the ant.

A minimum landing fee of $100 for peak periods would also have *some* effect on the movements of air carriers, since all fees at KIA would be raised (except the 747) and clearly many fees would be increased at La Guardia and Newark. We have no useful data to observe the effects of changes in landing fees on the behaviour of airlines. One is driven to synthesise (or I think a better word is fabricate!) values in order to obtain limits.

Assume that there is no possibility of substitution of one time for another in scheduled flights, that the load factors remain constant, that there is no substitution of airport outside the NYAS possible and that the only way to reduce the scheduled carrier demand is to suppress traffic. This will then give us a lower limit to the reaction of the increase in landing fee. The elasticity of demand for air carriage is of the order of $-1{\cdot}0$ to $-2{\cdot}0$, so we take the lower absolute value. For intercontinental carriers the landing fee constitutes about 2 per cent of total costs. Applying Marshall's Law, therefore, we find that the elasticity of demand with respect to landing fee will be $-0{\cdot}02$.[10] For domestic carriers the landing fee element probably is of the order of 5 per cent for the main airlines and as much as 10 per cent (at $100) for the feeder airlines. This suggests an elasticity of about $-0{\cdot}05$ to $-0{\cdot}10$.[11]

Now let us ask what would be the effect on scheduled airline operation of the increase in the minimum landing fee to $100. Although the average increase in fee both absolutely and proportionately is greatest for KIA the elasticity of demand, for the intercontinental flights in particular, is lower. For the three airports combined there

[10] Using the rule elasticity of demand for landing =
(fraction of landing costs to total costs) (elasticity of demand)

[11] For general aviation the elasticity implied by the $25 rate change is in the region of $-0{\cdot}4$.

would be a reduction in the number of operations of between 12 and 20.[12] Many of these would be the small short distance operations such as Alleghany, Piedmont and Mohawk.[13]

The question is whether $100 minimum during the peak hours would be an appropriate price to charge. The rule is simply that, in order to allocate existing capacity among competing users, the price should be fixed so that the amount of capacity purchased is just a little less than the amount available. Then there will be always a capability of coping with another operation. The situation at NYAS is complicated by (*a*) the fact that considerable congestion has inhibited the demand for operations, (*b*) there has been a 'quota' or rationing system in operation, and (*c*) the CAB regulations on competition giving rise to over-scheduling on the dense traffic routes.

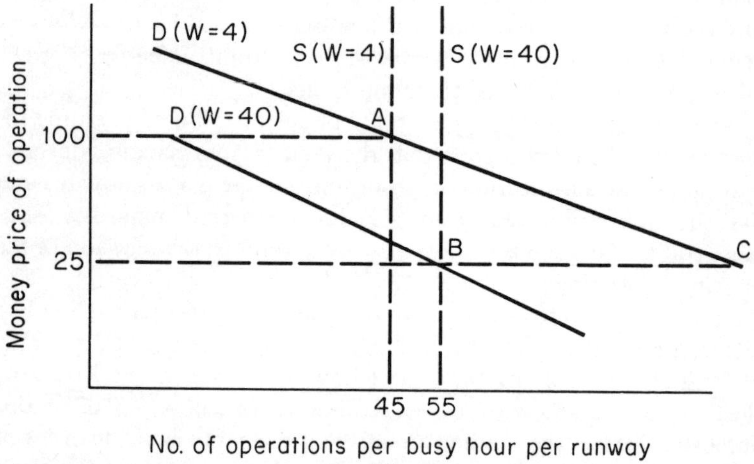

FIGURE 8.2.

The influence of congestion on demand can be simply described as in Fig. 8.2. For a particular runway we may find a whole spectrum of operating conditions which we have represented on the figure by only two. With 4 minutes' average delay ($W = 4$) the runway can achieve 45 operations an hour, and this is represented by the vertical 'supply curve'. With 40 minutes ($W = 40$) average delay the achieve-

[12] The detail of these calculations will be reported in another paper.

[13] These airlines receive Federal subsidies for providing services on lightly trafficked routes. It is conceivable, although quite silly, for the Federal government to underwrite these additional expenses.

ment is 55 operations. Demand varies according to price and expected delay and we have shown two such demand curves. The present 'free demand equilibrium' is represented by *B* (assuming for the time being that there is no effective quota system). The desired situation is described by point *A* (assuming that the 4-minute delay is best, that is to say assuming that the addition of another operation is worth just a little less than the additional delay caused to all aircraft). When we talk about the 'free demand' at say $25, we mean the demand illustrated by the point *C* on the D ($W = 4$), or 4 minutes' delay, demand curve.

At present the situation is that there is excess demand (at the $25 minimum) and the 'scheduling committee' of participating airlines allocate a number of specified slots among themselves. To some extent the scheduling committee is a phoney exercise since the quota, fixed by the FAA, is far in excess of what can be handled under IFR conditions, as can be seen in Table 8.2.

Table 8.2. NYAS

	FAA quota	Actual 1800–1900 July 1969
Air carrier	158	155
General av.	42	25
Total operations	200	180

(It seems, however, that for general aviation the price was the dominant factor since there was a significant shortfall of actual from quota.)

One may also be surprised at the large allocation of general aviation in the quota. One may provisionally conclude that the quota was not a dominant discouragement to the demand for services. Perhaps the main effect was to keep out the airlines who did not appear on the scheduling committee under the 'grandfather clause'.

It is possible, of course, to limit demand by means of an effective quota or rationing system rather than by using a price system. Whether an *effective* quota system is politically or even administratively feasible in NYAS, I do not know. But I prefer to use the price system for the following reasons.

First, the price system does not discriminate, as does both the present and various alternative rationing systems between aircraft or airlines. Discrimination occurs when services which have the same cost have different prices. Since all flights using duty runways occupy approximately the same space and time during the peak period, they should be charged the same price. Second, it avoids the discrimination inherent in the scheduling committee arrangement. The existing airlines on the committee would not have grandfather rights to the exclusion or discouragement of new competitors; nor would there be an inhibition on certain efficient existing operators growing at the expense of the less efficient. A pricing system applied uniformly to all users will avoid many of the problems of international diplomatic negotiation and offering of reciprocal landing rights.[14]

Third, the pricing system appropriates the value of the scarce facilities for the Airport Authority rather than, in the case of the rationing arrangement, leaving this equity in the hands of the lucky grandfather airlines. Such an increased revenue to PONYA could be devoted to a wide variety of purposes designed primarily to ameliorate, or compensate for, the deleterious environmental effects of the airport, such as subsidising insulation of buildings, compensation for depreciation of house values due to noise, purchase of property and relocation of residents affected by noise, the positive creation of amenities, etc. Such a fund could be channelled into the provision of parks and waterside recreation for those residents who have suffered a loss of amenity from the airport location and expansion – but, of course, this does not necessarily constitute the best use of such resources since such residents may be better off with some other arrangement. A fifth advantage is that the pricing system would give decision-makers a much better idea of the real demand for a new fourth jetport – a demand that they can properly compare with the long-run costs of expanding airport capacity (by building and operating the fourth jetport or by expanding the capacity of KIA). With the existing levels of user fees one has little or no idea of the true demand for airports. Existing fees were developed to recover the historical costs of the airport – and they are high when the airport was recently constructed (as at La Guardia) and low when the airport was constructed before the great inflation (as at KIA). The irrationality of such arrangements is obvious; such pricing procedures give very misleading indicators of the desirability of expansion of airport capacity.

[14] A recent example of this occurred when the Turkish Airline wanted to use London Heathrow at a peak period, but the British Government offered only the use of London Gatwick. The Turks replied by withdrawing BOAC and BEA landing rights in Turkey. Eventually, an accommodation was achieved at Heathrow but only after months of acrimony.

For these reasons, therefore, I reject any significant reliance on the quota system for rationing runway space. But, it may be argued that such economic regulation and rationing is so inherent in the air-transport industry that it is irrational to use the price system in one part of the system while the other part is regulated to 'sub-optimal'. An account of the effects of CAB regulation, however, will soon demonstrate that this is not so.

The method of regulation by the CAB creates its own artificially inflated demand for runway space. The CAB specifies the fares for the route and permits the airlines to offer as many flights as they wish. Thus the airlines are induced to offer a flight if the additional revenue they get from it exceeds the costs of operations. Consequently each airline will put on flights – stealing passengers from its own alternative flights and those of its competitors, but also generating more traffic as service frequency is increased – until the loadfactor is lowered to a figure near the break-even point. This loadfactor is very low for long-distance operations between main cities such as New York–Los Angeles.

The fact that virtually all competition is channelled into service, and not price, means that (*a*) intensive overscheduling occurs on many routes, and (*b*) there is no proper incentive to adopt larger aircraft – more pointedly to fill the airplane with seats as an alternative to providing 'service competition' in the form of leg-room. No doubt overscheduling of flights and the use of small rather than larger aircraft would be discouraged, at least to some extent by the increase in landing fees. But there is undoubtedly still some additional incentive needed for schedule consolidation. A good move would be for the CAB to reduce its controlled fares on the medium- and long-distance heavily travelled routes.[15] It is, however, more likely that the competing airlines will 'get together' to eliminate excess frequencies – and this has been recently suggested by the Chairman of the CAB.

The quantitive significance of this may be gauged from a calculation made by John Kain and Arthur de Vaney. Using the criterion of half-hourly service and 80 per cent load factor, it was shown that at least thirty-five operations would be eliminated from the peak NYAS hour.

The question arises now whether the extension of KIA into

[15] The irony is that the CAB maintains high fares on these dense routes because the airlines will then maintain services on the highly trafficked unprofitable routes!

Jamaica Bay or a fourth jetport can be justified on a usual cost-benefit analysis. No such study has been carried out. It would indeed be a demanding task. But at this stage one can give some broad estimates of the costs of such construction and so, with an estimate of the traffic to be accommodated by the new construction, one can make some estimates of the long-run marginal cost of catering for the additional traffic. The motivation for this calculation is to find the landing fees which must be charged in order that the investment and other expansion costs must be covered by revenue. I must emphasise that these numbers are very rough and ready and can only serve to give an orientation to the problem.

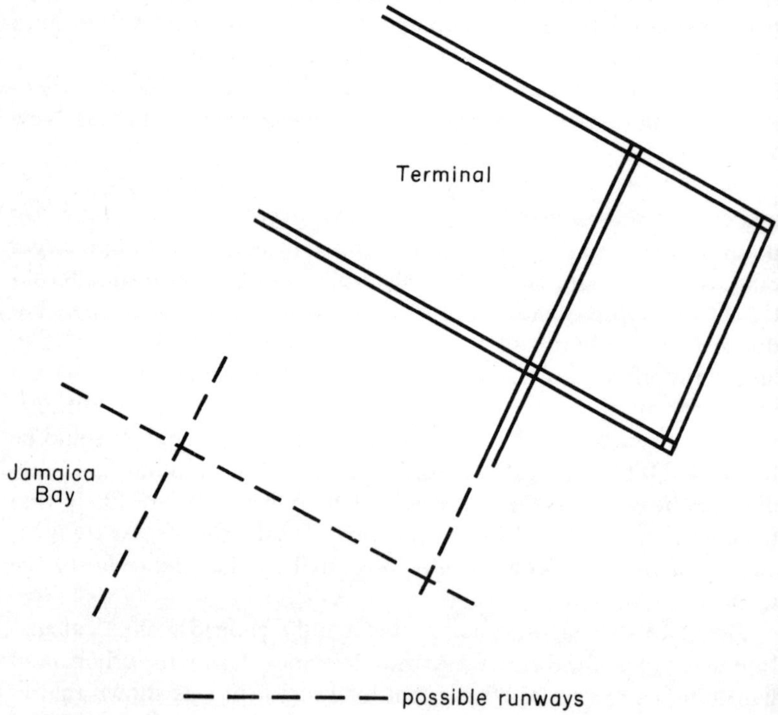

FIGURE 8.3.

The suggested extension of KIA into Jamaica Bay was apparently never put forward as a firm proposal by PONYA but the main ideas appeared publicly in August 1970. KIA was constructed some twenty years ago by reclaiming part of Jamaica Bay.[16] Two new runways were proposed for Jamaica Bay on more land to be reclaimed. This would mean a substantial reduction in the Bay – from some 12,000 to 8,000 acres. But it would give KIA at least two independently operable landing or mixed runways whatever the wind conditions. This would help considerably during the critical peak period when KIA has a great excess of arrivals.

The increase in capacity is not easy to calculate, but certain simulations of the system by ATC consultants have suggested that these improvements will expand the capacity of NYAS by as much as 40 per cent. For various reasons, however, this seems to me to be excessive and I would conjecture that a figure of 30 per cent is more appropriate.[17] This means that some fifty additional operations per hour will then be possible under IFR conditions – or approximately 200,000 operations per annum.

The capital cost of the extension into Jamaica Bay must be reckoned in the region of $200 million to $300 million, so we have taken a figure of $250 million for this purpose. The annual cost of this sum, amortized over 25 years at 9 per cent, may be taken as nearly $30 million or at 10 per cent with no amortization it is $25 million. Let us take the $25 million figure as an appropriate approximation. (Note that this does not include any 'rent' for the Bay – but this, in accounting terms would be a nominal sum.) Adding to this the current cost of maintaining and operating the runways will probably bring this figure near to $35 million.

This $35 million must be associated with approximately 100,000 landings for which fees are levied. To recover *all* these costs by landing fees one would require to charge an average of $350 per aircraft. In practical airport economics, however, revenues are derived from leasing terminal facilities and selling concessions. What non-landing-fee *net* revenue one may expect per average aircraft depends on the average size of airplane. It is unlikely to exceed $100, however, and a realistic figure would be less than $50 in view of the forecast traffic composition. Thus some average $300 per aircraft would be needed to recover the long-run costs of extension.

I would not claim that this figure is at all accurate but I do think it is indicative of a range of $150 to $450 which, in all probability,

[16] It took the form of excavating the fill from part of Jamaica Bay and compacting it to form KIA. This gave rise to a stagnant pool ('Grassy Bay') which has been troublesome ecologically.

[17] The explanation of the difference partly arises because of improvements to Newark.

contains the appropriate figure. This is far in excess of existing changes and it even exceeds by a substantial margin our proposed $100 minimum for the use of the runway during peak periods.

This provides an additional rationalisation for increasing the peak hour landing fee to $100 at KIA before any extension is undertaken into the Bay or, indeed, before a fourth jetport is begun. It may be conjectured that such a rise in landing fee may well dampen demand so much that New York may manage comfortably with its existing runways for many years. In fact the forecasts by PONYA suggest that from 1970 to 1980 there will be great expansion of general aviation movements in NYAS but air carrier operations will increase by only about 11 – the other 66 movements are in general aviation – to make a total additional movement of 77. If our calculations are correct then these general aviation movements, which were predicted in 1966–7 long before the $25 fee was introduced, will be largely put off by the high fee. The very much larger number of passengers (almost a doubling) will be accommodated in larger aircraft on the existing runway complex of NYAS.

It seems then that the extension of KIA may not be justified on these back-of-the-envelope calculations. But it may well be urged that it could be justified by:

1. Noise reductions due to the superior location of the new runways,

2. The social need to cater for general aviation at low subsidised landing fees, or

3. Other social costs and benefits not reflected in anyone's accounts.

The cost-benefit issue remains open.

REFERENCE

[1] A. Carlin and L. R. E. Park, *The Efficient Use of Airport Capacity in a Time of Scarcity*, RAND RM 5817 PA.

9

The Use of Cost-benefit Analysis as an Aid to Allocating Government Resources for Research and Development[1]

P. M. S. JONES[2]
Programmes Analysis Unit, Chilton, Berks.

SUMMARY

The application of cost-benefit methods to the allocation of R & D resources is described by reference to three main case studies with support from others. The importance of frames of reference, the methods of goal identification, the treatment of uncertainty and the application to real decision situations is described. Problems in benefit estimation are discussed with particular reference to the value of international trade, opportunity costing of resources and the treatment of social benefits in the amenity and health field.

Seven benefits to be gained from evaluation of R & D programmes are listed. These relate to identification of goals, decisions on the level and pattern of resource investment, the value of time and the value of uncertainty reduction.

1. INTRODUCTION

The Programmes Analysis Unit was established in February 1967, by the Ministry of Technology and the United Kingdom Atomic Energy Authority specifically to test and to develop methods for the appraisal of research and development programmes and to undertake practical evaluations as a step towards the more rational deployment of R & D resources[1]. The central theme of most of the evaluations performed (and these number about seventy) has been one of com-

[1] The author gratefully acknowledges the helpful discussions held with many members of the PAU, in particular with the Director, Mr R. L. R. Nicholson, and with members of the author's team, Messrs A. G. Hamlin, G. I. W. Llewelyn, K. Taylor and D. J. Storey.

[2] The author has now succeeded Mr Nicholson as Director, PAU.

parison of the net benefits expected to be derived as a result of the research with the costs of the R & D resources expected to be deployed in their attainment. The benefits have to be regarded realistically and due consideration given to the chance that they will be achieved in practice. Similarly the costs are likely to be uncertain so that unique values cannot be ascribed. This uncertainty is the main difference between cost-benefit analysis in the R & D field, which is essentially a speculative and medium- to high-risk activity, compared with the major capital investment projects for which the approach has been conventionally employed.

Cost-benefit analysis alone is not a sufficient tool; it has to be augmented by other techniques derived from the management sciences such as systems analysis, modelling, operations research and decision analysis in order to determine the proper objectives and fully explore the implications of the decision[2, 3, 4, 5].Technological[6, 7] and social[8] forecasting are also an integral part of the evaluation process. The only techniques that have been found inapplicable in the PAU environment to date have been the mathematical approaches to R & D portfolio selection[4, 5], the treatment of uncertainty using the concept of credibility developed by Allen[9, 11] and the numerical ranking methods of project appraisal[12] although it is recognised that the first and last of these may have application in special circumstances.

In this paper some of the problems associated with the use of the cost-benefit approach will be highlighted and discussed with reference to practical examples. Some of these problems are common to all evaluations whilst others have implications for the use of cost-benefit criteria in any decision process. There are very considerable benefits to be derived from the logical evaluation of the costs and benefits of research and the concentration of attention on the problem areas should not be allowed to obscure these.

2. THE COST-BENEFIT APPROACH TO R & D EVALUATION

Several distinct types of problem have been referred to the PAU for evaluation. These range from the analysis of specific individual project proposals or the selection of portfolios of projects, to the analysis of technological sectors or industries on a broad basis to determine the relevance of and benefits from initially unspecified R & D. These problems involve two different uses of the cost-benefit technique. In the specific project case or the portfolio both the benefits and costs may be determined and a direct comparison made between the two. For sector studies the benefits of attaining specific goals may be derived and used to set an upper limit to the level of R & D investment leaving it to the research manager to decide whether the target is practicable within the derived resource constraint.

In general, an evaluation of applied R & D begins with the determination of plausible objectives or goals. This is followed by the examination of each postulated goal to determine the benefits associated with its attainment. The alternative routes to attainment of the goal are then explored and costed, some of which may not involve R & D at all. Lastly, the chances of attaining the benefits in full or in part can be considered and the worthwhile objectives selected together with the preferred route or routes to their attainment. Both the level of benefit and the chances of realising it will be critically dependent on the attitudes of all those involved in the process of exploitation and no evaluation can be complete without separate appraisals from the viewpoint of each of those involved. This approach is discussed at greater length elsewhere[4, 5] and specific examples drawn from appraisals have appeared in a number of publications[4, 5, 12, 13, 14, 15, 16, 17, 18, 19, 20].

The most appropriate measure of benefit for Government-sponsored R & D has been taken to be the overall net benefit expected to be received by all sectors of the community. Transfers between sectors of the economy are thus eliminated, e.g. between Government and industry in the form of grants or taxation or between individuals and firms in terms of the split between price reduction and increased profit following increases in productivity. So long as the resources released as a result of an innovation are small in relation to gross domestic product it is assumed that they can be re-deployed elsewhere in the economy or absorbed by further growth so that the overall net benefit is equatable at its simplest with creation of real wealth. The true situation is clearly not this simple for several reasons; firstly, some changes are non-marginal and re-deployment of resources will not be instantaneous, i.e. economic and social penalties are incurred; secondly, transfers between individuals in the exploitation chain may affect the size of the market for or use of the innovation and hence change the level of benefit; thirdly, there are social and notional benefits to be derived from R & D that need to be included in the decision process but which are not normally included in the gross national product. These points and the concept of benefit at the national level have been discussed elsewhere[1, 5, 20, 21]. They will be further highlighted in relation to the practical cases considered below.

3. THE SIMPLE CASE OF A NEW PROCESS

A new versatile metal forming process, hydrostatic extrusion, was under development which offered the prospect of producing conventional semi-finished metal products more cheaply than existing processes. An evaluation was required in order to determine whether the programme merited continuation and the relative importance of different forms of the process. The latter would be dictated by the benefits attached to different types of product.

3.1. *The Method*

The method of appraisal adopted was that of comparing the economics of the new process with those of the processes it might displace and deducing from this comparison and other factors its potential utilisation by industry.

In the first place the unit cost of product produced by the new process was calculated on the basis of the expected capital costs of plant and buildings, labour and maintenance costs, throughput rate, scrap rates, the cost of pre-treatment of the feedstock and replacement of specialised short-life components. All of the cost elements were uncertain to a greater or lesser degree so that the final unit cost was also uncertain and could only be expressed as a range within which the true figure would lie. The sensitivity of the unit cost to variations in the individual contributory factors was explored and throughput rate and specialised component life identified as the most significant elements.

The costs of similar products produced by alternative processes were derived from either a similar analytical approach or directly from experienced industrial sources using these processes. The former was preferable but only applicable for one process and our own costings and costing methods were therefore discussed fully with industrial firms in order to minimise the risks of incompatibility. The comparisons took into account potential improvements in the competing processes prior to the new one reaching the factory floor.

The full costs arrived at in the above way are not necessarily a good guide to subsequent events. The users of the new process would be likely to receive investment grants and tax reliefs which would make the capital element of any process look smaller relative to the labour costs. (The saving was up to 50 per cent in present worth terms when this study was undertaken.) Furthermore a new process will only be compared with the full costs of an established one if a new plant is needed to maintain or increase output. In a static market or where surplus capacity was installed the marginal costs of running the existing process would be compared with the full costs of the new.

Taking these factors into account together with the size distribution of metal processing firms, the demand for metal products, etc., it was possible to forecast the market for the new process and express this both in terms of sales of equipment and output of semi-finished products using the process.

3.2. *The Benefits*

The gross benefits to the United Kingdom resulting from internal development of the process arise from:

(*a*) Sales of equipment by UK firms in the UK.
(*b*) Avoidance of need to import machinery.
(*c*) Exports of equipment by UK firms.
(*d*) Royalties and licence fees earned by UK firms from patents and know-how.
(*e*) Avoidance of royalties to overseas firms.
(*f*) Resource saving by UK firms utilising the process.
(*g*) Increased export of semi-finished or finished metal products resulting from lower prices or improved quality.
(*h*) Avoidance of increased imports of better and cheaper metal products.

The import and export of metal products of the type produced by the new process were too small to be of significance so (*g*) and (*h*) can be ignored. Internal royalty payments are transfers and so these too can be ignored. External royalties were impossible to estimate but were certainly small compared with the value of press sales so that (*d*) and (*e*) could be ignored in relation to (*a*), (*b*) and (*c*). The resources utilised in equipment manufacture were regarded as redeployable at comparable return elsewhere if the development was not undertaken so that no overall net benefit was attributable to sales of equipment other than attaching to the earning or saving of foreign currency. This is the first of the 'notional' benefits and one of the most difficult to quantify. At periods of serious imbalance between the inflow and outflow of goods and services from a country there will be benefits to be derived from rectifying the situation insofar as the imbalance may force a government to adopt growth-restricting policies or to devalue its currency with the resulting decrease in standards of living and relative wealth that this entails. In the opposite direction, acquisition of too much unusable foreign currency may itself carry disbenefits. These problems are not immediately relevant to R & D, however, since R & D programmes take seven to ten years[7] to reach fruition and hopefully the UK will have left her economic difficulties behind her. The real value of exports or import avoidance can then be measured solely in terms of what is gained in exchange. The transfer of resources to exports from alternative production for home consumption or avoidance of one import so that another can be obtained is only justified if it increases internal UK welfare. The problem is one of determining by how much internal welfare is increased.

Ideally, in project evaluation, one would like to associate the product of the project with a specific import but this is impracticable now and even more so when one has to look to the future. All exports have to be regarded as parts of a whole; it matters little whether imported fruit is paid for by machine tools or garments. On this basis it would seem appropriate to treat all imports and exports in terms of averaged values unless a baseline of imports and exports can be identified that one can be certain will exist at the appropriate future date. In this case the average should be over the remaining uncertain items only. One method of determining the benefit associated with exports would be to determine the extra level of resources that would have to be utilised to produce substitutes for the imports within the UK. Since the resource cost of domestic production must be higher relative to the exported commodity, than that of the import, the quantity of import substitute available must be less for a straight transfer of resources, or alternatively, the resources must be obtained from some other sector of the economy. Either way there is a net loss which can be measured best in terms of the resources needed over and above those made available from the export activity[8]. This is illustrated in Fig. 9.1. If the initial level of imports was B in exchange for exports utilising resources BD and domestic production of B would need resources BE then either additional resource DE has to be obtained from somewhere else in the economy or supply of import substitute has to fall to A such that $AC = BD$ and $OA = OB \times BD/BE$ assuming no scale effects occur. The actual level of resources wasted therefore will be less than DE but more than $BD \times ED/BE$, the precise value depending on the market readjustments that would occur.

The benefit arising from the manufacture and sale of a future export could be equated, as a first approximation, to something lying between the extra resource cost (£x) that would be incurred on average by domestic production of a substitute for the imports to a value equal to that of the export (£y) and $xy/(x+y)$. The averaging base would vary to embrace all potential imports in the distant future but for decisions relating to the very short term might reduce to the marginal import. Insufficient information is available at this time to permit a true evaluation of trade in these terms and an arbitrary weighting factor has conventionally been employed. This is a problem that merits much deeper attention than we have been able to devote to it[9].

An alternative approach could be to take the average duty levied on imports as a minimum measure of the consumer surplus vested in the imports, since the duty itself is an internal transfer payment. Again, the averaging base would be dependent on the timescale and the figure would be a minimum value.

The greatest benefits from development of hydrostatic extrusion arise from the resource savings resulting from its use by industry. These can be quantified on the basis of the comparative economic studies and estimates of market penetration and converted to net present values by discounting. However, these benefits will accrue regardless of where the development takes place and UK R & D is only justified if it increases the benefit over and above that which would result from the activities of others. Examination of the overseas situation led to the conclusion that abandonment of the UK programmes would delay introduction of the technique by several years, n, and this would decrease the net present worth benefit B_0, by an amount related to the discount factor d.

$$\text{Net present worth benefit without UK R \& D} = B_0/(1+d)n$$

3.3. *Uncertainty*

The benefit figures arrived at cannot be expressed as single values. Uncertainties in unit production costs, total markets, market penetration, lead time, etc., have to be taken into account. Where the uncertainty distribution for each component is known they can be combined mathematically or by Monte Carlo methods to arrive at a probability distribution for the overall benefit (Fig. 9.2.). Alternatively, one can assume distribution forms such as the rectangular distribution, with all values of a parameter between defined limits regarded as equally probable, and combine these. The sensitivity of the outcome to the assumed distributions can always be tested. In

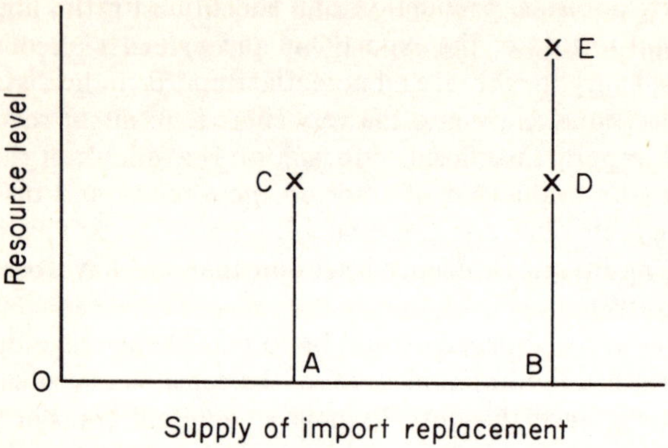

FIGURE 9.1.

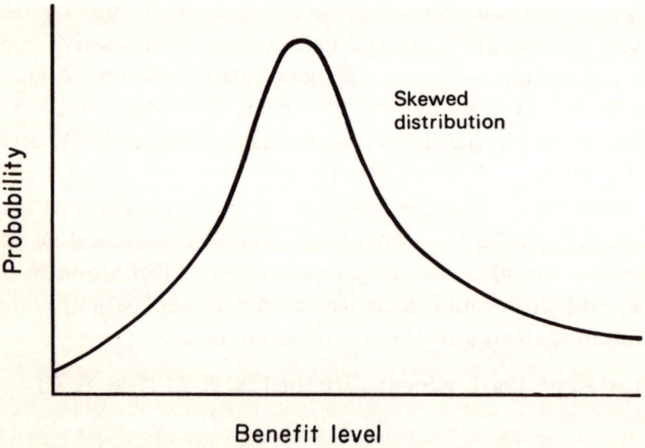

FIGURE 9.2.

many instances, however, and this study was one of these, it suffices for decision purposes to examine only the extreme limits of possible outcomes and compare the minimum net benefit level with expected R & D costs. These costs can also be explored in greater depth and expressed in probabilistic terms if the uncertainty looks significant.

In general, R & D resources are costed at direct real costs plus overheads but because of the existence of other uses for the resources (which are unlikely to have been evaluated fully) it would be more appropriate to use opportunity costs in the decision process. This difficulty is recognised by demanding benefit/cost ratios significantly above unity before deployment of resources is recommended; minimum figures in excess of 3/1 or 5/1 would be in line with experience to date both in PAU and in industry. The benefit/cost criterion appropriate for R & D decisions will be discussed later.

3.4. *Output*

The output of this particular study contributed to a decision on overall project viability, it identified the relative economic importance of different process types and the significance of the success of specific technical developments to process economics, hence helping with the balance of R & D investment, and it indicated the significance in economic terms of development timescales. A separate cost-benefit evaluation was also possible on alternative optional routes for speeding the adoption of the technique in industry via creation of industrial confidence in its reliability and product quality.

4. NEW MATERIALS

Several studies have been mounted on the benefits of development and use of new materials and some of the conclusions and principles involved have been described elsewhere[18, 19]. Contrary to popular opinion, new materials are rarely developed because of their intrinsic cheapness; it is the cost savings consequent on their use and the consumer surplus that they generate that provide the main stimuli to technological progress.

Two problems of particular interest in relation to benefit estimation have arisen and it is on these that attention is concentrated.

The fate of a technologically advanced industry may hang on the development or application of new materials and failure to pursue a vigorous R & D programme may result in an irrevocable loss of business. This loss would force the transfer of productive resources to other activities which are likely to be less profitable than the original use. For small industries these effects can be regarded as marginal and ignored but for major employers like the aircraft or vehicle industries the re-deployment is likely to lead to a significant decrease in net output per unit of transferred resource, i.e. a decrease in gross domestic product. Some estimate of the likely consequences of such forced transfer can be made by reference to the Census of Production and comparison of the output of the specific industries affected with the average of other industries employing similar labour. Subcontractors of the main industry may be similarly affected. There is, therefore, a defensive benefit to be gained by undertaking R & D to minimise the risks of loss of business and this benefit is taken to equal the consequences of the loss, evaluated as described above, multiplied by the probability of its occurrence. This probability can at best be a consensus of subjective estimates. The loss of business will also affect the international trade position which could be appraised as indicated in section 3.1. Care has to be exercised to ensure that resource re-deployment described above and that described in section 3.1 are complementary to avoid double counting.

The second problem lies in apportioning benefits between technical programmes. A specific goal, such as the development of a new engine, may be critically dependent on several features, e.g. design, special materials, fuel availability, etc., each of which is indispensable. In comparing benefits with costs in such instances it is only sensible to treat the development as an integrated whole but the sponsors of an evaluation may themselves only have responsibility for and control over one aspect. None of the benefit will accrue without their action yet they alone cannot achieve any benefit. In such a case the only sensible approach is to apportion the benefit between the individual contributory programmes in relation to their individual chances of success, the available alternatives and the overall expected benefit. For the hypothetical case in Fig. 9.3 there are two optional routes for design, material and fuel, each with its independent probability of success.

The overall probability of designing a competitive engine if these are the only uncertain elements is $(p1+p2-p1\,p2)\,(p3+p4-p3\,p4)\,(p5+p6-p5\,p6)$ so that the expected project benefit is $(p1+p2-p1\,p2)\,(p3+p4-p3\,p4)\,(p5+p6-p5\,p6)\times B$ where B is the estimated net present worth benefit if successful. The benefit dependent on development of Material A would be $Bp3(p1+p2-p1p2)(p5+p6-p5p6)$ but if this or the equivalent benefit were used for each route the total benefit from pursuing all routes would be three times the true value since there are three critical elements. Thus the benefit apportionable to an individual route for decision purposes ould be normalised to pB_e/n, where p is the probability of success of he specific development being considered, B_e the expected benefit if he specific route is successful (taking account of other uncertainties), nd n the number of uncertain elements in the overall development. The value of undertaking a second or further route to a goal follows rom the same approach and can be determined by the increase in xpected benefit, e.g. in the above example the expected benefit from leveloping material B in addition to material A would be $(p4-p3p4)$ $p1+p2-p1p2)$ $(p5+p6-p5p6)B$ with one-third of this sum apporionable on a normalised basis. This is less than the apportionable um if B were pursued alone in the absence of A. This approach has een applied in a simplified form for a material development[22] and n relation to the value of parallel strategies systems[12].

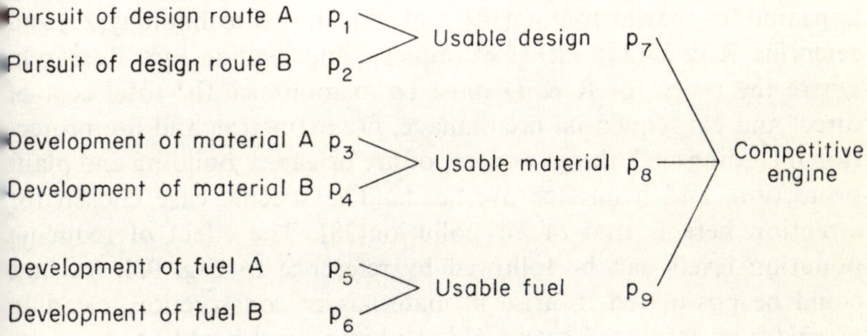

p = probability of success

FIGURE 9.3.

5. PROJECTS WITH SOCIAL BENEFIT

5.1. *Goal Identification*

In projects with social as well as economic benefits the goals may not clearly be defined and one of the principle roles of cost-benefit analysis is their clarification. Instances of this type clearly arise in the field of public policy[20]. For example, the policy on control of environmental pollution may be one of minimising the total economic plus social costs of pollution and its control, it may be one of maximising returns on Government investment bearing in mind other options competing for the resources, it may be one of ensuring that no one suffers any disutility due to the actions of others and it may be cast in a regional, national, or international framework. Cost benefit analysis cannot determine the policy, it can only help to set out the costs and benefits of such policies and social indicators. If the policy-maker chooses to pursue a superficially costly course the implication has to be that the analysts values are wrong, indeed the very act of decision changes them.

It is essential that goals are identified in relation to the whole system of direct and secondary effects they can produce. To impose narrow confines on a study can only result in a solution that is suboptimal and possibly wrong when seen in the broader context, furthermore, it is likely to bring the whole subject of cost-benefit analysis into unjustified disrepute.

Goal identification is greatly facilitated by use of qualitative or quantitative modelling techniques and examples of these have appeared for marine mining[14], and educational technology[23] and scientific R & D[24]. Other examples could include Fire Research, where the object of R & D must be to minimise the total cost of direct and consequential fire damage, fire extinction and fire protection including such things as costs of fire brigades, building and plant protection, and insurance overheads. The specific case chosen for attention here is that of air pollution[38]. The effect of reducing pollution levels can be followed by reference to Fig. 9.4. Savings could be postulated to arise in materials of construction, cleaning expenditure, increased crop yields and improved health. Extra costs might be incurred in control of emissions. Climatic effects might be avoided in the long term and general amenity increased. These changes will affect individuals directly, will change the demands on manufacturing industry and services of various types and would be likely, if beneficial, to release resources of manpower, materials, plant and capital, which could be redeployed elsewhere in the economy to advantage.

In principle, it should be possible to attach values to the direct changes following a postulated change of pollution level and to follow these through the system to determine the net change in available resources. Only the avoidable costs in product manufacture or labour utilisation can be regarded as real savings in the short term since fixed costs will still be incurred and profits can be regarded as intersector transfers. Furthermore, if the released labour and materials could not be re-deployed they would represent no gain to the economy.

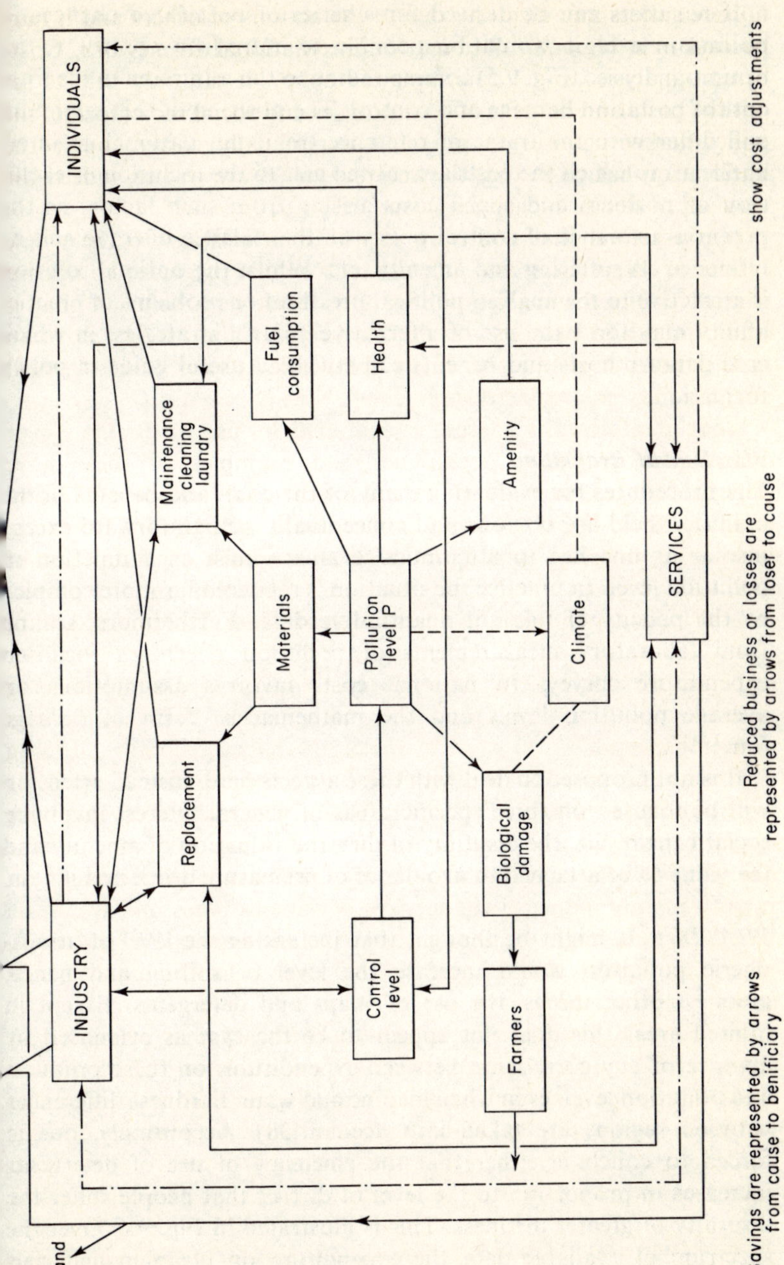
INDIVIDUALS
Fuel consumption
Health
Maintenance cleaning laundry
Amenity
SERVICES
Materials
Pollution level P
Climate
Replacement
Biological damage
INDUSTRY
Control level
Farmers
Land
show cost adjustments
Reduced business or losses are represented by arrows from loser to cause
Savings are represented by arrows from cause to benificiary

FIGURE 9.4.

If net costs can be derived for a series of postulated changes i pollution level it would be possible to introduce control to a optimum degree (Fig. 9.5) corresponding to the minimum in the tota cost of pollution damage and control. The position of this minimun will differ with the frame of reference (regional, national or inter national) to which the costs are related and to the inclusion or exclu sion of notional and social costs arising from such factors as th potential influence of control policy on the balance of trade and it influence on suffering and amenity, etc. Whilst the optimal solutio is attractive to the analyst, political pressures or problems of practic ability may force the use of alternative control strategies, in whicl case data on costs and benefits can still be a useful guide in polic formation.

5.2. *Benefit Evaluation*

The procedures for evaluating many of the costs and benefits in the pollution field are obvious and conceptually straightforward excep insofar as one has to attempt to evaluate both as a function o pollution level. In practice the situation is rendered far more comple by the paucity of relevant quantitative data. Furthermore, scaling from laboratory measurements of pollution effects or localised expenditure surveys to national costs involves assumptions on average pollution levels and the mathematical form of damage functions.

It is not proposed to deal with these aspects here. Instead attention will be focused on three specific areas of general interest involving social benefit, viz. the disutility of dirt, the valuation of amenity and the value to be attached to avoidance of premature death and illness.

5.2.1 *Dirt*. It might be thought that increasing the level of atmospheric pollution would increase the level of soiling and hence, amongst other things, the use of soaps and detergents. Except in limited areas this does not appear to be the case as evidenced by absence of any correlation between expenditures on these products and pollution level, even when income and water hardness differences between regions are taken into account[38]. Accordingly, one is forced to conclude either that the efficiency of use of detergents increases in proportion to the level of dirt or that people suffer the disutility of greater dirtiness. This is illustrated in Fig. 9.6. Over the spectrum of available data the expenditure on cleaning materials follows the lower curve to the right of *A*. For uniform cleanliness the

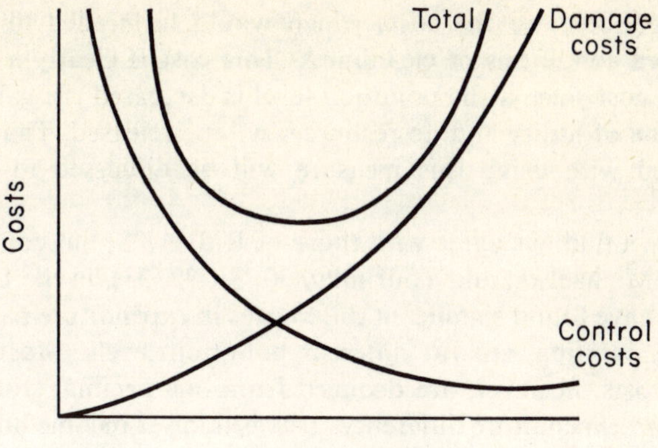

FIGURE 9.5.

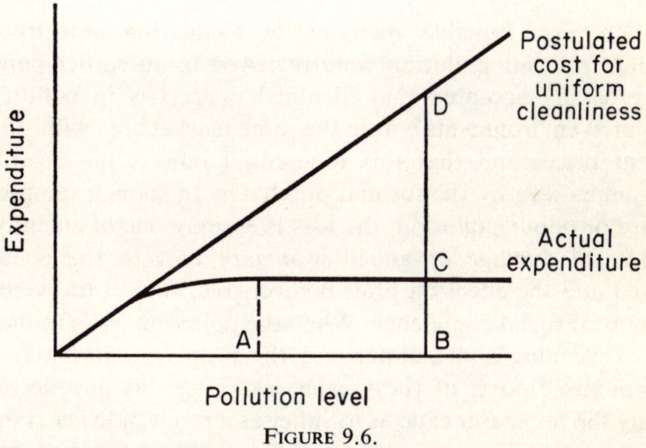

FIGURE 9.6.

curve might be expected to take a form similar to the upper line. At pollution level *B* expenditure patterns indicate that the individual is not prepared to spend the minimum sum, *CD*, necessary to gain the utility of extra cleanliness; he has other preferred uses for his resources. However, he is clearly suffering a disutility and it has been suggested by Prest and Turvey[26] that the disutility be measured by the minimum cost needed to rectify the situation, i.e. the sum *CD* the individual is unable or unprepared to spend unless some cheaper alternative exists. This concept has been applied by the Beaver Committee[27] who equated the costs of pollution in black areas (highly polluted) to the costs which would be needed to produce white area conditions of cleanliness. This cost is clearly a notional or social cost since if the pollution level is decreased the gain will be purely one of utility and no resources will be released. The problem associated with using this measure will be discussed in the next section.

Our own findings agree with those of Ridker[28] but conflict with those of Michaelson and Tourin[29, 30, 31, 32, 33], in the USA who claim to have found significant differences in expenditure patterns on cleaning, painting, etc., at different pollution levels. Most of their quoted costs, however, are deduced from one original study which showed no expenditure differences between lower income households and based all its conclusions on averaged data from higher income households with no allowance for possible social, climatic or other factors.

5.2.2. *Amenity*. Possible methods of evaluating amenity losses resulting from air pollution were reviewed in an earlier paper[34]. It is generally accepted that identical properties in polluted and unpolluted environments within the same market area will command different prices and that this differential reflects the disutility of pollution as seen by vendor and purchaser. In some instances, as in the case of odour pollution, the loss is entirely one of amenity since no physical damage or added monetary cost to the resident is incurred and the effect on price is reversible, subject to overcoming problems of social confidence. When the pollution leads to increased costs of cleaning and maintenance the property value may reflect the capitalised costs of these expenses as well as any decrease in amenity the purchaser expects to suffer as a result of lower standards. In economic terms the price of a property would equal the sum of the discounted stream of net benefits derivable from it, provided the vendors and purchasers are fully aware of all pertinent facts. However, it seems unlikely that the average man is aware of all the facts, a view that is supported by a survey by Ridker[28] in Philadelphia which suggested that people did not realise maintenance costs, or pollution effects on vegetation and health could be affected by moving home. At the same time people do recognise that residential areas differ with regard to dirt, soot and odours[28, p. 13*a*] and take these into account when moving house[28, 35, 36].

Jaksch[37] argues that one is less likely to be able to transfer costs from one market to another where land or property are concerned and 'proves' via indifference curves that changes in market price truly reflect changes in the utility derivable from the property.

Three studies relating to property values and air pollution appear in the literature. Jaksch[37] and Ridker[28] have performed cross sectional multiple correlation studies in Toledo and St Louis, USA, respectively based on earlier work by Brigham[39] who satisfactorily correlated land values in Los Angeles county with accessibility to centres of activity, local amenities, topography and present and future use. He found serious measurement problems and numerous intercorrelated proxies for amenity and accessibility. Ridker's study correlates property value with property characteristics (age, density, size); location characteristics (distances from work, highways, shops, etc.); neighbourhood characteristics (school quality, crime rate, residents occupations), taxes, public services and submarket variables including racial origins of occupants and family income, and finally pollution level due to customary urban sources. The property values were based on owner valuations. Jaksch[37] studies actual property sales over a 6½-year period in a situation with a single industrial dust source and correlated price with size of property, a depreciation factor, dustfall and a measure of local payroll which normalised for inflationary effects. Jaksch chose his area to minimise many of the social and amenity differences encountered by Ridker. A further study by Ridker[28] examined the time dependence of property values relative to a control area following introduction of a new point pollution source in a neighbourhood.

In the United Kingdom the same sources of property values (census data) are not available nor are there convenient records of sale prices. For this reason the PAU pilot study of property value relied on the opinion of estate agents. A first questionnaire identified and ranked spontaneously volunteered factors that affected property value, without identifying the purpose of the study. A second then invited opinion on the price differential between hypothetical identical properties with identical amenities in smoke controlled and uncontrolled areas, for properties within defined price brackets. The respondents were selected from fourteen towns where there was known to be a good mix of controlled and uncontrolled areas with data available on pollution levels, so that a real market existed and so that the question was meaningful to the respondent and numerically significant to the analyst. Questions relating to times for price adjustment following a change in pollution level, property rentals, and other factors were also asked.

Only 10 per cent of respondents voluntarily mentioned air pollution as a factor in property value and all valued it low. Smoke control was thought to enhance the value by 34 per cent, have no effect by 59 per cent, and 7 per cent thought values might fall slightly. In high pollution areas the average differential on a £5,000 house was 1·05 per cent whilst in low pollution areas it was 0·4 per cent with an overall mean of 0·8 per cent. In both areas the percentage magnitude of the differential increased with the value of the property. The lag between a change in pollution level and adjustment of the market had a mean value of 1·7 to 2·0 years. The values were surprisingly close to those of Jaksch and Ridker when normalised for pollution level and property value.

If these values are accepted as a measure of the value attached to the amenity of clean air and a cleaner environment by house purchasers they can be applied to all properties, including those where no true market can exist, to estimate the total national costs of pollution. In practice the capitalised figure has to be converted to an annual figure of £4 per household in a polluted area for comparison with control costs and annual expenditure on cleaning, etc. In view of the findings of the Ridker survey[28] concerning factors taken into account on house purchase, it was not surprising that this figure was close to the notional extra annual expenditure on maintenance and cleaning and only one of these two pollution costs should be included so as to avoid double counting.

There can be little doubt that property values are affected by pollution but the effect is small and masked by many larger items. Furthermore, decisions on house purchase are really a series of complex trade offs between a large number of factors – outlook *vs.* neighbours, schools *vs.* distance to work, etc. Also the types of property in heavily polluted areas tend to differ from those in cleaner areas partially as a legacy of the industrial revolution, but more particularly because the domestic coal fire is still far and away the most important source of pollution damage. For these and many other reasons the results of any survey have to be treated with caution.

In one respect pollution is easier to deal with than noise. In the pollution field the trend in the United Kingdom has been towards improvements for well over a decade. The forced removal situation which necessitates regarding removal expenses and lost consumer surplus as an integral part of the cost in the Roskill study[40] does not occur. Market value more truly reflects the gains and losses as seen by the purchaser and vendor and the current national situation is such that the effects are reasonably uniform. One is not faced with the problem of trying ante-hoc to deduce the impact of future changes (new airports, reservoirs, etc.) from narrowly specific post-hoc studies of equilibrium markets which may differ greatly from the real decision situations.

5.2.3. *Value of Life and Health.* In attempting to set values to the costs of ill health and premature death there are three prime categories to consider. The economic costs which appear in GNP, e.g. resulting from lost production, treatment costs; the non-GNP production losses from loss of housewives' services, students, etc, and the social costs not involving any output function at all.

Loss of output due to illness is usually valued by taking a worker's wage as equal to his marginal product. There are problems in estimating days lost from national statistics because of uncertified sickness and the opting out of some married female workers. Treatment costs can be assessed by estimating the demands on the General Practitioners' time and from statistics on the demands on hospital services. The economic costs of premature death will look different depending on whether the decedent is regarded as a part of society making the decision or not. Current opinion favours his inclusion, so that his foregone consumption is not deducted from his foregone wage. In our own studies[38] net product foregone was used to avoid double counting since consumption was also included in the method of 'determining' a social cost of premature death.

The housewife could be valued at 'replacement' cost for all her many duties but we preferred to set the value of housewives' time as being at least equal to the average wage she could have earned in alternative female employment. A similar policy was adopted for students. Both were on a weekly basis rather than hourly. For both illness and premature death of housewives gross notional income was employed compared with the net figure for premature death of an employed person. This was because a housewife's services would need to be replaced following death at a full rate for the job.

Following the thoughts of Professor A. Williams[41] the social value of illness or premature death could be assessed by either:

(*a*) looking at the value attached by society as evidenced by court awards;
(*b*) looking at the implications of public expenditure;
(*c*) asking people; or

(*d*) selecting a plausible value and working towards a consensus. The PAU study considered alternative (*c*) as impractical since few people can imagine chronic illness prior to having it and the chronically sick cannot be expected to recall how they felt when fit. Furthermore, it is the price society is prepared to pay for the welfare of others rather than that which the individual is prepared to pay in his own interests that is relevant to public decision. Attempts by US workers to explore this objectively through insurance concepts have not met with much acceptance[42].

Court judgements (*b*) are as arbitrary in many ways as self-selection (*d*) and are in any case only applicable for disablement since no allowance is made for suffering in fatal accident cases. Based on recent awards to road accident victims and deducting in the case of employed people the income losses, gives values ranging from £500 to £3,000 per annum for severe incapacitation. The figures have been deduced from capital awards on the basis of life expectancy at age at time of accident and a discount rate of 10 per cent.

Society could be argued to be willing to pay sums at least equal to pensions or unemployment pay plus supplementary benefit plus rate relief and other fringe benefits to keep the disadvantaged or old at some reasonable standard of comfort. Alternatively society would appear to be willing to meet the full cost of hospitalisation and treatment if an individual would benefit. These expenditures again suggest that the social value attached to avoidance of suffering and preserving life lies in the £500 to £2,000 per annum category. In other areas of public expenditure on safety, etc, there is little consistency in expenditure patterns.

The magnitude of social cost could lie anywhere from £100 per annum to £5,000 per annum but for calculation purposes it has been set at £1,000 per annum for chronic disablement or premature death. We do not believe this figure to have great validity, the more so for reasons to be explained later, but it suffices to put social costs, which include a consumption element, in perspective in relation to social costs in other areas. This represents an average current valuation, however, and any change in expenditures should be treated in terms of marginal incremental valuation, which would be considerably lower.

5.3. *The Use of Social Cost-Benefit Data as a Decision Aid*

The brief and partial treatment of pollution costs outlined above gives some picture of the complexity of one study. What has not been stressed is the uncertainty of all the derived values. They are dependent on uncertainties in the effects of specific pollution levels, uncertainties in actual pollution levels and the areas over which they are relevant, uncertainties in extrapolation of damage beyond level of current experience and uncertainties in the values attached to the various forms of disutility. The decision-taker has to be presented not only with median estimates but also with a picture of the possible range of costs and benefits that could occur in practice. This can be done crudely by attaching distributions to each element of uncertainty and combining these statistically. Where the precise form of contributory uncertainty distributions is not known, a range of alternatives can be used to test the sensitivity of the outcome.

The second and very important factor that is widely ignored in cost-benefit analysis is the need to keep growth investment and consumption based benefits distinct. That this is true in principle can be seen from Fig. 9.7 which is based on a model developed by Medford[23] for the value of education and extended by Jones[24] to R & D. Economic activity can bring about growth in the upper wealth-producing production cycle or one can withdraw monetary and other resources to improve the quality of life either directly or (as in the case of production) through an R & D/education chain which hopefully multiplies the potential value. Social costs and benefits (including consumption) are felt in the quality of life spur. In principle, if all the interactions and parameters were known, the rate of syphoning from the production cycle could be adjusted to maximise the quality of life, which is after all what everything is all about. The correct time-values would be taken into account using social time preference discount rates. Too much syphoning will clearly decrease the 'summed present worth' of the quality of life. For a complex cycle system of the type shown in Fig. 9.7 it is clearly quite inappropriate to suppose that adding the monetary and non-monetary benefits deduced without exploring the interactions in the model can constitute any guide to overall optimisation.

The argument that the transfer between growth-inducing and consumption spheres are marginal may suffice as a crude sub-optimisation if the benefit greatly exceeds the cost but this implies a decision criterion well removed from benefit-cost ratios of unity. Furthermore whilst any individual decision may appear marginal the sum of all social benefits or costs, as currently determined, resulting from pollution, noise, accidents, etc. may well exceed GDP and will vary with the baseline adopted for measurement; let us postulate a national plan with new roads, airports, factories covering the whole country and picture the total social costs we would derive. If the whole is non-marginal to the economy then even decisions on the marginal elements need to be adjusted otherwise they might represent a serious misuse of resources. If B_e and B_s are the economic and social benefits of a project and C_e and C_s its costs, and if:

$$\Sigma B_e + \Sigma B_s = n(\Sigma C_s + \Sigma C_s)$$

then $B_e + B_s \geqslant C_e + C_s$ can scarcely represent an efficient use of resources.

On the basis of these two lines of argument it would seem that the use of simple benefit-cost criteria must be treated with great caution and the impacts of transfers from wealth-producing to non-productive areas should be explored. Only where a decision has to be made between alternatives, one of which is certain to go ahead, can the second difficulty be ignored and even here the monetary and non-monetary elements should be considered separately.

5.4. *Application to R & D*

The above comments have related largely to general decision processes whereas the PAU study on pollution was aimed at R & D. The aims of R & D can be explored by reference to Fig. 9.5. assuming the overall cost optimisation philosophy to be appropriate. It is clear that one can aim either to reduce control costs or to reduce damage costs and that either course would be beneficial. Having defined the functions the effects of changes in them on total system cost gives a measure of potential benefit for comparison with R & D costs.

More important, however, is the value of R & D to decision processes via the reduction of uncertainty. This topic is still under study[43] but the principles will be seen from Fig. 9.8. For a fixed control cost function (in this instance) the damage function can lie anywhere between curves *A* and *B* with a total cost curve lying between *C* and *D* for different control levels. The decision-taker has no idea where the true costs are between these limits but if he follows a minimax strategy he will control to the mean level between extremes and minimise his maximum error. His average error in cost terms will then be roughtly 0·25 of the range *EF* between the extremes, the exact value depending on the form of the uncertainty distribution in the damage function. Reduction of uncertainty has value since it reduces his average error and application of Bayesian concepts enables one to set a benefit to the uncertainty reduction. The level of benefit will be dependent not only on uncertainty distributions but also on the policy to be adopted by the decision-taker. We have so far only attributed values in a simple overall manner and future work is aimed at isolating the relative importance of the individual contributions to uncertainty and the consequences of different control philosophies.

6. THE USE OF COST-BENEFIT METHODS IN R & D EVALUATIONS

Any cost-benefit appraisal is aimed at giving the best advice to decision-takers and R & D appraisal is no exception. In this paper we have sought to identify factors that have arisen from practical appraisals and deal with them by reference to specific examples. Of particular importance are the frame of reference for the study, its goals, the treatment of uncertainty and the logic of application of the outputs of analyses to decision processes. Particular problems also appear in trying to set values to benefits and instances in the field of trade, opportunity costing of resources and social benefit valuation have been given. All of these have implications in the wider sphere of cost-benefit analysis.

The most important features are probably those of goal identification and the use to which the results of analysis are put. As stated in section 5.3.3. if the total potential benefits from all postulated projects are many times the costs of gaining them, then investment on a unit benefit-cost ratio project would be wasteful. This point was also brought out in section 3.3. Ideally one would like to cost all resources at opportunity cost but this demands a body of background data on other opportunities which is rarely available. This background is gradually being built up in the government R & D resource field by the author and his colleagues, and opportunity cost for resources of three to five times their nominal cost seem appropriate. With social projects, however, there is no such data base yet available, neither is the model for the effect of transfer of resources from the economic cycle to social wellbeing and improved quality of living (Fig. 9.7). In the absence of the latter and with present methods of cost-benefit evaluation, the opportunity for resources cost in social terms can be expected to differ from that in economic terms, possibly by a large amount. Further work will help to elucidate this point. If the model or some variant were usable there would still be difficulties since the values for benefits need to be those values which will apply when they are realised, and social values in particular are subject to change. Some attempt to estimate future values by forecasting techniques is therefore essential[9, 24] although present efforts are rudimentary. Observations of current situations can also be misleading when applied to decision processes. The fact that society is currently prepared

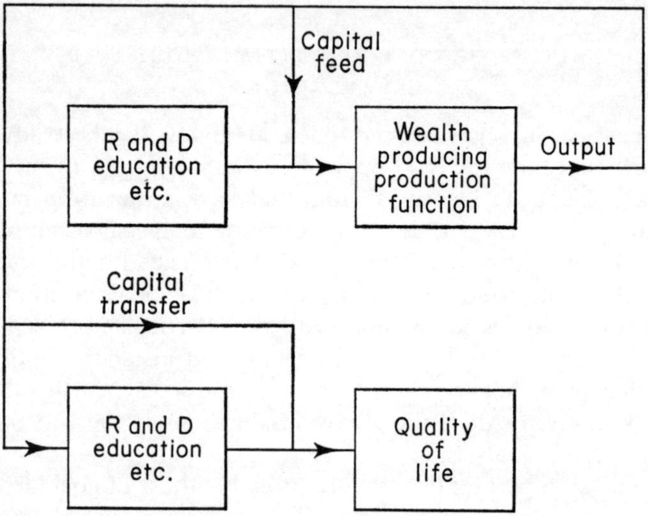

FIGURE 9.7.

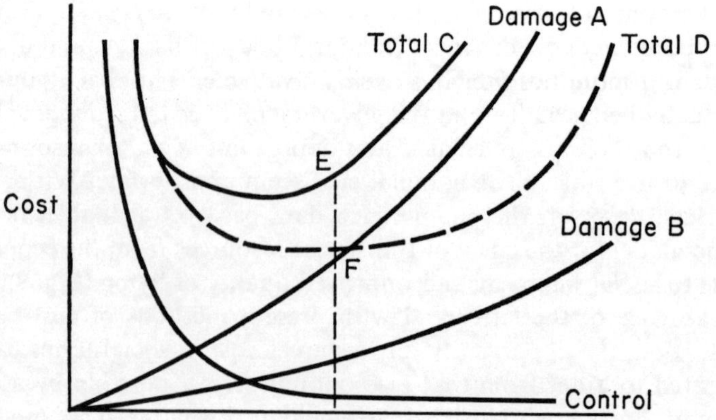

FIGURE 9.8.

to pay a sum of money to alleviate a social disutility does not necessarily mean that they would be prepared to pay ten times as much when some equivalent but hitherto unrecognised difficulty involving ten times as many people is identified.

The inevitably arbitrary nature of the baseline in socially oriented projects means that the outcome can never be objectively correct except by reference to defined standards or objectives which frequently lie in the political sphere.

Despite these difficulties, and the similar but much smaller problems which arise in solely economic project evaluation there are undoubted benefits from cost-benefit appraisals of R & D. These may be listed as:

(*a*) Questioning and close identification of goals.
(*b*) Assistance with decisions on overall worthwhileness of projects or project portfolios in relation to other options.
(*c*) Assistance with decisions on justifiable overall levels of resource investment.
(*d*) Assistance with decisions on balance of investment between sub-elements of programmes.
(*e*) Evaluation of the importance of timing on project viability.
(*f*) Identification by sensitivity analysis or other means of the importance of features in the development and exploitation process so that they get due attention from the outset.
(*g*) Identification of the value of reduction of uncertainty in decision processes.

There are still many problems to be overcome but it is only by perseverance that the methods can be tested and progress made towards a more rational and optimal means of resource allocation.

REFERENCES

[1] *The Programmes Analysis Unit 1967–70*, PAU, Chilton, Didcot, Berks.
[2] R. L. R. Nicholson, The practical application of cost-benefit analysis to R & D investment decisions, In NATO Symposium on cost-benefit analysis, The Hague, July 1969, English Universities Press, 1970.
[3] P. M. S. Jones, *Project Evaluation – Decisions on Levels of Investment in Research, Feasibility Studies & Market Surveys*, PAU Report M.8, HMSO, 1969.
[4] P. M. S. Jones and H. Hunt, *Programme Evaluation as Practised by the Programmes Analysis Unit with Three Case Studies*, PAU Report M.12, HMSO, 1969.
[5] P. M. S. Jones, *The Evaluation of Government R & D Programmes, R & D Management*, **1**, 81, 1971.

[6] R. L. R. Nicholson, *Technological Forecasting as a Management Technique*, PAU Report M.7, HMSO, 1969.
[7] P. M. S. Jones, *Technological Forecasting as a Management Tool*, PAU Report M.10, HMSO, 1970.
[8] P. M. S. Jones, *Preliminary Thoughts on Social Forecasting*, PAU Report M.16, HMSO, 1970.
[9] D. H. Allen, *O.R. Quarterly*, **19,** 25, 1968.
[10] P. M. S. Jones, *O.R. Quarterly*, **20,** 496, 1969.
[11] P. M. S. Jones, Contribution to *Decision Making in Practice*, IMRA Seminar, Nov. 1969, Industrial Market Research Association, London, 1970.
[12] P. M. S. Jones, *Ranking Development Options*, PAU Report M.14, HMSO, 1970.
[13] R. D. Medford, *Futures*, **1,** 510, 1969.
[14] R. D. Medford, *Mining Magazine*, **121,** 396 and 474, 1969.
[15] H. Hunt, *Futures*, **1,** 328, 1969.
[16] K. M. Hill, *Technological Forecasting in Some Basic Industries*, Ninth Commonwealth Mining and Metallurgical Conference, May 1969.
[17] P. M. S. Jones, Investment in Innovation, IEE Conference on electro-machining, March 1970, *IEE Conference Publication* No. 61, 181, 1970.
[18] P. M. S. Jones, *J. Mat. Sci.*, **5,** 796, 1970.
[19] P. M. S. Jones, The evaluation of R & D with particular reference to new materials, SCI Symposium on chemistry in the 1990s, Lancaster, July 1969, Society of Chemical Industry, London, 1970.
[20] P. M. S. Jones, *Lessons from the Objective Appraisal of Programmes at the National Level*, Research Policy, **1,** 11, 1971.
[21] P. M. S. Jones, The idea of national benefit, Civil Service Department Seminar on the evaluation of R & D, Sunningdale, May 1969.
[22] P. M. S. Jones and A. G. Hamlin, Unpublished studies on a materials R & D programme, Programmes Analysis Unit.
[23] I. McMullen, K. M. Hill, P. M. Ash, J. D'Arcy, R. Morris, R. D. Medford and P. McLaren, *Computer Based Learning Systems*, National Council for Educational Technology, London 1969.
[24] P. M. S. Jones, *Policy Sciences*, **1,** 299, 1970.
[25] Based on a study by P. M. S. Jones and G. I. W. Llewelyn, Programmes Analysis Unit.
[26] A. R. Prest and R. Turvey, *The Economic Journal*, **75,** 683, 1965.
[27] Report of the Committee on Air Pollution, HMSO, London, 1954.
[28] R. G. Ridker, *The Economic Costs of Air Pollution*, Praeger and Sons, London, 1966.
[29] I. Michelson and B. Tourin, Public Health Reports, **81,** 505, 1966.
[30] I. Michelson and B. Tourin, *Household Costs of Living in Polluted Air – Twin Kansas Cities*, Environmental Health & Safety Research Associates, New York, January 1968.
[31] I. Michelson and B. Tourin, *New York – New Jersey Metropolitan Area*, EHSRA, N.Y., March 1968.
[32] I. Michelson and B. Tourin, *Connecticut*, EHSRA, N.Y., October 1968.
[33] I. Michelson and B. Tourin, *Upper Ohio River Valley*, EHSRA, N.Y., Feb. 1968.
[34] P. M. S. Jones, Land, amenity and infrastructure in cost-benefit studies of air pollution, Treasury Management Accounting Unit Seminar on the valuation of land, amenity and infrastructure, Sunningdale, September 1969.
[35] W. S. Smith, J. J. Schuenneman, and L. D. Leidberg, *J. Air Pollution Control Association*, **14,** 418, 1964.

[36] Report of the Committee on the Problem of Noise, HMSO, London, 1963.
[37] J. A. Jaksch, The effects of air pollution on residential property values in Toledo, Oregon, M.Sc. Thesis, University of Washington, Seattle, 1969.
[38] From an unpublished study by P. M. S. Jones, K. Taylor, and D. J. Storey, Programmes Analysis Unit.
[39] E. Brigham, *Land Economics*, **41,** 325, 1965.
[40] Committee on the Third London Airport, HMSO, 1970.
[41] A. Williams, private communication, PAU Seminar, Durley Hall, Bournemouth, October, 1969.
[42] T. C. Schelling, Contribution to *Problems in Public Expenditure Analysis*, S. B. Chase (Editor), Brookings Institute, 1968; London, George Allen & Unwin, Ltd.
[43] Current studies by P. M. S. Jones, K. Taylor, and J. Raby, Programmes Analysis Unit.

Part Four

FRONTIERS

10

The Gains from Regional Policy

C. BLAKE

Professor of Economics, University of Dundee

I

It is generally accepted that our regional problem in the United Kingdom is attributable in part to spatial imperfections in the labour market. In some areas of the country the market price of labour has failed to reflect its shadow (social opportunity-cost) price, or – where the price signals are correctly shown – labour and capital have failed to relocate in the appropriate directions. This presumably provides an economic case for differential subsidies to development areas.[1] But subsidies are, under present arrangements, offered indiscriminately on a simple geographical test, without regard to the extent (if any) to which they bring about a welfare gain. It can not surely be sensible to imply that the advantages are alike between subventing, e.g. aluminium smelting in Angelsey and shipbuilding on the Upper Clyde. I believe that cost-benefit thinking offers an appropriate conceptual framework within which a *selective* policy for regional subsidies might be applied. To illustrate this, I propose that we think of the higher rates of investment allowance in the development areas as triggering marginal claims on capital resources, and thereafter generating a series of benefits in the form of outputs obtained at zero opportunity cost.

The position is complicated by the fact that the subsidy represents an implicit burden on the Exchequer, thus indirectly blocking consumption or investment opportunities in the public or private sectors. At the same time, to the extent that investments qualifying for subsidy absorb idle resources, there will be both a fall in unemployment benefit paid and a rise in direct taxation receipts. These can be seen as future inflows to the Exchequer which will have real con-

[1] I assume that the criterion of regional policy is the maximisation of national income per head. If some other criterion were adopted, e.g. the minimisation of inter-regional differences in income per head, then the following argument would have to be modified.

sequences for the national product in the same sense, but the opposite direction, as the fiscal burden. It is therefore possible to contain this complication within the cost-benefit framework, provided that future fiscal flows are discounted at appropriate rates.

II

An indiscriminate regional subsidy to capital investment will lead to its being paid in three distinct situations:

(i) Where a similar investment would otherwise have been made elsewhere in the UK.
(ii) Where the same investment would have been made, in the same location, even without subsidy.
(iii) Where all or part of the investment would otherwise have been made outside the UK, or not have been made at all.

We may characterise these three possibilities as, respectively, 'subsidy-diverted', 'autonomous', and 'subsidy-created' investment. In order to see how selectivity could be applied to the application of subsidy, let us now consider the various headings under which costs and benefits may be expected to arise.

First, there are capital outlays which are directly attributable to the subsidy. In the autonomous case, of course, these costs do not occur. The subsidy-created case will differ from the subsidy-diverted one, in that the entire resource cost of investment in the former case is attributable to subsidy whereas, with the latter, there will be only those costs which are incurred as a result of selecting the alternative location. (Some expenditures, e.g. on plant and machinery, are presumably unaffected by the location of the project; differential elements will arise in site preparation, building and the provision of mains services, particularly if the diversion means opening up a 'greenfield' site rather than extending an existing factory elsewhere.)

Second, there are consequential gains from the employment of otherwise idle resources in the assisted regions. Although these may include idle or under-utilised plant, in industries other than that in which the investment is made, the measure of spare capacity is assumed to be the availability of labour already in the region. With the subsidy-created case, the extent of the gain is the difference between market price and shadow price for all labour units employed. With the subsidy-diverted case, it is the relatively greater extent of this difference in the host region over alternative locations. With the autonomous case the gain is nil.

Third, but only in the subsidy-diverted case, there may be relocation economies or diseconomies from regional differences in labour quality or in transport costs, or from scale effects. At the same time, a subsidy-diverted investment may gain or lose external economies or diseconomies as a result of the move. It may also carry with it external benefits which accrue to other firms in the form of lower transport costs, specialist services, or a generalized 'sophistication' effect.

Fourth (and again for subsidy-diversion only), relocation towards the development areas may reduce congestion costs elsewhere, and lower the marginal cost of social capital for the country as a whole.

Finally, subsidy-creation through the attraction of foreign capital which would otherwise have avoided the UK, or of British-owned capital which would otherwise have gone overseas, generates a real benefit corresponding to the fiscal transfers from home country to host.

In constructing this list I have placed no cost on the social consequences of chronic localised unemployment, nor have I made allowance for any gains or losses in amenity due to diversion of manufactures. In general, intangibles have been excluded from both the 'cost' and 'benefit' sides. Again, I have not dealt with the redistributional effects of a subsidy which rewards capital creation. These effects will occur as long as there is non-zero elasticity of substitution between factors in response to a subsidy to one of them. Lastly, I have assumed that the administrative costs of any scheme of subsidy, which fall on eligible firms as well as the government service, are unlikely to affect the arithmetic to a significant extent.

Then, the analytic framework must be recognised as excluding certain dynamic effects. For instance, any subsidy to regional production may yield benefits through a process comparable to that of devaluation in a country. The argument is complicated by interregional linkages; nevertheless a regional subsidy may bring about an 'export-led' expansion in those areas where it is available, and this in turn may bring to the same areas those productivity gains which follow a sustained higher rate of growth.

According to another school of thought, re-structuring a regional economy is only the first stage of a dynamic sequence. It is sufficient, on this view, to relocate a 'strategic' manufacturing plant, having a network of linkages with supplying industries, for offshoots from that network to cluster round the migrant in its new site.

III

When we come to consider measuring the costs and benefits analysed in the previous section, it will help if we place them in the context of a specific region, let us say Scotland. For simplicity I propose to ignore linkages between Scotland and the rest of the UK. I propose also to concentrate the discussion on subsidy-diverted investment, as presenting both the more interesting problems and (presumably) the more common type of case. (The following arguments can be adapted to deal with the subsidy-created case.)

The basic tool for measuring the impact on Scottish production of a new project in Scotland is the 'regional preference function'.[2] We start by assuming *a priori* that markets for industrial materials exhibit a more or less smooth gradation from purely 'local' to predominantly 'national' markets, although the former category will probably be confined to certain services, fuels and raw materials (including agricultural products). We assume further that this is revealed by the coefficient of localisation for an industry, such that industries showing a low coefficient sell in mainly local markets, while national markets are served by industries which are regionally specialised.

Then, for any given degree of regional specialisation we postulate that the share of Scottish demand going to Scottish producers is a positive function of the Scottish share of UK capacity. In other words, the higher the coefficient of localisation the larger the Scottish sector has to be (relatively speaking) in order to obtain a given share of the Scottish market, and the less the strength of regional preference (which, however, is always present to some degree). Here, as in later stages of the argument, it is assumed that 'industries' (however defined) are homogeneous as between regions. Also, we ignore any preferences for established suppliers which may be retained by immigrant firms, and also those linkages which are dictated by common ownership within vertically integrated groups.

In order to construct particular regional preference functions, three limiting cases are defined intuitively as follows:

(a) Where the coefficient of localisation is less than a certain value, the industry is regarded as truly local and the Scottish share of Scottish demand put at 100 per cent.

(b) For all index values above this minimum, if the Scottish share

[2] See: 'Unemployment, Idle Capacity and the Evaluation of Public Expenditures' by R. A. Haveman and J. V. Krutilla (Johns Hopkins Press, for RFF Inc.).

of UK capacity is less than 1%, its share of Scottish demand is zero.

(c) Where the Scottish share of UK capacity exceeds the coefficient of localisation by 10 per cent (so that Scotland must be the only region specialising in this industry), the Scottish share of Scottish demand is again put at 100 per cent.

From the resultant preference map, Scottish shares of Scottish demand can be calculated.

If we then make a crucial assumption: that the technical relationships of production in Scotland mirror those for the UK; it is possible to derive a matrix of 'direct requirements from Scottish producers per £100 of Scottish output' from each industry by each industry. From this one may compute, by the familiar Leontieff methods, the direct and indirect impacts upon the Scottish economy due to either the construction or the subsequent operation of any hypothetical project.

To complete the multiplier calculation, we have to estimate the induced (consumption-based) effects of these increases in Scottish outputs. From the total of direct and indirect output increments in each industry, we calculate an incremental wage and salary bill paid by Scottish producers. This figure is then augmented to allow for dividends paid from increased trading profits, and the whole of the resultant additional earnings allocated to Scottish households.

These incomes are then broken down into the following six component parts:[3]

	%
Direct taxation	13
National Insurance contributions	7
Personal savings	10
Indirect taxation	13
Services	13
Goods before tax	44

It is recognised that National Insurance contributions are not deducted from dividends; to compensate for this, we attribute a higher savings propensity to dividend-earners.

If we then allow that (say) 25 per cent of the sales value of goods before tax represents traders' mark-up, all collected in Scotland, and that consumer services bought in Scotland are all provided from

[3] This analysis is derived from the *National Income Blue Book*, and the *Family Expenditure Survey*.

Scottish sources, we can re-group the foregoing components of incremental earnings in Scotland as follows:

	%
Leakages into taxation and savings	43
Consumer goods at ex-factory cost	33
Incomes re-circulated in Scotland	24

It then follows (from the familiar multiplier argument) that the eventual rise in incomes in Scotland will equal the incremental earnings due to direct and indirect output increases, raised by a factor of 1·31. There are, however, two gaps in this calculation. On the one hand it ignores the fact that some of the increased earnings will be paid to those previously receiving unemployment benefits, which will now cease. On the other, it ignores the fact that a proportion of the consumer goods bought out of these increased incomes will be produced in Scotland, thus giving a further turn to the income multiplier. However, the possible effects of these two distortions would seem to fall roughly within the same range of magnitude, i.e. between 10 and 20 per cent. Since they work in opposite directions, and in view of the overall crudity of the estimates, we may be allowed to regard them as having cancelled each other out.

IV

We may now sum, industry by industry, the direct, indirect and induced output changes to be expected in Scotland following the building or operating of any project for which the construction costs and production rates are known. The methods used will be familiar enough to anyone who has delved in the stony ground of regional multiplier theory. For the next step in the argument, we move closer to the central purpose of cost-benefit thinking. That is to say, we try to measure the extent to which incremental outputs in Scotland are obtained at lower social cost than in some hypothetical alternative location. In other words, we try to impute shadow prices to marginal labour inputs in Scotland, assuming that in the 'alternative location' these are reflected in labour's market price, then to make an adjustment for locational advantage or disadvantage.

We start with a postulate that the extent to which any increase in regional output is met by drawing from the pool of regional unemployed will depend partly on the occupational structure of the relevant industry, and partly on the extent of the unemployment in that industry in the region. For example, we may assume:

(i) that unskilled labour can always be recruited, in Scotland, from the pool;
(ii) that skilled trades will either have to be detached from other industries in the region, or attracted from other regions; and
(iii) that the availability of semi-skilled, managerial, technical and clerical labour will be a function of the differential regional unemployment rate for the industry. If that rate in Scotland is less than, or equal to the national rate, then all vacancies in the appropriate categories will be filled by transfers from other jobs. Thereafter, the proportion so filled will fall to 50 per cent where the regional unemployment rate is twice (or more) the national rate. The residual 50 per cent is taken to be a reflection of geographical immobility within the region.

Mostly, these assumptions err on the safe side. For instance, they ignore the likelihood of local 'pockets' of unemployment amongst skilled tradesman. On the other hand they do ignore the tendency for higher-paid managerial posts to be filled from within the parent company or – if the project is a new enterprise – from the national pool of mobile executive skills.

Applying these rules we can construct a vector of crude shadow prices, one for each industry, for marginal labour inputs in the Scottish economy. (Thus: if the unemployment rates for the industry in Scotland and Great Britain respectively imply that X per cent of its incremental needs for semi-skilled labour in Scotland will come from the pool of unemployed, we say that the shadow price of this labour is $(100\text{-}X)$ times its market price.) These shadow prices may then be used to impute values to the outputs in Scotland due to the construction of any project; and (given that unemployment will remain the sole alternative for a constant proportion of labour inputs in the future) to the outputs due to its operation as well.

However, the whole difference in the comparative social cost of output, as between Scotland and the rest of the UK, will not be determined by the shadow prices of the labour resources employed. Some account must also be taken of locational advantages or disadvantages, which follow from its re-siting in Scotland. I believe that it is impossible to deal with these complex 'efficiency' considerations satisfactorily.[4] We may, however, adopt the device of adjusting any im-

[4] They might of course be deduced from the observed response functions of different industries with respect to subsidy.

plied benefits, in the form of 'free' inputs, according to the difference between labour productivity per industry in Scotland and in the UK.[5] This kind of adjustment rests on two critical assumptions: that new projects will import neither scale economies nor superior technology into a previously disadvantaged region; and that the original (alternative) location outside Scotland offered a level of labour efficiency corresponding to the UK norm. If these can be accepted, then we may put a cost-benefit ratio on the incremental output of any industry in Scotland, as compared with the same output obtained at some least-private-cost site elsewhere, as follows:

Let V_i = cost-benefit ratio for incremental Scottish outputs in industry i

L_i = ratio of wages and salaries to total costs in industry i

P_i = relative shadow-price ratio of labour inputs going into incremental Scottish output in industry i

O_i = value added per man in industry i (UK)

Os_i = value added per man in industry i (Scotland)

So that

$\frac{Os_i}{O_i}$ = The labour-efficiency ratio of Scottish output in industry i.

Then:

$$V_i = \frac{Os_i/O_i}{[1-L_i\,(1-P_i)]}$$

We are now in a position to consider the kind of cost-benefit criterion which might be applied to projects eligible in principle for subsidy if located in a selected region. Two factors in particular seem to determine the appropriate form of test. In the first place, of the many assumptions required to support the calculations of cost and benefit (particularly of the latter), the most hazardous would seem to be that observed contingent relationships will continue into the future. In the second place, it is not easy to see clearly the political context in which such selective subsidies might be applied. For instance, would they be compared in terms of net present value, or internal rate of return, with the construction of highways, or support of R and D? Given the rapid decay from which the reliability of our

[5] The most up-to-date data for this, unfortunately, are to be found in the *1963 Census of Production*.

estimates must suffer, and a presumption that applications for regional subsidy can reasonably be compared with each other but not so easily with other candidates for public funds, I should suggest a model in which the agreed criterion would take from the form of minimising the 'pay-back' period. Thus:

Let K_1 = Differential inaugural costs of this project due to alternative location.
K_2 = Initial Exchequer outlay (e.g. tax rebate, or cash grant).
$(Bi)_t$ = Incremental regional output generated in industry i during year t as a result of relocation.
V_i = Cost-benefit ratio for incremental regional outputs in industry i.
E_t = Net Exchequer savings during year t as a result of relocation.
r_1, r_2 = Appropriate rates of discount.

Then we have to find the value of N which satisfies the criterion:

$$\left\{ \sum_{t=0}^{N} \frac{\sum_i [Vi \, . \, Bi_t]}{(1+r_1)^t} + \sum_{t=0}^{N} \frac{E_t}{(1+r_2)^t} \right\} = K_1 + K_2$$

In words: what is the value of N, such that the discounted net future benefits in the form of relocated production, plus the discounted net future receipts to the Exchequer in the form of increased tax inflows or reduced transfer payments, together equal the sum of the inaugural resource costs of relocating the project and the Exchequer outlay required to achieve it?

The previous section outlined methods by which we may arrive at estimates for the real gains. These can also be used to provide estimates of increases in regional personal income, and reductions in regional unemployment, such as are necessary to compute the flow of future returns to the Exchequer.

In order to complete the quantification of the model, we must choose appropriate values for the alternative discount rates. In principle, I should argue for the application to future net real benefits of an agreed social time preference rate. There would seem to me to be implicit in the policy of offering regional subsidies a genuine social option in favour of 'jam tomorrow' rather than 'jam today'. For the fiscal receipts I should propose rather the application of that discount rate currently laid down by the Treasury for capital projects in the public sector. It was noted earlier that the fiscal options closed off by regional subsidies might embrace not only public investment, but also all varieties of public consumption, not to mention the private consumption foregone as a result of taxation. However, it requires a governmental lead to identify the proper alternative; and without that the 'Treasury' rate would seem to offer the best compromise. In any case, for our model it would obviously be appropriate to vary the discount rates as part of a controlled series of sensitivity tests.

V

Given regional data to feed the kind of computational programme which I have described, it should be possible to apply the above model to preparing, for any region, a ranking of industries for development according to the length of period required for a new project to generate net social benefits which, suitably discounted, cover its inaugural costs. Apart from the many arbitrary assumptions required to set up the calculations, the major shortcoming of such a ranking would stem from the degree of inter-dependence that may exist between any two (or more) candidates for subsidy. Putting the point in a more general way, the danger is that analysis of costs and benefits appropriate to the individual project may fail to take account of the phenomenon of agglomeration.

There is also the fact – accepted under existing policies, and probably inescapable – that a selective policy of the kind proposed would still be indiscriminate in another sense: *ex ante*, it could not distinguish subsidy-created and subsidy-diverted investment from the autonomous variety. Yet if a subsidised investment could have gone ahead without assistance, because it justified itself to the owners on profitability grounds, then were the subsidy given on the strength of the foregoing cost-benefit test we would still be better off than if subsidies were totally indiscriminate or – worse still – if there were no regional subsidies at all.

11

The Journey to Work and Cost-benefit Analysis

M. E. BEESLEY
London Graduate School of Business Studies
and
M. Q. DALVI
University of Manchester

1. INTRODUCTION

Journeys to work assume greater importance the larger the urban agglomeration in which they take place. Characteristically, they govern peak demands on transport systems in urban areas. In the long term over which most urban planning aspires to look, two sources of increase of these demands exist: there may be more journeys (through increase of population or participation in the labour force) or the journeys may, on average, get longer. Wise planning for urban transport investments would seem to infer explicit knowledge of the behaviour of these components. One basic objective of this paper is to improve upon the remarkably meagre information now available about the journey length component.

Planners are interested in journeys to work in at least three phases of their task: first, the positive phase, of understanding what governs change in journeys to work, and in performing the task of forecasting further demands on transport systems; second, the normative phase, of valuation of alternative policies, often involving investments; and, third, in the selection from structural variables those for which planning measures can be devised and effective action taken, i.e. planners can hope to affect more easily some aspects of decisions taken by people and firms than they can affect others.

Planning systems are not characterised by consistency or completeness in these phases. The journey to work was once (and perhaps to some extent still is) a leading candidate in planner's minds, or as a relevant structural variable. Other things being equal, it was argued, the shorter the journey the better, and planning sought to increase the juxtaposition of jobs and homes. A very simple normative stance was of course involved in this.

Again, prediction in a form acceptable to social scientists was virtually zero. Now, of course, all conurbation planners have the assistance of the large-scale transportation and land use study to aid the formulation of proposals, and the big investment in it assures its great influence in at least the immediate future. But the large scale transportation and land use study has not yet noticeably contributed to a greater balance between, or effectiveness on the performance of, the three phases of the planner's job to which we have just referred. Predictively, not only is it typically rather naïve (one example among many is simple extrapolation of a single date's calibrated behaviour in traffic generation) but the job of prediction is incompletely done and even rather simple precautions not taken. Thus, in the London Transportation Study, to quote a sophisticated example of the genus, explicit prediction about journeys to work, as in all large-scale urban transport studies, centres on numbers of journeys only: what is anticipated about their length emerges only as a by-product of, in this case, a complicated generation, assignment and constraint of traffic procedure[1]. It was this curious neglect which led to one of the author's revived interest in journey to work length, and to some further observation about elementary, but desirable checks, and additional constraints to be fed into that kind of model.[1]

Evaluation has not kept pace with the expanding aspirations of the transport land use model. Some form of cost-benefit appraisal of investment proposals is of course now often attempted. Not surprisingly, this turns out to be partial, in the sense that measured benefits and cost are confined to changes in travellers' and infrastructure suppliers' costs, and benefits, but more often simply to relatively minor indications of the priority in locational terms, of a given set of investments. In the London case, for example, it is doubtful whether one can get much guidance from the evaluation techniques for even the latter problems – as has been argued elsewhere[2].

It seems to us that the aspirations for using cost-benefit analysis here must still be modest, for the simple basic reason of its being a partial equilibrium technique. One can indeed in principle evaluate alternative land use plus transport proposals for a large urban area, but only in the context of a more comprehensive inter-area model, which will enable one to isolate variation in the effect of the pro-

[1] Compare[1] pp. 145–9.

jected proposals in the subject area by reference to a relevant measure benefits and costs – for example the gain or loss in income per head in the subject area. The problem in evaluating proposals for large urban areas is thus not only constructing a plausible workable model of land use and transport for the area itself – though this as the last fifteen years has shown, has proved difficult enough in all conscience, but also in placing the model in an equally plausible larger system. The upshot of this is that there is likely to be a useful pay-off to improving evaluation with necessarily limited objectives, in the broad framework of the present land-use and transportation study. (This should of course have a beneficial spin-off to research on more comprehensive models.) Thus, for example, if prediction is improved, we may be able to formulate, even if not evaluate comprehensively, more relevant land use strategies; whether by a necessarily arbitrary total investment in transport projects we can hope to improve returns by more careful scrutiny of travellers' evaluations, in conventional terms, of differing modal conditions. ('Necessarily arbitrary' because we cannot evaluate the expenditure at the requisite level.)

Study of journeys to work may, then, contributed to cost-benefit evaluation in this area in two main ways – as a source for improvement of the measurement of traveller's benefits and costs directly; and as a means of improving explanation of structural relationships in, and the forecasting inputs to, plans to be formulated; and thus indirectly, helping to guide the search for improved evaluation. (For example, how important will the journey to work be in ten or more years' time in total transport demands? Since peaks govern costs, evaluation will be much concerned with them, but how far will journeys to work still dominate choice of investments?) And since the acceptance of the adoption and development of cost-benefit analysis quite importantly depend on its relevance to the objectives of those by whom it is used, closer attention to structural variables is likely to enhance the use of, and lead to an increased flow of resources into, this kind of analysis.

We shall be concerned in this paper with reporting work relevant mainly to these aspects of developing CBA. As practitioners in the use of journey-to-work material for the direct evaluation of elements in current CBA work, we would have liked to have commented at some length on the great potential still left, for example, in using such material for evaluation of time of travel by mode, which we suspect may now be somewhat underrated relative to other approaches. But this will have to be taken up on another occasion. Here we present some preliminary work based on journey-to-work lengths over the period 1951–61 in sixty boroughs selected at random in the SE England.

2. THE PURPOSES AND STRUCTURE OF THE MODELS

The starting point for this work was the realisation that though the journey to work is perhaps the most critical point at which land-use planning and transport interact, very little was known about its development over time, in spite of the traditional concern of planners with it. Journey-to-work length in particular had rarely been systematically measured in the sense of examining the structural relationships in either cross-section or time series data. As explained earlier, it is typically left to emerge as a by-product from transport models rather than being an explicit concern therein. Of the two components of changing travel demands arising from the journey-to-work, the number of journeys – the relatively easily predicted element – is given some attention; the second and much less easily explained journey length component is neglected. The only comprehensive source for information about the length of journey to work to cover a series of years is the Census of Population, and it is that material with which we work, for this yields cross-section and, though at rare intervals, at least some time-series observations.

The sole English estimates of long-run changes in journey to work lengths to come to our notice are Warnes'[3]. He measures journey length by crow's flight distances in a manner very like that to be explained later, and found that in 221 Lancashire authorities, the median distance travelled by workers to work rose from 0·86 miles in 1921 to 1·33 in 1931 and to 1·70 in 1961, or a 55 per cent rise in the thirty years to 1951 and a 28 per cent rise in the ten years from 1951 to 1961. It seemed appropriate to start our own enquiries in respect of the South-east area, selecting a random sample of sixty local authorities. The problems of data and measurement are discussed in the next section.

We would like to know, first, just how much journey lengths have changed in recent years. The obvious periods to take were the Censal ones of 1951–61–66, and ease of access to data led us to begin with 1951–61. Journey length may of course be measured by lineal distance, by distance by mode, by time taken, by cost of journey; or some combination. In terms of explanation and prediction the most satisfactory measure might well be some version of 'behavioural' or 'perceived' cost – i.e. an attempt directly to measure the cost of distance as seen by decision-makers. We had no choice in the time available; crow's flight distances were the only feasible measure, and it is for speculation how far this simplification affects the results. It is known of course that such distances are good proxies in general for road mileages, and thus were close, at least, to a relevant measure of demand on transport systems. Of course, a model dealing with crow's flight distances is unlikely to throw much direct light on the influence of many changes in transport provision (e.g. by altering the times taken for travel between home and work). But the focus of our interest was in any case to get a feel for the major determinants of change in journey to work length with transport cost fixed, and so the measurement of work journeys from residences in local authorities to work places in and outside the boroughs by crow's flights seemed appropriate. In fact, the main change in transport provision over 1951–61 in our subject area was the growth in motor car ownership – public transport altered very little in terms of the quality of provision or its supply. We hope to take up the matter of differential effect of changes in car ownership later on.

Viewing the change in the average journey-to-work length, in the local authorities, 1951–61, as the dependent variable, then, we wished to consider a form of explanation of the observed authority variance in experience which would say something about the influence of factors of most concern to planners and susceptible to influence by planning decisions. Journey-to-work length is affected by economic decisions on the one hand by households, who presumably wish to maximise utility to members by trading off the satisfaction provided by jobs, the cost involved in getting to jobs, the utility derived from, and the cost of, residence; and on the other hand, by firms and other organisations similarly attempting to maximise returns by locating or changing the scale of activity according to accessibility to markets and the costs, among other things, of labour supplies. Viewed from the point of view of residents (or potential residents) in one authority among many, the action of firms in changing the jobs available, can as a first approximation, be regarded as unaffected by the action of those residents. So we regard the change in the availability of jobs (measured by the product of their numbers and distance) as exogenous to individual borough experience, and the actions by firms that prompt the changes outside our ken also. This has some parallel in conurbation planning reality, in that it has, in the main, to adapt to the economic forces of firm location; or, to take a less extreme view, that such forces are amenable to planning measures only to the extent that the supply of total jobs can be markedly affected – a much more feasible task, one supposes, in a relatively isolated town, and much less so in the London area. There seemed to be good sense, then, in distinguishing a variable which measured change in employment opportunities as viewed from the borough. With due allowance for the imperfection of the distance measure used, there ought to be a clear connexion, we thought, between the effect of this variable and the appropriate constant in normal gravity model explanations of trip distance for it purports to measure residents' reaction to varying costs of taking suitable employment.

The rest of the model form focusses on other components of residents' decisions. Broadly, a change in work distance may result from one of three kinds of shift – of job with residence fixed; of house with job fixed; and a shift of both. Part of the first source of change we have dealt with, i.e. the change in employment distance from given residences. However, independently of employment distance shifts, people change their jobs from a given home – to better themselves, because they learn more about job opportunities, etc. We can see no convincing reason to suppose this element to have, in general, systematic effects on journey length, so we regard it as entering at random – provisionally at least. Shifts of house with job fixed are of course extremely important, and systematic in their net effect. A large literature on suburbanisation attests to the importance of people's preferences, on average, inclining in recent years particularly towards the consumption of more housing space. This is important to distinguish both because of its significance in household decisions and because the siting of houses is, in principle, and in practice, most amenable to planning decisions. Thus we distinguish a variable which we hope is a reasonable proxy for house shift. The third source of change: shifting both house and job, is, we believe, of less frequent occurrence, both because of very high cost of a simultaneous shift of this kind for the household, and because market change in economic opportunity or, more likely, change in the ability of persons concerned to take that opportunity (as when a professional qualification is achieved) would have to be present. From the point of view of the planner this would also, we thought, be a factor in what we might term the 'amenability to planning influence scale' intermediate between the general shift of employment factor and the housing shift factor. For these last two sources of change – housing shift and housing-plus-job shift, we devised proxies from the Census migration tables, as described later. As we also suspected that the household decision would be markedly different as between male and females we decided to run separate models for them, using the same explanatory variables.

All this is very much of a first attempt to structure the problems. The initial models are in simple regression form. Clearly if the approach looks worthwhile after some testing there are obvious refinements of specification and data which would then be worth following up. There are possibilities, for example, of splitting the housing-shift component into new household formations, distinguishing between public and private housing, etc., and in the employment shift variable between types of work. We did indeed incorporate in some runs of the models a 'blue collar' employment shift measure, with results to be reported below. Again, the job-plus-housing shift component, as it is clearly related to long-distance migration, might well be split into sources of migration in a more detailed fashion. All this, however, imposes costs in the form of data generation, and improvements of further specification of the dependent variable have also to be considered. It seems to us important, first of all, to investigate the likely stability of components already recognised; in particular, the employment and housing shift variables because of our interest in forecasting. This of course cannot be done within the ambit of a one-period model, and we hope to report soon as a result of further work on alternative time periods and the structure at 1951–61 and separately.

To summarise so far: we specify two model types, one for men and one for women, where the dependent variable is the change in the average journey to work for sixty SE local authorities, 1951–61, and the independent variables are employment opportunity shift, housing shift, and job-plus-house shift. Appendix I lists the authorities. After describing the data and the problems to which they give rise, we shall examine in more detail the expected performance of our variables and then present and discuss the results of the first runs of the models.

3. THE DATA AND VARIABLES USED IN THE MODELS

The dependent variable of the models is the change in the average length of the journey to work (ΔD) between the two census points (1951 and 1961 Censuses in the present exercise), calculated separately, for male and female workers. The average journey length has been computed for each census by using the data on 'workplace movements', which are available on a 10 per cent sample basis. The smallest area unit on which these data are collected is the local authority area – boroughs and urban and rural districts, which implies, in effect, that only the flows across local authority areas are recorded. Workplace movements which take place entirely within the boundaries of a local authority area are concealed. Since the majority of the economically active residents in the area work within its boundary we decided to include these within-boundary movements along with the movements across the boundaries for computing the average distance of the journey. The average journey distance has been calculated for each local authority area as follows: the workplace tables report for each area the total number of persons (males and females separately) who are economically active and, amongst these persons, those who are resident in the area but work elsewhere in England and Wales, the difference between these figures indicating the numbers of those who reside and work in the same area.

The first step in these computations was to get a measure of total journey-miles, for each area, by multiplying the total number of journeys (one journey per person) by the distances from the area of origin to each of the terminal areas, i.e. workplaces. For computational convenience it was decided to exclude terminating areas which involved less than $\frac{1}{2}$ per cent of the total journeys, the aim being to compute at least 95 per cent of the journeys for the area. Journey distances were computed by using the maps of the administrative areas from ordnance surveys. For municipal boroughs and most of the urban districts the calculation of these distances presented no problem as the focal points for them were easily identified, but for rural districts a convention was established to take the central point on the map for calculating them. The total journey-miles so calculated for each area were then divided by the number of 'economically active residents' of the area to arrive at a measure of average journey distance. ΔD is simply the difference between the average journey distances for 1951 and 1961 censuses. As pointed out before in the absence of any information about the choice of travel miles and travel routes actually used by the sample population, the computations of journey distances presented in this exercise indicate broad orders of magnitude only.

The following six independent variables have been identified to explain the variation in the average distance of work journey.

1. ΔE. The change in the spatial distribution of employment opportunities for the residents of a given area between the two censuses. This variable measures the change in the average distance at which jobs are located, as viewed by the residents of the area. Two

problems were faced in computing it. The first problem was concerned with the decision about where to stop in counting job opportunities for the residents of a given area. In theory one could, in arranging spatial distribution of jobs, start counting the number of jobs available in the same area and then proceed as far as the areas on the periphery of the region. But this procedure is unacceptable because job accessibility must be defined, in practice, by taking into account the marginal disutility attached by people travelling to work together with the nature of transport facilities available and the institutioned constraints within which the daily jobs must be performed. Besides, it would have been a difficult task computationally to get for each area a spatial distribution of jobs available in all the 227 local authority areas of the six counties included in our exercise. Hence, we decided to define a 'catchment' area for each borough such as to capture job opportunities open to the residents of that borough which are accessible by modern means of transport and subject to the institutional constraint that a job of a given time duration must be performed within a single day. This boiled down, in effect, to counting the number of jobs available in those local authorities where the residents of a given area were already working on census dates *supplemented* by the number of jobs available in the authorities in which the workers working in that area were resident. In other words, we have taken those authorities which were listed in the workplace tables under each area as those in which workers resident in that area were working and those in which the worker working in that area resided. This choice limited our count of job opportunities to those which were already accessible to the residents within the existing technological and institutional constraints.

The second problem related to the availability of data on the number of jobs in each local authority area. The 1961 census data give for each area the numbers of male and female workers with employment in the area. These figures are considered as providing the best approximation to the numbers of jobs in the area. No such data were published in the 1951 census reports. However, area-wide figures are available on occupied resident populations. These figures were used along with the figures on workplace movements to arrive at the number of jobs in the area as follows: From the total number of occupied residents population working in the same area to which we added the number of workers working in that area but resident elsewhere, the total being considered as providing job data comparable with those available in the 1961 census.

The variable ΔE is computed in terms of job-miles, the difference is the distribution of job opportunities between 1951 and 1961 census data. As ΔE has not been deflated by the number of jobs, changes in it may be due either to changes on the total number of jobs or the total distances at which they are located or both. The change in E due to the change in the total numbers of jobs at given distances will have no effect on the average length of work journey, but the change in E due to the change in the distances at which the jobs are located will have a positive correlation with ΔD. The implications of this hypothesis are as follows: if it is true, as has been hypothesised by Meyer, Kain and Wohl[4], that the recent developments in transport and communication technology have contributed to decentralisation within cities, by making different parcels of land increasingly homogenous for manufacturing, retailing and residential uses, then the effect of this change is to produce a positive change in E by increasing the average distances at which the jobs are located, and also a positive change in E, as people have to travel longer distances to get to work. There is also another force working with positive effect on ΔE and ΔD, viz. the rise in people's standard of living together with increasing appreciation of the quality of residential environment have led many persons to seek homes of modern design in open areas near to rural surroundings and farther from the noise and smoke of the industrial and commercial centres, thereby further separating peoples' residences from their work places.

2. ΔS. The change in the spatial distribution of the semi-skilled and unskilled jobs. This variable has been included to see if there is any specific bias in the spatial distribution of any particular categories of jobs in affecting the change in average journey distance.[2] We have singled out job opportunities for blue-collared workers for our analysis, assuming that they are mainly employed in semi-skilled and unskilled jobs, but the same exercise could be repeated for any other category as it would equally reflect any specific job-category bias if it exists. The procedure used in computing this variable is identical with the one used for ΔE.

However, there were a number of statistical hurdles in getting comparable data on skill distribution. Both the 1951 and 1961

[2] Since blue-collared jobs are part of the total number of jobs, there is a danger of high positive collinearity between ΔE and ΔS, unless the spatial distribution of blue-collared jobs is significantly different from that of the aggregate jobs. In the event of multi-collinearity it is not possible to discover the coefficient of either ΔE or ΔS, as both variables change together; only their sum is identified.

censuses provide data on the distributions of workers in some economic groups, but only the 1961 census data provide a breakdown of these for all local authority areas. (See the socio-economic group tables.) For the 1951 census, on the other hand, the area-wise breakdown by type of job categories is available in terms of classification by social *status* but this classification has been discarded for the 1961 census. The social status classification is in five categories: (1) professional, (2) intermediate occupations, (3) skilled occupations, (4) semi-skilled occupations, and (5) unskilled occupations. We have counted the job opportunities in the last two categories of the social status classification for 1951 census and compared them with the number of jobs in the two groups of semi-skilled manual workers and unskilled manual workers in the 1961 social-economical group tables. The 1961 census report gives seventeen social economic groups, but the two categories taken here account for nearly 20 per cent of the total job opportunities in the six counties. This compares with 22 per cent accounted by the semi-skilled and unskilled groups to the social status classification of the 1951 census.

3. H_1 and H_2. The average length of journey to work may change over time not only because of the change in the location of economic activity, and consequently of employment opportunities, but also because of the change in the location of population, either in search of new homes or new jobs. The shift in people's residential location is considered in two distinct ways. H_1 defines residential shift in terms of the number of persons immigrating into a given area from neighbouring districts which lie within twelve miles of its radial distance.* Each of these figures are expressed as a proportion of the total resident population (males and females separately) of the area. The migration tables were prepared in detail for the first time for the 1961 census for a sample of 10 per cent. Since a 'migrant' was defined as anyone whose usual address on census date was different from his usual address a year before, this not only provides a partial measure of the number of people who moved during this year but means that there is no information at all on the migration that has taken place during the whole census decade. Ideally our explanatory variables H_1 and H_2 should measure shifts in the residential location for the whole decade, because the dependent variable D refers to that decade. However, in the absence of any data on the year-to-year migration we had to confine our computation of H_1 and H_2 to the migration information for the year 1960–1 only.

* H_2 similarly measures persons emigrating.

4. J_1 and J_2. These variables indicate adjustments in people's location when they move into or out of the area to take up new jobs. J_1 measures job adjustment in terms of persons immigrating into the area from districts lying outside the twelve-miles' radial distance, from elsewhere in England and Wales, and from abroad; while J_2 measures such adjustment on terms of persons emigrating to the districts outside the twelve-miles' limit, elsewhere in England and Wales, and abroad. These variables are also expressed as a proportion of the total residential population of each area.

5. In the case of female workers, we compared two further variables to identify what to us were possible distinguishing factors, the first of which has been noted in other work as determinants of female employment, namely, the overall and widespread trend for women to become part of the labour force, a movement probably quite independent of shifts in employment opportunities, housing, etc., and having more to do with changing social attitudes than economic forces (and certainly not a realistic object planning influences) but nevertheless perhaps affecting our observations. This we label 'P', and is computed as the

$$\frac{\%\text{ of resident women of a borough employed in 1951}}{\%\text{ of resident women of a borough employed in 1961}}$$

As will be seen, the mean value for this is 0·90, denoting a secular shift towards the employment of women.

The second variable is the change in the percentage of females who are married, over 1951–61 in the boroughs. This, as we shall see in the next section, we thought might be important in interpreting the results, because there is a tendency in London for unmarried females to concentrate in certain boroughs (the 'bed-sit' areas). We also give reasons for supposing rather different effects upon change in journey to work for married and unmarried women. A change in the marriage composition of an authority, if it occurred, and turned up in our sample, was likely to disturb the expected relationships for females, governed in general by the widespread and more numerous married group. As we shall see, in the event, mean 'M', as it is labelled, is small, and its effect insignificant.

4. EXPECTATION OF THE PERFORMANCE OF THE PRINCIPAL MODEL VARIABLES

In both the male and the female models, we expect ΔE to be positively correlated with ΔD. How in detail it would perform in a linear model such as this was open to some doubt. We did not expect a shift in job-mile distance to have equal effects whatever the average distance from a borough involved. At some point in distance from the borough, the change in job opportunities is almost wholly irrelevant to the bulk of residents; and there is some possibility that a threshold distance beyond which commuting will not take place exists. Our method of computation insured that most shifts would be within a feasible range: however, it seemed wise to consider, as an alternative specification of ΔE, $\sqrt{(\Delta E)}$, and to provide for runs in which both forms of variable were included. The results are reported later.

The expected performance of the migration variables was somewhat more complex. As noted earlier, a movement into or out of a borough may take place in response to a decision to shift either the job location *and*, with it, the *residence* or a decision to shift the residence alone, with job location unchanged. If the distance of migration is very long, both job *and* residence must be involved, because of the high cost of commuting long distances. If it is short, both types of decision may be involved. Thus the difference between short- and long-distance emigration is that the latter does not include the effects of a residence shift alone. Generally, it will be true that the shorter the distance migrated, the more important will be the 'housing-shift-only' type of decision. This is the reason for calling H_1 and H_2 'housing' variables and J_1 and J_2 'job' variables. We expect the H's to be more mixed on average than the J's in their behavioural content, so shall not be surprised if, in general, the J's are relatively *better* explanatory variables.

What is the likely direction of the effect of the H's and J's on the average journey to work in a borough? A movement into or out of the borough will increase or reduce the average journey length in so far as it is longer or shorter than that average, so far as *immigration* is concerned, and vice versa so far as *emigration* is concerned.

Considering H_1: The boroughs most likely to be affected by this are, of course, the growing boroughs, the peripheral ones. In so far as immigration is a *housing* shift, one expects that immigrants will have a bias towards jobs at the dominant core (and thus expressing a shift of tastes towards more housing space) and thus *increase*, at par, the average journey to work length of the receiving borough. But clearly this will much depend on how much immigration the borough has already received over previous periods. When a borough is becoming a 'dormitory', the shift will be marked; when it is a mature dormitory suburb, the effects will be slighter.[3] (Notice that if we measured actual (e.g. time-based) rather than crow's flight distances, the effect of adding the marginal immigrant would be larger, because immigrants, on average, are added to the periphery of receiving boroughs.) For J_1, there is little reason to suppose that immigrants have very different preferences from the average of the commuters in the borough they are joining, except in so far as they may have, on average, higher incomes, and thus jobs at greater distances from their homes. So we expect a lesser marked, but still positive effect for J_1.

The discussion in this section so far has not recognised that more than one job is often involved in a shift of residence – specifically, that there may be different effects for men and women (and indeed for persons of different ages). On the whole, we expect that housing shifts decisions are taken with the head-of-household's (usually male) job distance principally in mind. More especially would this be true of long distance (J_1) shifts, which would affect principally married women.[4] Thus we would expect to find clearer effects in increasing women's average job length than men's; *if* (married) women retain a job in the shift of residence, they are likely to enter the local job-market somewhat, on average, at a disadvantage relative to existing female workers.

So far as H_2, emigration, is concerned, we recognise that the boroughs likely to be more affected are the inner and older boroughs. Emigration is likely to decrease average journey to work, because first, those who shift in response to housing decisions are likely to be of higher than average income, having longer average journeys, and those who also shift may well have, on average, a relatively long journey as part of their dissatisfaction with their present situation. So far as females are concerned, we should again distinguish between married and unmarried workers. We would expect that married women emigrants would on the whole be of higher incomes and skills, and therefore tend to decrease the female average; this would be specially true of long-distance emigrants. For short-distance female emigrants, we have, as noted above, the special feature of the concentration of female employment in specific 'bed-sit' areas of the West End. The effect of the growth of this on metropolitan boroughs would be to shorten journeys to work; unmarried women thus are

[3] So we might observe a residual variance for 'new' dormitories.

[4] Unmarried female workers tend to shift to, and cluster, in specific boroughs, not as it happens in the sample.

envisaged on average to enter the labour force from a parental home and then subsequently adjust to a more convenient residential location. H_2 and J_2 should thus be negative in sign; more certainly for women.

In the area we draw our sample from, emigration (but not so much immigration) includes an element of retirement from the labour force. In the fast expanding peripheral boroughs, these will tend to have shorter than average journey to work lengths and thus reinforce the earlier expectation; but we would not expect the effect to be marked.

5. THE RESULTS

Over the sixty authorities, average journey length increased for both males and females from 1951–61, as the following table shows:

	Males	Females
1951	4·32	4·05
1961	4·83	4·60

The averages for 1961 may be compared with the household data for the London Transport Study, whose field work fell in 1962–3. From that Study (vol. 1, table 6-34) average distances to work are seen to vary widely according to the area within LTS surveyed, ranging from 1·37 miles for the 'Central Area North' to 5·60 for Kent. Since we cover a wider area than did LTS, and it is clear that the nearer the central core, the shorter the journey length, the correspondence is close enough for us to be fairly confident that the crude measure of distance used here will not unduly distort broad comparisons over time. (In our data, ΔD is larger in outlying areas than is the centre.) If anything, however, our average lengths seem to be on the high side, probably due to the influence of the assumptions about trip length for employment within an authority.

That the figures are considerably higher than those for the NW authorities quoted earlier does not surprise us; for one thing, mean trip lengths to work are known to be greater than the median trip length used in that measure. Thus, whereas mean journey length for car-owning households in the London Study area in 1963 was 4·2 miles, the median was 2·8 miles (p. 118, table 6-34, and p. 117). And the Metropolitan boroughs are also known to have a longer journey-to-work length than most other areas because, of course, of the size of the very influential London core.

The percentage increases for men and women were 12 and 14

respectively. These provide an interesting contrast with the corresponding NW authorities change, of 28 per cent, reported above. Whatever forces were operating to increase the journey length, they were clearly considerably stronger in the NW than in the SE over that period. A sidelight is thrown here on the influence of growing car ownership, the major transport change in the period with car ownership rising in 1951–61 from one in twenty persons to one in eight countrywide. We know that in this respect, the London areas were similar to the rest of the country, so we may suspect that either rises in car ownership had little effect on total change, or that the influence of the growing car ownership was far greater outside the London area than within it. In fact, it is possible to surmise that perhaps not much more than a quarter of our SE authorities' increase is likely to have been due to the change in car ownership alone, as follows. At the end of the period, in 1961, 40 per cent of LTS households had cars, but only just over 40 per cent of these were used for work trips. Thus, about 16 per cent of work trip-making was done by car. In 1951 about 16 per cent of households had cars. If none of these was used for work journeys (as an impossible, limiting assumption) and if we attribute the difference in journey length to work by car and other modes reported in the survey – about 35 per cent – solely to the presence of a car, then the maximum possible influence would be about 6 per cent of the reported 12 per cent for males. (Women would be much less affected, of course.) It is not likely, we feel, to have exceeded half this in practice. Clearly, however, the addition of a variable measuring change in car ownership would be a most interesting addition to a model – or indeed an acceptable proxy for it, perhaps a measure of change in income. In view of the possibility mentioned above, we might expect the variable's influence to differ as between authorities near and authorities far from London, a possibility kept in mind when discussing the residuals in our models later.

As expected, there was considerable variation about the mean values, namely an increase of 0·51 miles for males and 0·55 miles for females, the coefficient of variation being 0·55 and 0·67 respectively. Regressions were computed for both males and females, all variables included, and then alternative specifications were used to test the effect of dropping variables. Tables 11.1 and 11.2 give the results, *A* for male and *B* for female workers. The general equation column gives that including all variables, and the 'Best Equation' columns contain results for the specifications which maximise $\bar{R}^2$ subject to

Table 11.1. Regressions on journey-to-work model, A. male workers

Independent variables	Mean values	General equation	Best equation 1	Best equation 2
ΔE	4700	0·000008 (2·61)	0·00001 (6·15)	0·000007 (3·53)
ΔS	15000	−0·0000003 (−0·004)		
H_1	0·046	4·65 (1·23)	7·83 (2·88)	
H_2	0·036	−15·51 (−2·94)	−13·78 (−2·72)	−14·02 (−2·78)
J_1	0·046	3·52 (1·08)		6·47 (2·99)
J_2	0·031	1·22 (0·44)		
constant		0·256	0·156	0·374
$\bar{R}^2$		0·50	0·51	0·51
d-statistic		1·72	1·77	1·71

Mean value of the dependent variable = 0·49, σ = 0·75, CV = 0·55, *t*-values in the brackets.

Table 11.2. Regressions on journey-to-work model, B. female workers

Independent variables	Mean values	General equation[a]	Best equation[b] 1	Best equation[b] 2
ΔE	58000	0·0000001 (0·018)	0·000007 (2·84)	
ΔS	17000	0·00014 (1·31)		0·000025 (3·71)
H_1	0·043	11·08 (2·58)	12·86 (3·09)	9·58 (2·36)
H_2	0·034	−13·30 (−1·48)	−13·90 (−1·82)	−12·52 (−1·65)
J_1	0·046	6·15 (1·68)	5·61 (1·66)	6·70 (2·10)
J_2	0·026	−18·85 (−2·04)	−17·46 (−2·54)	−19·42 (−2·31)
P	0·90	−0·114 (0·16)		
M	0·97	1·96 (0·68)		
$\sqrt{\Delta E}$	—	0·082 (0·55)		
Constant		−1·89	0·243	0·348
$\bar{R}^2$		0·44	0·44	0·46
d-statistic		1·59	1·67	1·50

Mean value of the dependent variable = 0·54, σ = 0·80, coefficient of variation = 0·67, *t*-values in the brackets.

[a] General equation indicates the equation which includes all the explanatory variables of the model.

[b] Best equations are those which maximise the value of $\bar{R}^2$ subject to the restriction that each regression coefficient is significant at least at the 10 per cent level.

the restriction that each regression coefficient is significant at least at the 10 per cent level.

In general, it can be seen that though the male model explains rather more of the total variation, the female model is the more successful in yielding information. (In this kind of cross-sectional analysis of change we were, of course, not expecting higher $\bar{R}^2$s than were achieved, especially in view of the possibilities of refining specification, and data, mentioned earlier. The results seemed, in fact, very encouraging.) For both males and females, ΔE and ΔS are very highly correlated and when entered separately perform in the same way. See the zero-order correlation matrices at Appendix 2.

In the 'Best equation' for males, the signs of ΔE are as expected, and the variable highly significant as an explanation. H_1 and H_2 have the expected signs also and are again significant. J_1 turns out to be rather highly correlated with H_1, probably accounting for its insignificance when run with H_1, though in 'Best Equation 2' and in the 'General Equation', it has the expected sign. J_2 fails in both sign and significance, and apparently not because of collinearity problems.

For the female equations, all signs of the chief variables are as expected, with, as said earlier, little significance to be attached to P and M, the participation rate and marriage effects. Alternative runs for females including $\sqrt{(\Delta E)}$ as a substitute for ΔE were less successful than those reported; high collinearity between $\sqrt{(\Delta E)}$ and ΔE (see Appendix 2) prevented any substantial improvement when $\sqrt{(\Delta E)}$ was run in conjunction with ΔE.

The contrasts in the performance of the male and female models seems to justify the initial separation and, to a large extent, our expectations of the differences. ΔE explains much more of the variance for males than for females (about 45 per cent as opposed to 25 per cent) and is the principal reason why the male models have more explanatory power overall. The H_1 through J_2 variables add much more to the explanation in the case of women. H_2, emigration, performs very much the same way for men and women. This, it will be recalled, affects inner London boroughs principally, and it may be that the movements in these cases reflect public rehousing exercises, a movement difficult to interpret in terms of market forces bearing on personal advantage and disadvantage. The striking difference between the male and female results is of course the larger effect, in lengthening journeys of the H_1 variable for women, and especially, the shortening effect of long-distance moves, J_2. The latter may well include movements, for example, to new towns. The notion that women, compared to men, are differentially affected by migration gets considerable support.

Selecting equation 1 in both cases, we may compute the contributions of the significant variables to change in journey length for an imaginary borough of mean size, 32,600 for males and 34,400 for females, by examining the elasticity of the dependent variables with respect to them. The results are shown in Table 11.3.

Table 11.3. Elasticity coefficients of journey to work

Independent variables	Male journeys	Female journeys
E	0·960	0·748
S	—	—
H_1	0·734	1·02
H_2	−1·02	−0·872
J_1	—	0·477
J_2	—	−0·840

Note: These coefficients are obtained from best equation (1) for male and female journey models reported above.

Comparing the coefficients for males and females, we interpret the difference to mean that a given shift away of job opportunities will lead to longer journeys for males than for females. This seems plausible. Faced with such a shift, both trade off the prospective extra disutility of travel against a possible sacrifice of incomes and/or job satisfaction. *Ceteris paribus*, we would expect a maximum of 1·0 for this coefficient, indicating that the maximum sacrifice in terms of extra travel required to maintain jobs unchanged would not normally exceed the amount by which the job had shifted away. Males would approach this, because of their likely preference for maintaining income relative to reducing travel disutility. Females, on the other hand, would not regard their income or job satisfaction so important to the family: they are relatively more content with less rewarding jobs, or even to withdraw from the labour force. (Since participation, however, did not prove significant in the general female model, the former explanation seems more likely.)

To judge from the H_1 and H_2 coefficients for males, and interpreting the variables as reflecting housing shift decisions, a given change in the immigrant population seeking fresh housing has a less than proportionate effect in increasing journey lengths (H_1). On the other hand, a somewhat larger effect is noticeable for emigrant moves (H_2). (As explained earlier, there will be some admixture of job shift in these effects.) Overall, the net effect of housing shift for males, for equal amounts of short-distance migration – as of course would tend to occur in authorities as a whole within a metropolitan area, as here – is, it seems, to lessen journeys to work. That is, for the period measured here, the costs or losses incurred to secure more satisfactory housing were more than offset by the gains through moving nearer to work (again, assuming that crow's flight distances are a reasonable proxy for these losses and gains).[5] For women, as expected, the proportional effect of the H_1 variable is greater than for males, and H_2 smaller; i.e. women on the whole 'lose' more and 'gain' less from housing shifts. Overall, these 'gains' are outweighed by the 'losses' in their case. Also, for women, the net effect of given amounts of long-distance migration is to shorten journeys to work; but this, of course, is the net effect of many different job shifts which, on the whole, do not involve the same set of boroughs; rather, they measure, as it were, the proportionate effect of the transactions of the SE with the rest of the country. We attempt some very tentative inferences from these results, for the planning tasks mentioned earlier, in section 6. There we also point out some dimensions of possible improvement to the models.

An inspection of the residuals of the 'best' equations for men and women do not reveal any readily discernible 'borough' effects. In particular, there is no indication that inner London boroughs (there are eight in the sample) display a 'bed-sit' effect for women. These boroughs' residuals were in general opposite to that which one would expect from such an effect, and, in any case, were similar to the men's for the same boroughs. Distance from the core plays no systematic part in explaining the residuals, it seems, and there are no obvious unmeasured public transport effects, such as specially good train connections. Effects of the differential changes in car ownership remain the most likely elements missing from the model. We are currently trying to add to the model along this line, for example, by including the effect of the change in proportion of blue-collared workers in boroughs as a (somewhat distant) proxy for income and, hopefully, therefore, car ownership changes.

[5] Authorities who gathered more population from short-distance immigration than they lost by short-distance emigration were a little smaller, at an average of 31,000 male workers, than those experiencing the opposite, at 35,000.

6. CONCLUSIONS

In terms of improving explanations of change of demand for transport systems models along the foregoing lines should help to decompose a measured change in journey length into factors important for planning. If our results are approximately right, we might expect work journey length to increase in the future overall; and if the 1951–61 rate is applicable, at about one per cent per year in the SE. We hope to do more work on the structure of the models and for the periods 1951–61–66, to get a better view of the rate of change over time. Such estimates could be entered as constraints to which land-use transportation models are required to conform, and by keeping to deeper explanations of the behaviour of trip length already used in them.

Apart from those mentioned in the second section, we see several dimensions along which further improvements in the specification of our models would assist in discovering the structure of journey to work lengths, and their forecasting ability; especially:

1. The effect of increases in car ownership, which are probably to increase journey length on average.

2. The effect of differential demands for skills on the work force. We attempted one version of this, but probably failed to specify it in an effective way. It remains likely that increasingly diversified demands for skills will on average increase journey-to-work length.

3. The effect of first entry into the labour force – especially the differential effect of the young taking jobs at the beginning of their careers, to see how far, if at all, parental decisions to locate are disfunctional for the young.

4. The effect of differential housing occupancy. This is principally interesting because of the possibility of long-distance immigration's being associated with 'ghetto' effects, i.e. longer journey-to-work because of constrained housing opportunities. Intensification of housing use, *ceteris paribus*, will cause rents to rise; and those affected may be expected to attempt to adjust their incomes to compensate. This, in itself, may have little effect, net, on journey-to-work lengths, though there may be some tendency to save on transport costs, i.e. to seek a job nearer at hand. But if housing constraints supervene, the lengths may well, on average, increase.

In such ways, then, may estimates of future demands for transport systems perhaps be improved. These new variables, as those already presented, may, as we have indicated, differ in the degree to which planners can seek to control them. We might conclude from our tentative results that the main focus of past planning activity, the siting of houses has, in conjunction with market forces, had a positive, but probably relatively small in total, effect in reducing journey length: other less controllable factors have outweighed housing shifts. Most of the variables just suggested are, again, relatively difficult for planning measure to affect directly. Planners, in turn, may view the problem as intensifying feasible conventional methods, or of inventing new ones.

There are, however, some possibly more interesting implications for attempts to evaluate alternative land-use transport plans in the limited framework now typically used. A current example of this is, we understand, to be found in the Freeman Fox study in the West Midlands. Here, alternative configurations of residence and work-place distributions are to be tested by comparing the total costs (infra-structure provisions and travellers' costs including time, measured in the fashion now conventional in transport studies) of alternative networks associated with them. A supplementary ranking of schemes by general accessibility indices is also to be provided. The full methodology has yet to be published. But, in general, it seems to resemble the evaluation procedures developed by the Roskill Research team in the CBA of the four Third London Airport sites in respect of passengers, namely to compare the costs associated with a 'base load' of passengers, common to all four, and then to calculate, by comparing relative accessibility, the extra passenger movements, and their net benefits, of lower cost sites.

Now, one major problem in this kind of approach is to be reasonably sure that the benefits of the services provided will, in fact, outweigh the costs being measured. In the Third London Airport case, this was in effect assured, for the sites as a whole, by calculating the costs of congestion associated with not providing a third airport, and in distinguishing between sites, by measures of the likely effect on demand of extra accessibility.[6] Moreover, the main interest in the evaluation process was what were suspected to be large and diverse external disbenefits such as noise, so that the choice of a fairly con-

[6] The checks could have been better of course. In particular, because one type of trip-making – air passengers – was involved, it would have been quite feasible to have fed estimates of elasticities of demand directly into the traffic model, instead of relying on rather poor accessibility measurements in conjunction with a conventional transportation model. Such an approach was indeed argued before the Commission, but the model was unfortunately mis-specified.

ventional treatment for passengers could be defended (though of course it turned out that passenger benefits and costs were very important in the total CBA). But in any case, where, as in the West Midlands example just quoted, the focus is on alternative transport networks, it seems a wise precaution to do one's best to distinguish between the costs incurred by travellers which are fairly clearly offset by benefits accruing to them, and those which are not. So, while an approach which focusses on travellers and associated costs must at best be a very partial guide to project selection, in the context of assessing these in alternative planning configurations, one especially needs to try to isolate the travel costs, broadly defined, necessarily associated with differing juxtapositions of houses and workplaces reflected in the rival prospective networks.

The kind of model we have presented seems likely to help towards this. By distinguishing elements of trip-making associated with housing shift, we are, in effect, isolating an element of cost presumably willingly incurred by residents to improve their housing conditions. In our results, this happens to be, for men, probably a negative cost on balance, but, of course, this does not affect the principle. On the other hand, the employment shift variable corresponds closely to what is the main cost effect of alternative configurations, though to regard it as pointing to a measure of *the* relevant cost may require, among other things, a strong interpretation in one respect in particular. This is that no elements of changing location rent complicate the picture. (Thus, ΔE might be expected to result in an opposite shift in location rents, and thus people's reactions not wholly captured by measured journey length change. We feel that this is not likely to have been a very important factor in our data because, among other things, of rent control. But, this is in fact why we are concerned to test the models over different periods and why we would like to include housing occupancy as a variable.) The additional variables we suggested for further investigation might be similarly classified: for example the differential costs arising from a shift to car ownership and the consequences of increasing demands for special skills belong in the first category; and the entry-to-the-labour force variable in the second. If we could establish a case for supposing the different configurations to be causally related to the first category of factors – for example, if we could establish that a more 'rural' configuration leads to greater car ownership, then we might consider not merely the elimination of some costs from the comparisons, but go further and treat them as measures of benefits to be attributed, though this is clearly a very speculative extension of the process of evaluation.

There must obviously be a great deal of development work on the models before they can be used with any confidence, and in this, the requirements for use primarily as a forecasting tool or as an evaluatory tool may well conflict in terms of research input. For example, to what extent ΔE should be regarded as a proxy for a shift in location rents is probably more important for evaluation than prediction. And the fact that the models throw no direct light upon trip numbers and related issues such as labour force participation underlines their limitations in evaluation. But in the present state of CBA work in this area the pay-off to a small gain in insight into evaluation is, we think, very possibly larger than a substantial gain in forecasting accuracy, and our future efforts should perhaps be distributed accordingly.

Appendix 1

LOCAL AUTHORITIES IN THE SAMPLE

County	
ESSEX	1. East Ham CB
	2. Barking MB
	3. Benfleet UD
	4. Brentwood UD
	5. Dagenham MB
	6. Ilford MB
	7. Thurrock UD
	8. Walthamstow MB
	9. Chelmsford MB
	10. Chigwell UD
	11. Canvey Island UD
	12. Epping & Ongar RD
	13. Hornchurch UD
HERTS	14. Barnet UD
	15. Cheshunt UD
	16. Hitchin UD
	17. St Albans MB
	18. Watford MB
	19. Hemel Hempstead MB
	20. Bushey UD
	21. Stevenage UD
	22. Hatfield RD
KENT	23. Ashford UD
	24. Chatham MB
	25. Crayford UD
	26. Gravesend MB
	27. Maidstone MB
	28. Orpington UD
	29. Rochester MB
	30. Tonbridge UD
KENT	31. Whitstable UD
	32. Stroud RD
	33. Bexley MB
	34. Erith MB
	35. Herne Bay UD
	36. Sevenoaks UD
LONDON	37. Bethnal Green MB
	38. Finsbury
	39. Hackney
	40. Lambeth
	41. St Pancras
	42. Chelsea
	43. Fulham
	44. Lewisham
MIDDLESEX	45. Acton MB
	46. Ealing MB
	47. Edmonton MB
	48. Tottenham MF
	49. Harrow MB
	50. Uxbridge UD
	51. Southall MB
SURREY	52. Dorking UD
	53. Esher UD
	54. Reigate UD
	55. Wimbledon MB
	56. Guildford RD
	57. Banstead UD
	58. Leatherhead UD
	59. Richmond MB
	60. Barnes MB

Appendix 2

ZERO-ORDER CORRELATION COEFFICIENTS

Males

	ΔD	ΔE	ΔS	H_1	H_2	J_1	J_2
ΔD	1·0000	0·6629	0·5452	0·0299	−0·3988	0·43/4	0·1913
ΔE		1·0000	0·8270	−0·2142	−0·3888	0·40/6	0·1800
ΔS			1·0000	−0·1864	−0·2948	0·3632	0·2509
H_1				1·0000	0·4569	0·5645	0·2116
H_2					1·0000	0·1925	0·2167
J_1						1·0000	0·5033
J_2							1·0000

Females

	ΔD	ΔE	ΔS	H_1	H_2	J_1	J_2	P	M	$\sqrt{DE}$
ΔD	1·0000	0·4886	0·5502	0·2774	−0·3088	0·3763	−0·0872	−0·0765	−0·2569	0·5114
ΔE		1·0000	0·6557	−0·0859	−0·3984	0·3013	−0·0195	0·0508	−0·3339	0·9553
ΔS			1·0000	0·1530	−0·2781	0·3688	0·1038	−0·0987	−0·3072	0·7392
H_1				1·0000	0·4742	0·5957	0·4995	−0·4421	−0·1642	−0·0137
H_2					1·0000	0·2095	0·5675	−0·3801	0·3051	−0·3664
J_1						1·0000	0·6085	−0·4716	−0·4590	0·3434
J_2							1·0000	−0·4615	−0·2337	0·0717
P								1·0000	0·0948	0·0240
M									1·0000	−0·3915
$\sqrt{DE}$										1·0000

REFERENCES

[1] M. E. Beesley, Transport in London and motorway planning, *Environment and Planning*, **2,** 137–51, 1970.
[2] M. E. Beesley and A. A. Walters, Some problems in the evaluation of urban road investments, *Applied Economics*, Jan. 1970, 241–59.
[3] A. M. Warnes, Changing work patterns – an indicator of metropolitan change. Salford Conference: Techniques in Urban Geography. Institute of British Geographers. September 1968.
[4] J. Meyer, *The Urban Transportation Problem*, Harvard University Press, 1965, Chapter 2.

12

The Valuation of Time in Cost-benefit Studies

P. WATSON

Department of Economics, Northwestern University, Evanston, Illinois

The late N. MANSFIELD

sometime Ministry of Transport

1. BACKGROUND

The application of the techniques of cost-benefit analysis to investment projects in the field of transport has without doubt reduced the random element of decision-making by providing the decision-maker with systematically presented information on the projects under his consideration. The difficulties of evaluating and enumerating all the benefits and costs of a given investment project led to the rejection, on pragmatic grounds, of sophisticated cost-benefit analyses, and the adoption of the more practical TAL (time and accident loss) method. By this method only the time and accident savings attributable to an investment project were considered. However, even this simplified technique ran into difficulties when the problem of valuing time arose, and it soon became obvious that the solution was not obvious. Nevertheless, it was a solution which had to be found, as the value of time savings can account for in the lowest estimate, 25 per cent of total benefits, and in the highest, more than all the other benefits combined. It will be clear, therefore, that the results of cost-benefit analyses of transport investment projects are extremely susceptible to the value which is placed upon time savings.[1]

A brief perusal of the literature might leave the reader under the impression that studies concerning the evaluation of time are few and far between. The reason for this strange state of affairs stems from the lack of attention directed towards the subject by academic economists. While the theoretical aspects of techniques like cost-benefit analysis have been relatively well covered by economists the

[1] The value to be placed upon time-savings is often referred to as the value of time.

practical details have been left, on the whole, to highway planners and traffic engineers, with the result that the student in this field is obliged to extend his scope to take in the literature appropriate to these and related fields.

In order to reduce the findings of such a literary search to the more manageable proportions appropriate to this paper, the procedure of considering the methods used to evaluate time one after the other in chronological order has been eschewed as time-consuming and tedious. Thus a more direct procedure has been adopted. The methods have been classified under a number of sub-headings corresponding to the different approaches to the subject. Each approach will then be considered in general terms and the more interesting and representative exponents will be examined.

1.1. A Priori *Evaluations*

Into this section fall all the evaluations which are based not on empirical research but on *a priori* reasoning. These evaluations are usually presented as being 'a reasonable view' or 'representative of current opinion'. In fairness to their exponents it must be said that, in the majority of cases, it is made quite clear that the suggested valuation is an 'assumed' valuation. In the absence of better or more reliable information cost-benefit analysts, realising the importance of time savings, have felt obliged to invent or 'assume' a value for the time saved; moreover, in the hope that their valuation will be widely accepted, they have, on the whole, avoided extreme valuations. Nevertheless, the variation between the different estimates has been considerable. American estimates range from the US Bureau of Public Roads (1925): \$3.00 per vehicle hour, to the American Association of State Highway Officials (1960): \$1.55 per vehicle hour. These valuations are from semi-official bodies, and the estimates of individual researchers vary even more.

The majority of British analysts have avoided simply assuming values for time saved. The approach of the M1 motorway study in providing multiple estimates of benefits given various evaluations of time savings is a clear improvement on providing a single estimate. Nevertheless, British analysts have estimated time values on *a priori* grounds, and 2s 6d was a common value in the late 1940s and early 1950s. The Road Research Laboratory in their publication *Research on Road Traffic* also recommended an *a priori* valuation, calculated at 75 per cent of the average wage-rate.

This type of valuation is reminiscent of some of the earliest attempts at valuation in which time was valued at the wage rate, on the grounds that, if people sold their time at that rate, they would be equally willing to buy time at the same rate. This type of reasoning has, however, fallen out of favour in more recent times, and valuers have usually assumed that a 'reasonable' valuation must be less than the wage rate, since the time saved is not productive. Valuation at the wage rate has been reserved for working-time saved, a procedure which is almost universally accepted, while the controversy over leisure time still goes on.

The idea that time should be valued at more than the wage rate has never received popular currency, yet *a priori* reasoning might well lead to this conclusion, since the over-time rate is the rate which must be paid to induce people to give up their leisure time. This view is supported by Bellis. It is, however, true, that, as a result of collective bargaining in the wages field, the additional payments received for over-time working may be considered as an economic rent, generated by the power of the organised labour. This argument is supported by the findings of empirical studies which do not support the view that time spent in leisure pursuits is, in fact, valued more highly than working time. Moreover, as pointed out by Glassborough, payment is made for both time and effort, and he claims, 'little value is placed on leisure and high price on effort'.

When the US Bureau of Public Roads recommended in 1925 that time be valued at $3.00 per vehicle hour, the absence of data on the topic made this a justifiable procedure. Since then, much work has been done in the field, and although no firm conclusions have yet been reached, it is arguable that it is no longer justifiable to simply 'assume' a value of time, while attempting to give greater weight to the assumption by claiming that it is 'reasonable' or 'representative' of current opinion. If such an assumption is required, it must be made on the basis of relevant empirical work, which, it is contended, is now available to cover most situations with a certain degree of accuracy.

1.2. *Valuations Based on Operating Costs and/or Toll Fees*

In the early 1940s H. Tucker reported two methods which had been used to measure the value of time. The first was based on the argument that, even though a car might be held up in a stream of traffic, the fixed operating costs still applied; if the fixed cost per mile was multiplied by the average speed, a cost per hour would be determined. This appears to be the first attempt to introduce a valuation of time based on operating costs, albeit a rather crude one. Tucker mentions it briefly and then moves on to consideration of a method based on route choices. It was noticed that drivers are sometimes willing to take a route involving additional mileage in order to save time. The value for time was calculated by calculating the cost of the extra distance and dividing it by the time saved:

$$\text{Value of time} = \frac{O\Delta m}{t}$$

O = operating cost per mile, m = mileage, and t = time. This approach was duplicated by Hennes in 1956.

A very similar method was developed by West in 1946 after he noticed that traffic was generated by the opening of a toll bridge. His argument was that people were buying the time saved at the price of the toll fee. The value of time, was therefore, calculable as follows:

$$\text{Value of time} = \frac{f}{\Delta t}$$

where f = toll fee, and t = time.

The operating-cost method was modified in 1958 by Vaswani who split the costs into highway costs and user costs. (Unfortunately, from available information, it is not possible to deduce exactly how these are defined.) The value of time is then defined as the marginal rate of change of costs per unit of time, and is expressed in terms of a differential

$$V = \frac{\partial(H+U)}{\partial t}$$

where H = highway costs, and U = user costs.

In 1959 Dawson, working with the Road Research Laboratory combined the operating-cost method and the toll fee method, and developed a method in which operating costs and toll fees jointly determined the value of time

$$V = \frac{f+Om}{\Delta t}$$

This attempt to include various elements of total cost was followed up by Cherniak, in his analysis of travel impedances, which were represented in the following way:

$$\Delta TC = C\Delta m + V\Delta t + \Delta f + e$$

where e = residual impedances.

The model is solved by the least squares method. In a similar treatment by St Clair and Lieder, an allowance for comfort and convenience was included for the first time. They were measured by the number and amount of changes in speed resulting from the route under consideration.

$$\Delta TC = O\Delta m + \Delta a + \Delta f + V\Delta t + W\Delta y$$

where a = accident costs, y = speed changes, and W = value of discomfort and inconvenience in $ per m.p.h. of speed change. Finally, this model was extended by Claffey who carried out test runs on toll and free roads and collected data on highway use, operating costs, toll costs, time, speed changes and accident costs. The model: $Wgr = -e(O\Delta m + \Delta a + \Delta f + V\Delta t + W\Delta y)$ where e = a residual value can be used to evaluate the values for time and discomfort and inconvenience by multiple regression methods.

The methods based on operating costs alone are subject to two main objections. First, they assume that the driver is aware of his operating costs and of the mileage involved in different routes. It is by no means certain, however, that motorists do in fact know what their operating costs are. While it is likely that they take account of the costs of petrol, it is argued that it is unlikely that they include wear and tear, taxes, insurance and depreciation in their calculations. It is also possible to postulate that, especially for short journeys, motorists do not accurately perceive small differences in mileages.

Second, this method of evaluating time depends heavily on the assumption that motorists base their decisions exclusively on cost, time and mileage difference. While these variables appear to be the most important influences on the motorists' decision-making process, and while arguing as if each motorist constituted an 'economic man' can be justified, it is arguable that other factors such as safety or comfort should be taken into account.

The later models which attempt to build these factors into the models are a definite improvement on their less sophisticated predecessors. They are still based, however, on quite simple models and it is only in recent years that better models have been developed.

1.3. *Behavioural Models*

A behavioural model is one in which mathematical and statistical techniques are used to model or represent the behaviour of individual travellers. In this case the particular behaviour under examination is the selection of a travel mode or route from the possibilities open to the traveller. The basis for the model is the hypothesis that: 'The traveller will choose the mode (route) whose speed, cost and comfort levels, weighted by the relative importance of each factor, produce the most favourable combination relative to other modes. The weights will be in some part determined by the characteristics both of the traveller himself, his environment, and of the trip which he is making.' The mathematical model is no more than the representation of the hypothesis in terms of mathematical symbols, it being convenient to present the hypothesis in such a way in order to facilitate the use of statistical techniques to produce estimates of the weights attached to the variables and a measure of the significance of the postulated relationship.

It is inappropriate in this paper to consider in detail the forms of relationships which have been estimated or the statistical methods which have been employed. For the purposes of exposition, assume that the relationship which has been estimated is:

$$P(A) = a_0 + a_1 \Delta T + a_2 \Delta C$$

where $P(A)$ = probability of choosing a mode A, ΔT = time difference between modes, a_1, a_2 = weights, and a_0 = constant term. The value of time is the ratio a_1/a_2, since this ratio determines the amount by which, given a unit change in ΔC, ΔT must change in order to leave $P(A)$ unchanged. If ΔC is in pence and ΔT is in minutes, then a one penny change in ΔC will require that ΔT change by a_1/a_2 minutes, if $P(A)$ is to remain unchanged. In other words a_1/a_2 represents the rate of substitution between time and cost, and can, thus, be interpreted as the value of time. It should be noted that an analogous procedure operates for a non-linear model.

This type of derivation technique was applied to a number of commuting situations and values of time were derived. The choice of commuting trips for the early studies of this type was based on a number of factors. Commuting trips, of course, are one of the most frequent types of trip undertaken; most people make such a trip daily during the week. This being the case, it is likely that people will have clear information about the times, costs and other characteristics associated with their trips. This makes data collection much simpler, as does the fact that commuters can readily be isolated, either in a suburb or at a place of work, so that a group of people with similar trips can be identified. Moreover, as most traffic problems are caused by the peaking of commuting trips, it was reasonable to begin an investigation of mode or route choice behaviour with studies of commuting trips.

From the values of time derived from the commuting studies, a value was chosen for use in cost-benefit studies, but although this single value represented the current body of opinion on the value of commuter's time, doubts were expressed as to whether it was representative of any other type of time, and studies were set up to investigate different types of trip, e.g., medium range inter-urban trips, short intra-urban trips to recreational facilities, shopping trips. Thus it was acknowledged that the purpose of the trip and its length might influence the value of time in different circumstances. Moreover, it became clear that, in the same circumstances, different travellers might have different values of time, and so the personal characteristics of the traveller are now taken into consideration.

This brief description of the recent history of the derivation of values of time serves as the background to the problem to be considered in this paper, that is, the implications of these developments for cost-benefit analysis in the field of transport. The next step is to set out clearly the present state of the art and also the foreseeable developments. Then it is necessary to consider the problems of the cost-benefit analyst when confronted with these new developments and the steps which can be taken to solve these problems.

2. THE STATE OF THE ART AND FUTURE DEVELOPMENTS

As most of the studies investigating non-commuting trip-making behaviour are currently being undertaken, little can be said about the present state of the art beyond saying that it is in a state of flux. The old order based solely on commuting studies has been challenged and is in the process of being modified, but the new order has not yet come into being. Perhaps the best method of explaining the present situation is to expand on what was said above about the factors which might lead to modifications to the currently accepted value of time. Such an expansion involves borrowing from the taxonomies (classification systems) of Lisco and Thomas. Since there is at present some disagreement as to the content of the most appropriate classification system, and since the precise form of the system is not important in the context of this paper, a notional system will be used to illustrate the point.

Having drawn up a classification system of this type, it is possible to fill in some of the compartments, and to assign priorities to those which remain empty. It is then possible to approach the question of new studies from a rational starting point.

Table 12.1. Classification of values of time

Length / Purpose	Intra urban: Intra centre	Intra urban: Suburb to centre	Intra urban: Suburb to suburb	Inter urban: Centre to centre	Inter urban: Suburb to centre	Inter urban: Suburb to suburb
Social/ recreational						
Commuting						
Business						
Educational						
Shopping						

Although it is not necessary in this paper to enter into the controversy over the merits of different classification systems, it is appropriate to consider their content. In the 'non-controversial' system presented in Table 12.1, the values of time have been classified by length of trip and purpose of trip.[2] Other factors which could be used are the age and/or sex of the traveller, the frequency with which he makes the trip, the method of payment for the trip (e.g. personal or on expenses, expenses claimable in advance or in arrears, etc.), and, of course the income of the traveller. The present view on income seems to be that each compartment should be sub-divided by income. It will be clear from this description of the classification possibilities that, whatever system is chosen, the resultant value of time matrix will be quite complex. It seems doubtful whether it can be limited to a two-way matrix; it will possibly develop into a four-dimension matrix with sub-divisions of each element.

Clearly such a position does not exist at present, nor can it be envisaged in the near future, but it is, without doubt, the direction in which value of time thinking is moving, and it is with the implications of this movement for the cost-benefit analyst that this paper is concerned.

3. VALUE OF TIME AND COST-BENEFIT ANALYSIS

Cost-benefit analysis in the field of transport as in any other field, is an aid to decision-making, by means of making economic assessments of projects for which the market may not provide an optimum allocation of resources, as a result of the difficulties of deciding who the beneficiaries are and to what extent they benefit. In the case of

[2] It should be noted that the breakdown by purpose and length is not intended to be incontrovertible.

investments in roads, bridges, railways, etc., it is relatively easy to identify the costs and benefits; moreover, the evaluation of the costs is usually merely a question of obtaining engineering estimates. The evaluation of the benefits has always been a problem, given that the benefits are usually made up largely of time and accident savings. The derivation of a single value of time from commuting studies greatly simplified the task for the cost-benefit analyst: he simply had to calculate the amount of time saved and multiply it by the value of time. Clearly the developments described in section 2, above, will radically change this position.

In order to make use of the classification of values of time, the cost-benefit analyst will need to have access to detailed information about the travellers who save time as a result of the project which he is studying in order to match up the values of time with the different categories of traveller. For example, in a simple case where only four values of time existed as shown in Table 12.2, the analyst would have

Table 12.2.

	Social trips	Others
Intra-urban		
Inter-urban		

to divide his time-savers into these four categories, before applying the values of time in order to calculate the total value of the time saved. Obviously, the type of developments envisaged above will make the calculations considerably more complex.

How then is the cost-benefit analyst to deal with this problem? It would seem possible to approach it in two ways, both of which involve a new departure for the cost-benefit analyst, i.e. the collection of extensive data from the travelling public. In the past a cost-benefit study of an investment project has not necessarily involved contact with the public beyond that required for an origin-destination survey, which is by its nature, restrictive in the type of information collected. In order to make full use of a value of time matrix, it would be necessary to collect more complete data, including, e.g. income, age, household size, etc. There is little doubt that this type of information can without undue difficulty be collected even in the context of a roadside survey, but it must be allowed that the increase in costs resulting from collecting and processing the extra data may be considerable. Nevertheless, it should be stressed that such information could be collected by the cost-benefit analyst.

Having collected the data on the trip and personal characteristics of the travellers, the analyst can use them in two ways, in what might be called the disaggregate and the aggregate approaches:

(a) The Disaggregate Approach

The disaggregate approach involves nothing more complicated than the straightforward multiplication and summation of the time savings and values of time in each category. The procedure would be tedious but not difficult, and, given the use of a computer, not very time-consuming.

(b) The Aggregate Approach

The aggregate approach results from consideration of a factor which has so far been ignored, i.e. the fact that the use of a matrix of values of time may tend to confirm the value which is at present used.

The consideration of such a possibility indicates, it is contended, a preference for a single value of time. It is felt that a single value of time is easier both to understand and to manipulate than a multiplicity of values. It is suggested, therefore, that a 'standard' value of time could be defined as the value of time to be used in a setting which embodies 'standard' distributions for trip purpose, income, etc. To take account of the fact that these distributions could change from project to project, it would be necessary to define an adjustment factor by which the 'standard' value of time modified. For example, if commuters had a high value of time and a given setting had a higher than 'standard' proportion of commuters in its trip purpose distribution, then the 'standard' value would have to be adjusted upwards. It would not be difficult to base the adjustment factor on a number of distributions so that the adjustment factor could reflect the balance of a number of possibly conflicting influences.

(c) An 'Equity' Adjustment

Given a situation as described above it would be feasible, if thought desirable, to build into the analysis an element of income redistribution. By this it is meant that certain distributions would automatically modify the value of time used in order to benefit a certain group of the population. If, for example, it was discovered that the value of time varied directly with income, it might be thought undesirable to allow projects whose beneficiaries were in a high income group to be undertaken at the expense of those whose beneficiaries were in a lower income group. In other words where the time savings are equal it may not be a good thing to give preference to projects simply because the beneficiaries are wealthy, and value their time more highly. It is thought that this idea might be of particular importance in cases of urban redevelopment, where choices arise between the rehabilitation of slum areas, presumably at a low apparent value to the beneficiaries, and the development of facilities in high-income suburbs.

Similarly, it is possible that the transport infrastructure of a region could remain underdeveloped because the region always came off second-best in comparisons with more affluent regions, whose benefits were valued more highly simply because the region is more affluent.

If the value of time were to be modified whenever the income distribution indicated that social aims should over-ride economic goals, a useful tool would be available to the policy-makers who seek to produce a more equitable distribution of the country's wealth.

4. CONCLUSION

In conclusion it should be stressed that the aim of this paper has not been to present a polished, more up-to-date version of the technique of cost-benefit analysis. It has been to indicate changes which have been taking place and which will continue to take place, and to point out the implications of these changes. Tentative suggestions have been made as to the ways in which cost-benefit analysis can be modified to make full use of the more detailed information which is becoming available. It is hoped that these ideas will provide food for thought and that fruitful discussion, and action, will spring from them.

Index